CHILDREN, YOUNG PEOPLE AND SOCIAL INCLUSION

Participation for what?

Edited by E. Kay M. Tisdall, John M. Davis, Alan Prout and Malcolm Hill

First published in Great Britain in November 2006 by

The Policy Press
University of Bristol
Fourth Floor
Beacon House
Queen's Road
Bristol BS8 1QU
UK

Tel +44 (0)117 331 4054
Fax +44 (0)117 331 4093
e-mail tpp-info@bristol.ac.uk
www.policypress.org.uk

© E. Kay M. Tisdall, John M. Davis, Alan Prout and Malcolm Hill 2006

British Library Cataloguing in Publication Data
A catalogue record for this book is available from the British Library.

Library of Congress Cataloging-in-Publication Data
A catalog record for this book has been requested.

ISBN-10 1 86134 662 X paperback
ISBN-13 978 1 86134 662 9 paperback
ISBN-10 1 86134 663 8 hardcover
ISBN-13 978 1 86134 663 6 hardcover

Cover design by Qube Design Associates, Bristol.
Printed and bound in Great Britain by Hobbs the Printers, Southampton.

Contents

List of figures

Acknowledgements

This book arose from the seminar series, organised by the editors, titled 'Challenging "social inclusion": perspectives for and from children and young people'. The seminar series was funded initially by the Economic and Social Research Council (R451265206), with additional funds provided through The Children's Society and individual participants' organisations. Further, emerging ideas from the seminar were brought to a conference of European youth organisations and young people, 'Including young people: sharing good practice across Europe', organised by the Youth Education and Social Work Forum (http://www.yes-forum.org/) and hosted by The Children's Society Liverpool in late 2003. This book has thus benefited greatly from the collective contributions of all participants, at the seminars and beyond.

The editors would like to thank all chapter contributors for their patience and willingness to contribute to the book. The editors also wish to extend their appreciation to the commissioning and editing teams of The Policy Press, who have supported the book throughout.

Notes on contributors

Robert Bell is the Director of Carnegie Young People Initiative. He was previously at the UK government's Children and Young People's Unit in the Department for Education and Skills. Prior to this, he worked in the Cabinet Office, in the Women and Equality Unit. Between 1992 and 2001, he worked as a youth researcher at the universities of Edinburgh, Cambridge and London South Bank. He has written reports and articles in the areas of youth transitions, identity and policy. He also coordinates a consortium of organisations developing Participation Works, an online gateway to participation resources and information.

Johnston Birchall is Senior Lecturer in Public and Social Policy, Stirling University, and Co-director with Richard Simmons of the Mutuality Research Programme. He is author of several books, including *The International Co-operative Movement* (Manchester University Press, 1997); *Decentralising Public Services* (with C. Pollitt) (Macmillan, 1998); *The New Mutualism in Public Policy* (ed) (Routledge, 2001); *Rediscovering the Co-operative Advantage: Poverty Reduction through Self-help* (International Labour Office, 2003) and *Co-operatives and the Millennium Development Goals* (International Labour Office, 2004). His research interests include user involvement and governance in public services; cooperatives and poverty reduction; and a mutual incentives model of what motivates people to participate.

Liam Cairns has worked with children, young people and their families for more than 20 years, in a variety of social work posts, in different local authorities in Scotland and the north of England. Since 1997, he has been the manager of Investing in Children. Originally based in County Durham, and resourced by the local authority and the National Health Service, Investing in Children is concerned with the human rights of children and has developed a range of innovative strategies designed to create opportunities for children and young people to contribute effectively to debate and become active participants in democratic processes.

John M. Davis has carried out ethnographic research projects in the UK in the areas of childhood studies, curriculum innovation, disability, education, health and sport. He has published widely in such journals as *Children & Society, Disability & Society*, and *The International Journal of Children's Rights*. Formerly a senior lecturer in Childhood and Disability Studies at the University of Northumbria, he is currently a senior lecturer and Coordinator of the BA in Childhood Studies at the University of Edinburgh.

Rosie Edwards has worked for organisations such as The Children's Society and the Scarman Trust and is presently working independently. She has published articles on young people and social inclusion, working with communities and young people's participation. She studied mediating organisations for her Masters degree at the London School of Economics and Political Science and is interested in how the community sector can challenge the democratic deficit and in ways in which the community sector can develop and shape the local economy.

Michael Gallagher is a visiting fellow in the Institute of Geography, University of Edinburgh. His research interests centre on the connections between space and power in schools, particularly the ways in which teaching and research relationships construct the child–adult divide. Michael also currently works as a practitioner in secondary schools and in a range of youth settings.

Malcolm Hill is currently part-time Research Professor at the University of Strathclyde, working within the Glasgow School of Social Work. For 10 years he was director of the Glasgow Centre for the Child & Society. He has carried out studies on a wide range of topics related to children and families, with a specialist interest in looked after children and adoption. Recent and current research has covered young people who persistently offend, teenagers and their grandparents, inter-ethnic relations at school and children's views of services. Key publications include *Children and Society* (with Kay Tisdall) (Longman, 1997); *Effective Ways of Working with Children and Families* (ed) (Jessica Kingsley, 1999); and *Shaping Childcare Practice in Scotland* (ed) (BAAF, 2002).

Gerison Lansdown is an international consultant and advocate in children's rights, and Co-director of CRED-PRO, a new international initiative to develop child rights educational programmes for professionals working with children. Recent publications include *The Evolving Capacities of the Child* (UNICEF,

2005); *Can You Hear Me? The Participation Rights of Young Children* (Bernard Van Leer Foundation, 2005); and *Betrayal of Trust: An Overview of Children's Experience of Physical and Humiliating Punishment, Child Sexual Abuse and Violence when in Conflict with the Law* (Save the Children, 2006).

Berry Mayall is Professor of Childhood Studies at the Institute of Education, University of London. Her research work spans more than 30 years, and has had a focus on children and parents. Over the past 15 years, she has carried out a number of studies with children, within the sociology of childhood. In addition, she runs an MA in Childhood Studies with Priscilla Alderson and Virginia Morrow, which stresses links between sociological and rights agendas and issues. Among the many papers and books she has had published are: *Conceptualizing Child–Adult Relations* (with Leena Alanen) (RoutledgeFalmer, 2001); *Towards a Sociology for Childhood* (Open University Press, 2002); and 'Sociologies of childhood' (chapter in M. Holborn (ed) *Developments in Sociology*, Volume 20, Causeway Press, 2004).

Peter Moss is Professor of Early Childhood Provision at the Thomas Coram Research Unit, Institute of Education, University of London. His research interests include: services for children and relations between them; the workforce in these services; gender issues in work with children; and the relationship between employment and care, with a special interest in leave policies. Between 1986 and 1996, he was coordinator of the EC Childcare Network and he is currently editor of a multinational, multilingual magazine, *Children in Europe*. Recent books include *Beyond Quality in Early Childhood Education and Care: A New Deal for Children? Re-forming Education and Care in England, Scotland and Sweden* (with Bronwen Cohen and Pat Petrie) (The Policy Press, 2004); and *Ethics and Politics in Early Childhood Education* (with Gunilla Dahlberg) (Routledge, 2004).

John Pinkerton is Professor of Child and Family Social Work at Queen's University of Belfast, Northern Ireland, where he is involved primarily with post-professional qualification training. His particular areas of research and publication are young people leaving state care, family support and the process of relating research to policy and practice development. Recent publications include *Family Support as Reflective Practice* (Jessica Kingsley, 2006); *Evaluating Family Support: Thinking Internationally, Thinking Critically* (John Wiley & Sons, 2003); *From*

Parity to Subsidiarity? Children's Policy in Northern Ireland under New Labour (*Children & Society*, vol 15, no 1, pp 118-21); and *Developing an International Perspective on Leaving Care* (in A. Wheal (ed) *The RHP Companion to Leaving Care*, Russell House Publishing, 2002).

Alan Prout is Professor of Sociology and Childhood Studies at the University of Warwick and was formerly Director of the ESRC Children 5-16 research programme (1995-2001). Publications include *Constructing and Reconstructing Childhood* (Falmer Press, 1990, 1997); *Theorizing Childhood* (Polity Press, 1998); *The Body Childhood and Society* (Macmillan, 2000); and *The Future of Childhood: Towards the Interdisciplinary Study of Children* (RoutledgeFalmer, 2005).

Tess Ridge is a Lecturer in Social Policy at the University of Bath. Her research interests are childhood poverty and social exclusion, children and family policy, especially financial support for children and families. She has recently completed a three-year ESRC (Economic and Social Research Council) Research Fellowship developing a child-centred approach to understanding how children, especially low-income children, fare within the policy process. Publications include an article in the *Journal of Social Policy* and *Childhood Poverty and Social Exclusion* (The Policy Press, 2002).

Peter Seaman is a public health research specialist at the Glasgow Centre for Population Health, an organisation established to explore the origins underlying, and solutions for, Glasgow's distinctively poor health record. He worked at the Glasgow Centre for the Child & Society between 2002 and 2004 as a research fellow, exploring parenting in disadvantaged neighbourhoods in Glasgow. Prior to this, he worked at Edinburgh University, Department of General Practice, and completed a PhD, exploring parenting within changing notions of family, at the Medical Research Council Social and Public Health Sciences Unit in Glasgow. Pete specialises in qualitative research and has research interests in contemporary trends in family formation and social capital.

Richard Simmons is Co-director of the Mutuality Research Programme in the Department of Applied Social Science at Stirling University. Recent publications include a series of articles developing a theoretical model of what motivates people to participate in several different settings. He is currently working on a book on user involvement in public services, based on two major ESRC-funded projects. Research interests include the role of mutuality in social systems, human identities and relationships, and participative theory and practice (particularly in the governance and delivery of public services).

Anne Stafford is Deputy Director of the Centre for Research in Education Inclusion and Diversity (CREID) at the Moray House School of Education at the University of Edinburgh. She was previously Deputy Director at the Glasgow Centre for the Child & Society at the University of Glasgow. Her research focus is mainly on children's rights, child abuse and child protection, and children and young people on the margins. She has worked for many years in the children's voluntary sector.

E. Kay M. Tisdall is Programme Director of the MSc in Childhood Studies, and Reader in Social Policy, at the University of Edinburgh. Previously, she worked as Director of Policy & Research at Children in Scotland, the national umbrella agency for organisations and professionals working with children and their families. Current and recent research includes: school councils; training on research methods with children and young people; children's views in family law proceedings; and inter-agency services. Recent journal articles have been published in *Children & Society*, *Critical Social Policy*, the *European Journal of Social Work* and the *International Journal of Law, Policy and the Family*.

Katrina Turner is a Research Fellow in the Department of Community-based Medicine at the University of Bristol. She is experienced in using both qualitative and quantitative research methods, and is particularly experienced in conducting in-depth interviews and discussion groups with children and young people. Her research interests include teenage motherhood, young people's sexual health and mental well-being.

Moira Walker was until recently Senior Research Fellow at the Social Work Research Centre, Stirling University. Her current research involves evaluating a range of social work services for children and families. This includes the use of secure accommodation in Scotland, a parenting development project, family centre-based provision for families and children, and an advocacy project for children within the child protection system. Previous research has focused primarily on children looked after away from home. Before becoming a researcher, she worked as a social worker.

ONE

Introduction

John M. Davis and Malcolm Hill

Social inclusion and participation

This book arose from an interest in exploring, with respect to children and young people, the connections between two key concepts that became prominent in social policy during the 1990s and early years of the new millennium: social inclusion and participation. At a superficial glance, these two terms appear to have virtually identical meanings. Social inclusion is about being allowed or enabled to take part, while participation entails taking part. The former suggests a more passive stance and the latter a more active mode, but in each case it is possible to consider processes and factors that act as barriers or facilitators to inclusion/participation, at individual, local and societal levels. Of course, both beg the question – taking part in what?

Potentially, participation and inclusion can apply to any of a sizeable set of life domains: social activities and relationships; the labour market; consumption; education; recreation and leisure; decision making of various kinds that may be collective (for example, political voting; school councils) or personal (for example, where to live after parental divorce). The addition of the qualifier 'social' to inclusion implies a somewhat more restricted sphere, omitting some other types of inclusion, such as political inclusion. In practice, though, social inclusion and participation have mostly been used in narrower ways. For instance, participation has been most closely linked with decision making, while inclusion has more often referred to economic and social relationships and well-being. In the rest of this chapter, we first consider separately how each has been conceptualised and applied, then indicate potential connections. Later chapters examine some of the issues that emerge in greater depth.

Poverty and exclusion/inclusion

In policy and academic circles, social inclusion was adopted to describe in positive terms policy measures to combat social exclusion, regarded largely as an outcome of socioeconomic processes (Percy-Smith, 2000; Pierson, 2002). With roots in continental European usages (Hantrais, 1995), social exclusion became popular in the UK under New Labour as a means of describing and also redefining poverty. It referred to individuals or families having incomes and resources that are inadequate in the context of an advanced economy. Drawing on notions of relative poverty (Townsend, 1979), social exclusion in this sense encompasses financial hardship compared with the minimum expectations of society. It takes account of the capacity not only to meet 'basic' requirements (food, clothes, accommodation and so on), but also to cover socially normal items and activities. What was once a luxury or innovation can come to be seen as a social necessity within particular social and temporal contexts. Television and mobile phones exemplify such a transformation. As Room (1995) pointed out, social exclusion more than poverty takes account of the social processes involved in both defining and reacting to financial deprivation, with stigma being a key element. He suggested that whereas poverty is about the distribution of material resources, social exclusion refers to 'inadequate social participation, lack of social integration and lack of power' (p 5). This makes an explicit link between exclusion and participation, but rooted in material disadvantage.

Like poverty previously, social exclusion in the financial/material sense has been subject to many differing explanations at several levels, with corresponding policy strategies. These range from the macroeconomic and societal to the sub-cultural, familial and individual. Levitas (1998) has argued that the UK New Labour government's interpretation is based largely on a notion of social circumstances limiting access to employment opportunities, to which the response has been policies designed to integrate the unemployed and non-employed into paid work. Levitas and others have argued that the focus has therefore been on promoting opportunity rather than redistributing resources or creating equality (Cockburn, 2002). Both social integration and redistribution approaches contrast with 'moral underclass' discourses that place responsibility and often blame onto families living in 'sink' estates or on the 'edge of society' and their presumed failings in socialisation (Murray, 1990; Leisering and Leibfried, 1999). By blaming parents and communities for the failure of children and young people, this perspective overlooks the evidence that many children and young people (for example, those who are working class, disabled or from a minority ethnic background) are unable to fulfil the requirements of educational institutions and social norms or laws, not because they themselves are inherently 'delinquent' or do not receive sufficient support from their parents, but because they experience discrimination within these social settings or because wider social issues and economic constraints impact on their everyday choices (Ridge, 2002; Davis et al, 2003). It also disregards the positive aspirations and strategies adopted by many parents and children living in disadvantaged areas (Seaman et al, 2006).

Social barriers and exclusion

From the above perspective, social exclusion refers to people being unable to afford to participate in socially expected purchasing and activities. Emphasis is placed on financial reasons for being excluded but, in both everyday and sociological language, exclusion from mainstream activities and social groupings can occur for many other reasons. Notably, acceptability and exclusion are often crucially affected by membership of a particular status group based on personal characteristics, including gender, disability, ethnicity, age or appearance. Attitudes and policies based on equality and respect for diversity can help counter such tendencies. For instance, The Social Model has enabled disability to be recharacterised as a form of social oppression that prevents disabled people's inclusion in society (Barnes et al, 1999).

Individual and group behaviour may also lead to various forms of exclusion. Indeed, French policies of social 'insertion' have been fortified by the desire to manage youth crime and urban conflicts by reducing alienation related to both poverty and lack of social acceptance (Pitts, 1992). These forms of differentiation are generally the product of informal though powerful processes, but may be embodied in the law. That is particularly true of children as a class excluded from a range of activities and arenas on the basis of age. They are not legally allowed to take part in many activities, such as voting, full-time employment and driving. The law also sanctions more individualised exclusionary measures, including exclusion from school and compulsory placement away from home, which tend to promote stigma and separation from mainstream peer associations (Triseliotis et al, 1995; Munn et al, 2000).

It is also important to recognise that children can be perpetrators as well objects or victims of social exclusion. Bullying and racism by peers are major causes, not only of distress to the children who are picked on, but also of the isolation of individuals or the segregation of peer groupings that often results (Davis and Watson, 2002; Arshad et al, 2005). Gang activity both reflects and reinforces territorial boundaries, restricting children's safe movement and access to activities (Seaman et al, 2006).

Social ties and inclusion

Just as social relations can disregard or isolate individuals and groups, so they can also serve to integrate people not only into support networks but also into social and economic institutions (Granovetter, 1973). This has implications for inclusion in both the material and social senses. Over the past decade and more, the concept of social capital has been a popular means of expressing the link between properties of personal and neighbourhood networks and varied types of engagement and achievements, as with regard to employment, political activity, education, voluntary work and pro- or antisocial behaviour (Putnam, 1993; Portes, 1998). Close ties, trust and norms of reciprocal help are seen as crucial elements of social capital, which is usually framed in terms of positives, although close-knit groupings can sometimes be exclusive and oppressive (Portes, 1998). Statistical analyses have been carried out, leading to certain generalised conclusions that stereotype and blame (Morrow, 1999a, 1999b, 1999c). Deficiencies in children have been attributed to inadequate resources in, for instance, lone-parent or one-child households (Coleman, 1988), while other writers have explained lack of community cohesion in terms of local defects (Putnam, 2000).

A number of writers have suggested that this social capital perspective, which has often dominated writings in the US and UK, has been very male-orientated, has failed to consider the positive impact of children on parents, ignored different types of communities (especially those that are not related to geographical location), misunderstood multi-community membership and homogenised children by class or ethnic background (Backett-Milburn et al, 2000; Morrow, 2000). Another criticism concerns the emphasis on the parent–child (usually mother–child) bond and the importance of nuclear families at the expense of understanding the relevance of other family forms and relationships developed through wider kin, peer group, family, friends and neighbours (Morrow, 2000). This failure means that social capital theorists have been unable to consider whether 'non-traditional' families open a child up to more differentiated resources (Prout, 2000). In a globalised and liquid society, critical adaptability is arguably as crucial for children to acquire as conventional qualifications (Bauman, 2005).

On the other hand, Bourdieu's formulation of social capital emphasised the role of available resources, both external and internal, as reproducing inequalities. This draws attention to the importance of money, environment and services in accounting for the hardships and exclusions faced and the consequences for health and well-being (Wilkinson, 1996; Campbell et al, 2000; Seaman et al, 2006). A connection can be made here to the resource-based account of exclusion and redistributive approach to inclusion discussed by Levitas (1998).

Children's inclusion and exclusion

Children have been central, though also passive, in discussions of poverty and exclusion for several reasons. There is particular concern for their well-being, but also they are seen as a key target for intervention to modify socialisation processes that, in the eyes of many, will otherwise replicate in the next generation factors responsible for poverty. This may be criticised on two counts: from a more material distribution explanation of financial exclusion and from a social analysis of childhood perspective.

By emphasising the role of children as future adults and workers, social exclusion theorists have been guilty of ignoring the skills of children in the present and arguably placing too much emphasis on parents' roles in reproducing social capital. The concept of socialisation (top-down learning from adult to child) has been privileged at the expense of viewing children as present beings capable of agency and choice. For example, by explaining negative health outcomes in terms of adult perspectives of health and psychosocial stress that are related to economic insecurity, health writers play down children's own experiences of stress (for example, stress that is generated through peer relational inequality). Similarly, children's material, emotional and social resources are not confined to those they gain from parents. Children have the capacity to act independently of family and peer group (James and Prout, 1990; Waksler, 1991). Much writing on childhood and health inequality has overlooked the fact that children and young people often do not want to replicate their parents' belief systems and patterns of behaviour (Allatt, 1993). This has meant that there has been a failure to recognise different children's ability to manage a variety of locations (such as home and school); negotiate their own capital; and provide support for parents (Mayall, 1996; Backett-Milburn et al, 2000; Davis, 2000).

Little account has been taken of children's own definitions of poverty and inequality. In the rush to combat social exclusion, children have sometimes been left behind as participants. The rare studies that have explored children's experiences highlight the social relational aspects of children's lives in poverty (Davis et al, 2000; Ridge, 2002). Aid from relatives and others can mitigate the impact, whilst commercial, school and peer pressures often divert expenditure away from what parents or even children themselves see as essential (Middleton et al, 1995; Ridge, 2002). Poverty not only restricts current social lives, but tends to limit future horizons and the ability to fulfil career aspirations (Attree, 2006; Seaman et al, 2006). Children in low-income families may feel excluded for a number of reasons, for example:

- their home is not suitable for friends to visit;
- they live far away from their friends;
- they do not have efficient transport links to their social networks;
- they cannot afford specific clothing;
- they do not have access to school trips/events, books, project equipment, stationary, bags and meals (Ridge, 2002).

Children see schools and services as having a vital part to play in affecting their life chances through complementing what parents can do. A survey of young people living in 'underprivileged areas' showed they wanted, among other things, improvements in after-school care, homework assistance, sports provision and adult education facilities (De Winter et al, 1999). Besides such local resources, they also suggested that national policies (to encourage shorter working hours, for example) could help their parents more, so that they in turn could do more for their children.

Other research has shown how children's lives can be severely restricted not only by financial and service resources, but also by hazards in their local environment, related to both physical dangers and threatened or actual violence by young people or adults (Morrow, 2000; Seaman et al, 2006). Although not necessarily income-related, poor people are most likely to be living in high-stress neighbourhoods, while lack of money makes it harder to afford safe transport and recreation in such contexts. Children (and parents) deploy a range of knowledge and strategies to cope and keep safe in such areas, but that does not reduce the need to tackle the adversities they face.

In/exclusion have spatial dimensions (Vanderbeck and Dunkley, 2003). This applies to physical or geographical space, as well as to the more abstract social and political space. Poverty limits the financial capacity of children (and adults) to travel locally and over distance.

Families on low incomes tend to be overrepresented in neighbourhoods with poor-quality housing and amenities, often with higher levels of environmental hazard, so that children or their parents regard certain places near their homes as off-limits on safety grounds (Borland et al, 1998; Valentine, 2004). Likewise, exclusion resulting from social attitudes and behaviour can express itself in the failure to use spaces perceived as risky. For example, girls are often reluctant to enter areas in playgrounds used by boys for playing football (Blatchford et al, 1991), while fear and experience of bullying can lead to children avoiding locations where they may be at risk in and out of school (Rigby, 2002).

A key point made by children and young people living in disadvantaged circumstances is the lack of respect and choice they experience (Backett-Milburn et al, 2000; Davis et al, 2001), which means that there are few spaces and decisions over which they feel they have some control, at least outside the home (Prout, 2000). This corresponds with concerns voiced by children more generally about being excluded from central decision-making processes affecting them (Sinclair, 2004). In this sense, the notion of exclusion fits with the growing attention being paid to participation by children and young people.

This multidimensional view links material inequality with inequality based on a lack of access to social rights and relations. It requires us to examine the range of power relations that create exclusion:

> In these and other respects, social exclusion emerges as more dynamic, actor-oriented, multi-faceted and methodologically plural than poverty. The sources of social exclusion may therefore be found at the macro level in the consequences of mass unemployment, mass migration or de-industrialisation. Or they may be traced at the micro level in the particular experience of (sometimes self-) exclusion of individuals and groups which lack feelings of membership in and loyalty to their community: not only because of the scarcity of material resources or deprivation of social and legal rights, but rather because the contexts people live in and/or their personal biographies have not given them any motivation or chance to belong (Saraceno, 2001, p 2).

Participation

Unlike exclusion, 'participation' in policy discourses encompasses domains other than access to material resources. Attention has been given to political participation, usually in relation to voting proclivity, party and interest group membership and so-called apathy with conventional political processes. Another important strand has been with regard to service user participation, associated with lobbying to make the welfare state more responsive and accountable to those accessing its provisions and more recently procedures to give users a say, in local health services for instance (Beresford and Croft, 1993). A few of these initiatives have included children and young people (Wheelaghan et al, 1999; Lightfoot and Sloper, 2003). In relation to school, this trend has mostly been framed in terms of parental engagement, although school councils and other mechanisms have been developed with the aim of giving pupils opportunities to express their views.

Interestingly, the growing trend to involve consumers has not been very apparent in the field of poverty, where the views of 'the poor' in general have rarely been taken into account (Lister, 2003) and children's perspectives have been largely absent, though a few researchers have attempted to remedy this (Middleton et al, 1995; Ridge, 2002).

The past decade has witnessed a rapidly growing interest in participation by children and young people in collective decision making (Prout, 2000; Hill et al, 2004). For the most part, this has not centred on allowing children to vote as recommended by some (Holt, 2004), although there has been some support for the proposal to reduce the threshold for voting to 15 or 16 years. Instead, both government bodies and advocates have tended to concentrate on collective decision making about issues that directly affect children, including education, recreation, transport and the local environment (Sinclair, 2004). The Council of Europe has published a number of documents that set out how children can be involved in service planning. It has also funded European youth centres and foundations to act as resource/educational institutions and encouraged non-governmental youth organisations to enable young people to contribute to decision making. Consultations with children across Europe revealed that children were deeply aware of discrimination against other groups of children, felt that they were given 'lesser' status than adults and were disregarded during the development of public policy. In response to this experience, children wanted to play a greater part in contributing to policies and legislation that could impact on their lives (Lansdown, 2001).

Both bottom-up and top-down mechanisms have been introduced to promote children's participation, ranging from one-off events and consultations to involvement in institutionalised bodies through representation on adult decision-making bodies and the establishment of separate youth forums intended to feed into policy making (Stafford et al, 2003; Sinclair, 2004). Certain actions have involved particular groups of young people, notably those who are disabled or looked after (Thomas and O'Kane, 2000; Badham, 2004). All these developments can be seen as reflecting and contributing to a reshaping of adult–child relations more generally (Prout, 2005), with more acknowledgement given by adults to children's autonomy and expression rights.

Participation policies and practices have been criticised, mainly for being ineffective or misdirected, although less often for being wrong in principle. A number of authors argue that despite children having enormous enthusiasm for being involved in improving their life world, innovations such as school and youth councils often become undemocratic and fail to fulfil their original aims. Young people often regard them as tokenistic, unrepresentative in membership, adult-led in process and ineffective in acting on what children want (Alderson 1999a, 1999b, 1999c; Stafford et al, 2003; Tisdall and Davis, 2004; Hill, 2006).

The introduction of limited and context-specific participatory mechanisms can also be contrasted with what some see as a growing tendency to regulate children's activities, so that time that was formerly 'free' in the early years, after-school and during holidays is increasingly structured in ways similar to that of school itself (Moss and Petrie, 2002; Prout, 2002). From this point of view, a preferable approach is to tackle adult–child power relations more generally to support children's individual and collective self-empowerment (Cockburn, 2002).

Bringing together 'inclusion' and 'participation'

Connecting the concepts of social inclusion and participation as interrelated themes with respect to children offers the prospect of enhancing our understanding of the nature and consequences of several key interactions for children and young people. Social ex/inclusion debates and policies have centred on the importance of resources, mainly financial, with implications for resource distribution and redistribution among different groups in society and within families and households. To Lister (2002), a vital feature is power or its absence, while the consequence is the deprivation of citizenship rights, discussed further below. Discussion of participation has focused on power and influence in decision making. These are linked. Access to material resources is one of the major bases of power, while decisions made by state, commercial and voluntary organisations greatly affect the availability and cost of many particular services as well as incomes through setting the levels of remuneration for employment and government transfer payments. Linking these elements with respect to children are attitudes and beliefs held by adults, especially about children's capabilities, moral status and entitlements, which have tended to restrict children's involvement in the labour market, confer state benefits via parents, confine most collective decision making to those aged over 18 and limit the kinds of places where children can go.

Also participation opportunities can give young people knowledge and skills that make it easier for them to avoid or move out of poverty. For instance, a Danish project both promoted dialogue between adults and young people and gave the latter skills that helped them gain employment (Boukobza, 1998). There is, however, a danger in participatory programmes losing sight of wider goals about increasing children's power, influence and respect in general by concentrating on improving the life skills of a few contributors (Borland et al, 2001).

Rights and citizenship – a helpful link?

Examination of the position of children and young people in relation to social inclusion and participation is illuminated by ideas about children's rights and by recent debates about citizenship and children. The connection has been described by Lansdown (2001) as follows:

> Children are socially and politically excluded from most national and European institutions. They cannot vote. They have little or no access to the media. They have only limited access to the courts. They are not members of powerful lobbies that campaign and lobby governments such as the trade unions, the commercial sector or environmental groups. Without access to these processes which are integral to the exercise of democratic rights, children and their experience remain hidden from view and they are, in consequence, denied effective recognition as citizens (p 7).

Most formulations of children's rights, including the UN Convention on the Rights of the Child (UNCRC), distinguish between various kinds of survival and protective rights on the one hand and liberty and expression rights on the other. The first include rights to well-being and services (such as health), which require expenditure by families and governments. States are expected to prioritise provision for children in view of their vulnerability. Whereas children are privileged in these protective and provision rights, liberty and expression rights have traditionally been seen as either not applicable to children or as being qualified by age and understanding. The UNCRC and UK legislation tend to promote children's participation in decision making that directly affects them as individuals, though still subject to the age and capacity qualification (Archard, 1993). Involvement of children and young people in collective decision making has been slower to develop, usually taking the form of separate bodies like youth parliaments or limited consultations by or on behalf of government bodies (Sinclair, 2004).

Similarly, views about children as current or future citizens have been deployed with different implications for dealing with the material basis of social exclusion on the one hand and with participation in collective decision making on the other. Uncertainty exists about whether or not children should 'count' as citizens, depending in part on which of the several meanings of citizen is being considered, but also on ambivalent and changing ideas about children's status (Hill and Tisdall, 1997). In the broadest sense, the term citizen refers simply to membership of a particular community or nation, covering both children and adults. This seems to be the way in which the majority of both adults and young people conceptualise citizenship (Lister et al, 2003; Graham et al, 2005). On this basis, any child is entitled as a citizen to at least the minimum standard of living deemed appropriate in the society in which she or he lives, with appropriate policy mechanisms such as child benefit and the minimum wage aiming to bring this about. However, in another way, young people are sometimes excluded from ideas about the community, because of negative stereotyping of their behaviour as threatening to and hence outside the community (Hill and Wright, 2003).

In a second sense, common in political theory, citizenship connotes more specific responsibilities and rights that have often been seen as contingent on characteristics, especially age and ability, though in the past also gender and ethnicity. Notably, this has applied to voting to elect local or central governments, which in democratic societies has gradually been extended from a narrow base to all adults, but not children, who thereby become non-citizens, not full citizens or citizens 'in the making' (Marshall, 1997, p 25). This view of children as citizens in the making (Archard, 1993) has conventionally been taken to mean that children do not take part in adult decision making, but it is advocated that they be prepared for (full) citizenship by learning about democratic processes and practising some of the associated procedures and skills. Cockburn (1999a, 1999b, 2005) has argued that children's intellectual and moral abilities have often been underestimated in arguments for leaving them out of adult decision making. After considering the complexity of the issues, Lister (2005) concluded that it is helpful to consider which elements of 'being a citizen' apply to children and to what extent. She suggested that it is important that adults confer on children the rights to receive respect and to contribute to decision making that are associated with citizenship, though not necessarily all the responsibilities linked with adult citizenship. This highlights the layers of meaning within the word participation. Preparing for later decision making, contributing views and taking part in an actual decision-making process may all be seen as forms or stages of participation. Education programmes have mostly focused on helping children learn to be adult citizens, but some do promote the idea of children as current citizens, with rights and capacities to contribute to the improvement of schooling for themselves and others in the present (Holden and Clough, 1998).

Pupavac (2002) challenged current notions about citizenship as connoting certain kinds of participatory processes, which – she argues – privilege some groups (the politically and emotionally literate) over others (the reticent). She suggests that power is still central to participation and that those who organise participatory processes are incapable of using reflexive approaches to set aside their prejudices and control. Hence existing forms of participation are tokenistic and offer a false therapy for experiences that require more fundamental change. This raises questions about what kinds of processes can avoid reinforcing traditional power relations and enable children and young people to interact successfully with adults in ways that enable mutual interdependence. It also suggests that participatory processess require reflective practice by practitioners to examine assumptions about children, increase recognition of diversity and attune to children's own perspectives. Contrary to Pupavac, Davis and colleagues (2003) cite evidence that such awareness can develop and be effective in relation to disabled children. Similarly, Cairns (2001) described how adult service providers over time came to take more account of children's views about local transport through recognising the children's expertise as well as desires.

Creating spaces of inclusion, diversity and change

There are inevitable tensions in adult–child relations between adults' wish to control children and children's autonomy/self-realisation. These tensions owe as much to children's own interests (as perceived by the adults) as to issues of adult convenience. To optimise responses to this tension, changes are needed in age-related power relations as they affect all the social spaces of children's everyday lives. Reciprocal, mutually respectful interdependence does occur in some family settings and certain other contexts (Davis and Watson, 2000; Mayall, 2000; Shakespeare, 2000). Moss and Petrie (2002) were impressed with the practical application of such an approach in early years centres in Reggio-Emilia (Italy), which allowed children to give expression to their wishes and valued peer friendships as sources of fun, understanding and comfort.

Such an approach is applicable to help all children feel more 'included', but children brought up in low-income households and impoverished environments may require extra support and resources for their inclusion to be meaningful; and these need to be offered in ways that are sensitive to the wishes of the children themselves (Ridge, 2002; Seaman et al, 2006).

Conclusion

It has been argued that social exclusion takes many forms, some of which are rooted in the material circumstances of families and the economic conditions of societies, but others are connected with social relations, both intergenerational and intragenerational. One form of social exclusion describes the ways in which 'poor' children are marginalised through lack of material resources. Another refers to the ways in which all children are left out of most major forms of decision making outside family households, so that their preferences and wishes are not recognised by adults (Alderson, 1995).

Solutions to social exclusion may come in different forms; they may require a range of responses, including national policy changes, a development of local strategies and/or a shift in distributions of social, cultural and material resources. What is important is that the solutions are not simply defined by adults, be they parents, teachers, service providers or politicians (Davis et al, 2003). Any social policy related to children and young people should enable children themselves to define solutions to social exclusion. It is through such opportunities that children and young people will be able to promote more effective responses to their own life problems. At local level, too, it is necessary to encourage collaboration between adults, children and young people within a climate of listening, understanding and acting that is of mutual benefit to each group. This requires a complex and dynamic understanding of both exclusionary and inclusive processes. At the centre of this understanding should be a consideration of how participatory mechanisms reflect the interplay of economic, social and political relations affecting adults and children with multiple identities and roles, including but not confined to those of citizen, consumer and person.

References

Alderson, P. (1995) *Listening to Children*, London: Barnardo's.

Alderson, P. (1999a) 'Human rights and democracy in schools: do they mean more than "picking up litter and not killing whales"?', *International Journal of Children's Rights*, vol 7, pp 185-205.

Alderson, P. (1999b) 'Civic rights in schools', *Youth & Policy*, vol 64, no 1, pp 56-73.

Alderson, P. (1999c) 'Education and civic rights', *ChildRight*, vol 163, no 1, pp 6-9.

Allatt, P. (1993) 'Becoming privileged: the role of family process', in I. Bates and G. Riseborough (eds) *Youth and Inequality*, Buckingham: Open University Press.

Archard, D. (1993) *Children: Rights and Childhood*, London: Routledge.

Arshad, R., Diniz, F.A., O'Hara, P., Sharp, S., Syed, R. and Kelly, E. (2005) *Minority Ethnic Pupils' Experiences of School in Scotland (MEPESS)*, Edinburgh: Scottish Executive Education Department.

Attree, P. (2006) 'The social costs of child poverty: a systematic review of the qualitative evidence', *Children & Society*, vol 20, no 1, pp 54-66.

Backett-Milburn, K., Davis, J.M. and Cunningham-Burley, S. (2000) *Discussion of the Social and Cultural Context of Children's Lifestyles and the Production of Health Variations Relevant to Adult Risk of CVD*, London: National Heart Foundation.

Badham, B. (2004) 'Participation – for a change: disabled young people lead the way', *Children & Society*, vol 18, no 2, pp 143-54.

Barnes, C., Mercer, G. and Shakespeare, T. (1999) *Exploring Disability: A Sociological Introduction*, Cambridge: Polity Press.

Bauman, Z. (2005) *Liquid Life*, Cambridge: Polity Press.

Beresford, P. and Croft, S. (1993) *Citizen Involvement: A Practical Guide for Change*, London: Macmillan.

Blatchford, P., Creeser, R. and Mooney, A. (1991) 'Playground games and playtime: the children's view', in M. Woodhead, P. Light and R. Carr (eds) *Growing up in a Changing Society*, London: Routledge, pp 224-42.

Borland, M., Laybourn, A., Hill, M. and Brown, J. (1998) *Middle Childhood*, London: Jessica Kingsley.

Borland, M., Hill, M., Laybourn, A. and Stafford, A. (2001) *Improving Consultation with Children and Young People in Relevant Aspects of Policy-making and Legislation in Scotland*, Edinburgh: The Scottish Parliament.

Boukobza, E. (1998) *Keys to Participation: A Practitioner's Guide*, Strasbourg: Council of Europe Publishing.

Cairns, L. (2001) 'Investing in children: learning how to promote the rights of all children', *Children & Society*, vol 15, no 5, pp 347-60.

Campbell, C., Gillborn, D., Lunt, I., Sammons, P., Vincent, C., Warren, S. and Robertson, P. (2000) 'Developments in inclusive schooling', *Interchange 66*, Edinburgh: Scottish Executive.

Cockburn, T. (1999a) '"Children, fooles, and mad-men": children's relationship to citizenship in Britain from Thomas Hobbes to Bernard Crick', *The School Field*, vol x, no 3/4, pp 65-84.

Cockburn, T. (1999b) 'A historical perspective on the working contributions of children in Britain: 1800-1914', *Community, Work & Family*, vol 2, no 1, pp 33-50.

Cockburn, T. (2002) 'Concepts of social inclusion/exclusion and childhoods', Paper presented at ESRC Children and Social Inclusion Seminar, University of Edinburgh, December.

Cockburn, T. (2005) 'Children's participation in social policy: inclusion, chimera or authenticity?', *Social Policy & Society*, vol 4, no 2, pp 109-19.

Coleman, J.S. (1988) 'Social capital in the creation of human capital', *American Journal of Sociology*, vol 94, Supplement, pp 95-120.

Davis, J.M. (2000) 'The politics of the qualitative research role: researching children's perspectives of health and inequality', Paper presented to BSA/ESHM International Health in Transition Conference, York, September.

Davis, J., Watson, N. and Cunningham-Burley, S. (2000) 'Learning the lives of disabled children: developing a reflexive approach', in P. Christensen and A. James (eds) *Research with Children*, London: Falmer Press, pp 201-24.

Davis, J.M. and Watson, N. (2000) 'Disabled children's rights in everyday life: problematising notions of competency and promoting self-empowerment', *International Journal of Children's Rights*, vol 8, no 5, pp 211-28.

Davis, J.M. and Watson, N. (2002) 'Countering stereotypes of disability', in M. Corker and T. Shakespeare (eds) *Disability and Postmodernity*, London: Continuum.

Davis, J.M., Stewart, I., Adamson, L. and Cavanagh, S. (2001) *Young People's Concepts of Health and Wellbeing*, Greenhill Midlothian: Newbattle Cluster New Community School. .

Davis, J.M., Watson, N., Corker, M. and Shakespeare, T. (2003) 'Reconstructing disabled childhoods and social policy in the UK', in C. Hallett and A. Prout (eds) *Hearing the Voices of Children*, London: Falmer Press, pp 192-211.

De Winter, M., Kroneman, M. and Baerveldt, C. (1999) 'The social education gap: report of a Dutch peer-consultation project on family policy', *British Journal of Social Work*, vol 29, no 6, pp 903-14,

Graham, A., Shipway, B., Fitzgerald, R. and Whelan, J. (2005) *Children and Young People's Perspectives on Rights, Responsibilities, and Citizenship in Australia*, Australia: Centre for Children and Young People, Southern Cross University.

Granovetter, M. (1973) 'The strength of weak ties', *American Journal of Sociology*, vol 78, no 6, pp 1360-80.

Hantrais, L (1995) *Social Policy In The European Union*, Basingstoke: MacMillan.

Hill, M. and Tisdall, K. (1997) *Children and Society*, London: Longman.

Hill, M., Davis, J., Prout, A. and Tisdall, K. (2004) 'Moving the participation agenda forward', *Children & Society*, vol 18, no 2, pp 77-96.

Hill, M. (2006) 'Children's voices on ways of having a voice: children's and young people's perspectives on methods used in research and consultation', *Childhood*, vol 13, no 1, pp 69-89.

Holden, C. and Clough, N. (1998) *Children as Citizens: Education for Participation*, London: Jessica Kingsley.

Holt, L. (2004) 'The "voices" of children: de-centring empowering research relations', *Children's Geographies*, vol 2, no 1, pp 13-27.

James, A. and Prout, A. (1990) *Constructing and Reconstructing Childhood*, London: Falmer Press.

Lansdown, G. (2001) 'Children's participation in democratic decision-making', UNICEF (www.unicef-icdc.org/publications/pdf/insight6.pdf, accessed 1 February).

Leisering, L. and Leibfried, S. (1999) *Time and Poverty in Western Welfare States. United Germany in Perspective*, Cambridge, Cambridge University Press.

Levitas, R. (1998) *The Inclusive Society? Social Exclusion and New Labour*, London: Macmillan.

Lightfoot, J. and Sloper, P. (2003) 'Having a say in health services', *Children & Society*, vol 17, no 4, pp 277-91.

Lister, R. (2002) 'A politics of recognition and respect: involving people with experience of poverty in decision making that affects their lives', *Social Policy & Society*, vol 1, no 1, pp 37-46.

Lister, R. (2003) *Citizenship: Feminist Perspectives*, Basingstoke: Palgrave.

Lister, R. (2005) 'Investing in the citizen-workers of the future', in H. Hendrick (ed) *Child Welfare and Social Policy: An Essential Reader*, Bristol: The Policy Press, pp 449-62.

Lister, R., Smith, N., Middleton, S. and Cox, L. (2003) 'Young people talk about citizenship: empirical perspectives on theoretical and political debates', *Citizenship Studies*, vol 7, no 2, pp 235-53.

Marshall, K. (1997) *Children's Rights in the Balance: The Participation–Protection Debate*, Edinburgh: The Stationery Office.

Mayall, B. (1996) *Children, Health and the Social Order*, Buckingham: Open University Press.

Mayall, B. (2000) 'Conversations with children: working with generational issues', in P. Christensen and A. James (eds) *Research with Children*, London: Falmer Press, pp 120-35.

Middleton, S., Ashworth, K. and Walker, R. (1995) *Family Fortunes*, London: Child Poverty Action Group.

Morrow, V. (1999a) 'Conceptualising social capital in relation to the well-being of children and young people: a critical review', *Sociological Review*, vol 47, no 4, pp 744-65.

Morrow, V. (1999b) 'If you were a teacher, it would be harder to talk to you: reflections on qualitative research with children in school', *International Journal of Social Research Methodology*, vol 1, no 4, pp 297-313.

Morrow, V. (1999c) '"We are people too": children's and young people's perspectives on children's rights and decision-making in England', *International Journal of Children's Rights*, vol 7, no 2, pp 149-70.

Morrow, V. (2000) '"It's cool, 'cos you can't give us detentions and things, can you?" Reflections on research with children', in P. Milner and B. Carolin (eds) *Time to Listen to Children*, London: Routledge, pp 203-15.

Moss, P. and Petrie, P. (2002) *From Children's Services to Children's Spaces*, London: Routledge.

Munn, P., Lloyd, G. and Cullen, M.A. (2000) *Alternatives to Exclusion*, London: Sage Publications.

Murray, C. (1990) *The Emerging British Underclass*, London: IEA.

Percy-Smith, J. (2000) *Policy Responses to Social Exclusion*, Buckingham: Open University Press.

Pierson, J. (2002) *Tackling Social Exclusion*, London: Routledge

Pitts, J. (1992) 'Juvenile justice policy in England and Wales', in J. Coleman and C. Warren-Adamson (eds) *Youth Policy in the 1990s*, London: Routledge.

Portes, A. (1998) 'Social capital: its origins and applications in modern sociology', *Annual Review of Sociology*, vol 24, no 1, pp 1-24.

Prout, A. (2000) *The Body, Childhood and Society*, Basingstoke: Macmillan.

Prout, A. (2002) 'Researching children as social actors: an introduction for the Children 5-16 programme', *Children & Society*, vol 16, no 2, pp 67-76.

Prout, A. (2005) 'Children's participation: control and self-realisation in British late modernity', in H. Hendrick (ed) *Child Welfare and Social Policy: An Essential Reader*, Bristol: The Policy Press, pp 463-74.

Pupavac, V. (2002) 'The international children's rights regime', in D. Chandler (ed) *Rethinking Human Rights*, Basingstoke: Palgrave, pp 57-79.

Putnam, R.D. (1993) 'The prosperous community', *American Prospect*, vol 4, no 13, pp 35-42.

Putnam, R.D. (2000) *Bowling Alone*, New York, NY: Simon & Schuster.

Ridge, T. (2002) *Childhood Poverty and Social Exclusion*, Bristol: The Policy Press.

Rigby, K. (2002) *New Perspectives on Bullying*, London: Jessica Kingsley.

Room, G. (1995) *Beyond the threshold: The measurement and analysis of social exclusion*, Bristol: The Policy Press.

Saraceno, C. (2001) 'Social exclusion. Cultural roots and diversities of a popular concept', Paper resented at Social Exclusion and Children Conference, Institute for Child and Family Policy, Columbia University, (www.childpolicyintl.org/intpublications.html).

Seaman, P., Turner, K., Hill, M., Stafford, A. and Walker, M. (2006) *Parenting and Children's Resilience in Disadvantaged Communities*, York: Joseph Rowntree Foundation.

Shakespeare, T. (2000) 'The social relations of care', in G. Lewis, S. Gewirtz and J. Clarke (eds) *Rethinking Social Policy*, London: Sage Publications.

Sinclair, R. (2004) 'Participation in practice: making it meaningful, effective and sustainable', *Children & Society*, vol 18, no 2, pp 106-18.

Stafford, A., Laybourn, A., Walker, M. and Hill, M. (2003) 'Having a say: children and young people talk about consultation', *Children & Society*, vol 17, no 5, pp 361-73.

Thomas, N. and O'Kane, C. (2000) 'Discovering what children think', *British Journal of Social Work*, vol 30, no 6, pp 819-36.

Tisdall, K. and Davis, J. (2004) 'Making a difference? Bringing children's and young people's views into policy-making', *Children & Society*, vol 18, no 2, pp 131-42.

Townsend, P. (1979) *Poverty in the United Kingdom*, Harmondsworth: Penguin.

Triseliotis, J., Borland, M., Hill, M. and Lambert, L. (1995) *Teenagers and the Social Work Services*, London: HMSO.

Valentine, G. (2004) *Public Space and the Culture of Childhood*, Aldershot: Ashgate.

Vanderbeck, R.M. and Dunkley, C.M. (2003) 'Young people's narratives of rural–urban difference', *Children's Geographies*, vol 1, no 2, pp 165-80.

Waksler, F.C. (1991) *Studying the Social Worlds of Children*, London: Falmer Press.

Wheelaghan, S., Hill, M., Borland, M., Lambert, L. and Triseliotis, J. (1999) *Looking After Children in Scotland*, Edinburgh: Central Research Unit, Scottish Office.

Wilkinson, R. (1996) *Unhealthy Societies*, London: Routledge.

Part One
Children and poverty

TWO

Childhood poverty: a barrier to social participation and inclusion

Tess Ridge

Participation is a fundamental principle of social inclusion, and 'fitting in' and 'joining in' with the everyday activities and expectations of peers is a driving force in children's lives. Without satisfactory opportunities for participation, children's social lives can be disrupted and restricted. For children who are poor, gaining access to adequate resources and opportunities for social participation is a significant concern. Poverty can have a profound impact on participation, excluding children from social experiences available to other more affluent children, and encroaching on their capacity to develop and maintain satisfactory social relationships.

The voices of children who are poor are some of the least likely to be heard in policy and practice; they are doubly silenced both as children and as part of the constituency of the poor. Poverty is a stigmatised social position, and perceptions of child poverty are often informed by contradictory discourses of poor children as either vulnerable and at risk, or dangerous, out of control and socially threatening (Davis and Bourhill, 1997; Scraton, 1997; Lee, 2001). Therefore, to begin to comprehend the meaning and experience of poverty in childhood, it is essential that researchers, policy makers and practitioners develop an understanding of child poverty that is grounded in the realities of children's everyday lives and experiences.

In 2003/04, there were more than 3.5 million children living below the poverty line in the UK (Flaherty et al, 2004). For these children, poverty is an everyday lived experience, and research shows that the effects of being a poor child in an affluent society can permeate every aspect of that child's life (Ridge, 2002). This chapter explores the impact that poverty can have on children's capacity for participation and social inclusion. It engages directly with children's accounts of their social lives, and reveals some of the issues and concerns that they themselves identify as problematic. It is based on findings from qualitative child–

centred research carried out with children and young people who are living in low-income families in the UK.

The chapter draws on two main research studies: first, research carried out with children and young people living in families in receipt of Income Support (Ridge, 2002); and second, findings from the Families, Work and Care Study, a longitudinal, qualitative study[1] of the lives and experiences of children living in low-income, working, lone-mother households. Both studies used child-centred research methods that treated children as informed social actors in the context of their own lives and within their families (James and Prout, 1997; Christensen and James, 2000)[2].

Although based on findings from both studies, the chapter draws most heavily on new empirical findings from the Families, Work and Care Study. This research is ongoing and involves in-depth interviews with 61 children and their lone mothers (50), exploring their expectations and experiences of paid work over a period of two to three years. One of the main aims of the project is to explore how families negotiate the everyday challenges of sustaining low-income employment over time. The findings presented here are from the first round of child interviews carried out in 2004.

The children in the study were aged between 8 and 14 at the start of the project[3]. Their mothers had all recently come off Income Support and entered low-paid employment. They were also receiving Working Tax Credits – a low-income wage supplement[4]. There were 31 girls and 30 boys; six children came from minority ethnic backgrounds and a further five had dual heritage. Interviews were carried out in various areas of England – both rural and urban – in the North, the West and the Midlands.

The first stage of the study explored children's perceptions of their lives both before and after their mothers moved into employment. This chapter focuses on children's accounts of their lives before their mothers moved into employment, when they were living in families that were receiving Income Support (the lowest level of social assistance). Their accounts reveal the social and economic challenges that many of them faced on a regular basis, and highlight some of the effects that poverty and disadvantage can have on children's opportunities for social participation.

The impact of poverty on children's lives

To explore the impact of poverty on children's capacity for participation, the chapter focuses on three elements of social participation that previous research had revealed to be particularly problematic (Middleton et al, 1994; Shropshire and Middleton, 1999; Daly and Leonard, 2002; Ridge, 2002). These are: participation in social activities; sustaining and negotiating social networks and friendships; and inclusion and exclusion within the school environment. Each of these provides some textural insight into childhood itself, and highlights the importance of understanding and addressing children's experiences within it.

Participation in social activities and shared leisure opportunities

Opportunities for participation and the overall feeling of being included and valued are profound issues for children from low-income homes. Their concerns about social exclusion coalesce particularly around the issue of leisure opportunities. As the commodification of childhood intensifies, children's access to economic resources increases and they are now perceived as major consumers in their own right (Gunter and Furnham, 1998; Schor, 2004).

In the UK, as elsewhere, children's engagement with commodified leisure experiences is increasing with the growth of private leisure centres, expensive sports complexes, bowling alleys, multiscreen cinema complexes and so on (Mizen et al, 2001; Ridge, forthcoming). However, the costs of participating and sharing in these experiences are often high and poor children find it hard to gain access to them. Furthermore, not only do consumer goods and services play an important role in children's lives, they also act as a significant means of communication between children and young people (Willis et al, 1990; Miles, 2000; Hengst, 2001). The need to stay connected and identified with the prevailing trends and fashions of their peers presents particular challenges for low-income children who are caught up in the changing social and material conditions of childhood (Middleton et al, 1994; Daly and Leonard, 2002; Ridge, 2002).

Reflecting on their lives before their mothers moved into employment, children in the Families, Work and Care Study indicated that their social lives were often severely constrained by their financial circumstances. Like children in Ridge's previous study (2002), they experienced considerable difficulties gaining access to the social and leisure opportunities enjoyed by their peers. As Josie explains:

> I wanted to go swimming quite a lot, but couldn't and I wanted to go to the cinema but I couldn't.

Children report checks and exclusions at every level of engagement from initial difficulties in obtaining transportation to and from activities, to the attendant costs of entrance fees, and appropriate equipment and clothing. These financial hurdles prevent many low-income children from sharing in the everyday expectations of more affluent children – to go swimming, attend the cinema and enjoy the facilities of local sports complexes. The inability to participate in shared social activities is often exacerbated for children by the realisation of the opportunities available to their peers. In their accounts, children reveal an intense awareness that their friends and other children are enjoying a range of activities from which they feel excluded. This is Lewis talking about how he felt when his mum was out of work and his friends were off doing things at the weekends without him:

> Couldn't do nothing on the weekends, just stayed in, couldn't go out with my friends and go to the shop or anything like that, so ... bit boring.

When children want to participate in activities and opportunities that their more affluent friends take for granted, they can be faced with uncertainty and moral dilemmas within their homes. Children who are poor are acutely aware of the financial restrictions that operate within their homes and often try to tailor their needs accordingly (Ridge, 2002). However, this tends to conflict with the drive to be included and accepted by friends. This is Karen describing how difficult it was for her and her sister when their mum was out of work:

> At that time when we didn't have no money, yeah, because it was real hard to just do anything 'cos all our mates would be doing everything and we'd think – 'oh I want to do that'. We'd try and ask mum, but then we'd think no, because what if she says, 'well look I've only got a bit of money', then we'd feel guilty for asking, so we didn't ask her.

For Karen, the tensions between wanting to join in with friends and trying to deal with financial pressures within her family were an ongoing challenge. Special occasions and school holidays can also expose children's inability to participate, especially when others are going to the swimming pool, leisure centre or just into town. This can be compounded by the fact that many low-income children do not get the opportunity to go away for a summer holiday (Ghate and

Hazel, 2002; Ridge, 2002). This is Zoe talking about the rise of tensions in her house during the summer holidays:

> We always start rowing all the time 'cos I always ask for money all the time nearly, 'cos I want to go to town and there's nowt else to do ... just to go to town. And every time you go to town you need money.

Zoe is upset by the thought that her friends are getting things and having more money than her: 'That's what I hate about it ... mates getting and I don't'. There are clear tensions within Zoe's family, yet many low-income parents play a vital role in supporting children and working with them to negotiate the challenges of poverty and disadvantage (Backett-Milburn et al, 2003).

Access to adequate and affordable transport is also a key concern for many children. Living in a poor household adds an extra dimension to issues of mobility and access, particularly in rural areas (Davis and Ridge, 1997; Matthews and Limb, 2000). For children like Jason, his mother's unemployment had meant great uncertainty about getting out and about and visiting friends.

> When Mum didn't work, we couldn't go and see other people 'cos we didn't really 'ave a car or anythin', an' stuff.

Lack of transport can also affect reciprocity; without transport to share, children are often unable to play a full part in the everyday currency of shared transport commitments, including lifts to clubs and activities and participation in key social events like sleepovers. This can have a knock-on effect on children's friendships and social relationships.

Sustaining and negotiating social networks and friendships

Previous research with low-income children has shown that making and sustaining friendships is an area where children struggle particularly hard to maintain their social status and stay connected with their peers (Ridge, 2002). The capacity to develop desired friendships and extend social networks is fundamentally important to children's lives. Friendships represent valuable social assets for children, and can play a central role in the development and maintenance of human and social capital (James et al, 1998; Pahl, 2000). Peer friendship groups also play a significant role as arbiters of identity, providing the context, and parameters, in which teenagers construct and reconstruct their identities (Miles, 2000). Without secure social relationships and wider social networks, children are particularly vulnerable to social isolation and exclusion (Ridge and Millar, 2000).

Restricted access to shared social and leisure opportunities, coupled with limited access to affordable and suitable transport, and a weakened capacity for reciprocity, can all affect children's capacity to meet up with friends and widen social networks. Poor children can experience considerable difficulties maintaining their friendships, especially outside school. At school, secure friendships are also important, especially at times of transition between primary and secondary (Pratt and George, 2005).

One of the things that children appear to fear most is social isolation and being seen as different or 'other' because they are poor. The consequences of being singled out can be bullying, and children in previous research have reported a high degree of bullying (Ridge, 2002). For children like Clarke and Jake, the threat of bullying is very real. Clarke lives on a large estate in the north of England and, before his mother was working, he felt that his family was 'real poor' and often short of food. He has been badly bullied both at school and in his neighbourhood. Here he is talking about his experiences of going to the local shop:

> I went to the shop, I walked back the normal way we usually go and I was getting stones chucked at me and everything and it split open my cans.

Clarke is now very careful when he is out in his neighbourhood in case he gets 'battered' again. Jake has also experienced bullying in the street where he lives. He relates this directly to being poor. Here he is talking about what his life was like before his mother was working:

> It was really different, 'cos some of the other friends used to pick on us 'cos we didn't have enough money.

Since his mother has been working, their financial situation has improved and Jake feels that this has made a difference:

> Now lots has changed. These friends don't pick on us. They really like to play with us and everything. So a lot's changed.

The visibility of poverty can be particularly difficult for children to overcome, and even being able to conform to current fashion norms and expectations may make a difference to how children feel about themselves and how others view them.

Although unlikely to be identified by adults as an issue of importance with regard to the well being of low-income children, children themselves are highly likely to identify clothing and fashion expectations as a key issue in relation to inclusion and acceptance by peer groups (Morrow, 2001; Ridge, 2002). As Angie states, 'you don't feel very good when you haven't got much clothes'. For Angie, clothes are important and she wants to be able to dress like her friends; for her, wearing the 'right' clothes can make a difference to her overall well-being and confidence. This is Shannon talking about how essential it is to have similar clothes to her peers:

> I feel more confidence wearing something like everyone else is wearing and I don't really like going on the streets wearing like really old stuff.

Consumer goods, especially clothing, shoes and personal accessories, are culturally and symbolically powerful markers of both individuality and belonging (Willis et al, 1990). While 'taking part' and ensuring social participation and inclusion is a fundamental drive for children, 'looking the part' is also playing an increasingly meaningful role in their lives. These issues take on further significance in the social arena of school life, where feelings of inclusion and exclusion can be felt particularly acutely.

Inclusion and exclusion within the school environment

The school environment is a significant site of social encounters and ensuring that poor children have a satisfactorily inclusive school experience should be of fundamental concern, to both policy makers and educators. The opportunity to develop social capital and secure social identities should be an integral part of every child's school experiences. However, previous research has revealed that low-income children often feel excluded *within* their schools, and many children report feeling bullied, isolated and left out at critical stages of their academic careers (Ridge, 2002).

The costs of maintaining an adequate school presence and acquiring appropriate materials for examinations and school activities are problematic for children. Although education is considered to be 'free' in the UK, the costs associated with education are rising and present a substantial problem for low-income parents (Tanner et al, 2003). In many ways, wearing school uniform represents a real and symbolic marker of belonging and, in general, conforming to school uniform expectations is essential for secure participation in the shared school identity. This fundamental connection to school life is undermined for many poor children by the challenges presented by poverty. In the absence of government support in the form of school uniform grants, the costs of buying and maintaining school uniform has become prohibitive, and children like Hester are struggling to ensure that they are able to conform to their school's clothing codes:

> My dad he didn't really help with it because he was being a bit nasty at that time. So he was a bit, like, not helping my mum with the money so I was trying not to get my school uniform ripped or dirty or try not to grow so the trousers would get too small or something, you know.

School trips are also an essential component of shared school experiences, and children value them greatly. Previous research has found that many low-income children are missing out on school trips, with the costs of school trips particularly problematic for children in large families and in families reliant on means-tested benefits (Ridge, 2002; Tanner et al, 2003). In Ridge's previous study (2002), some children were excluding themselves from school trips by not taking letters home or asking their parents for the money to attend. This was again apparent in the Families, Work and Care Study as children like Ashia strove to protect their parents and reduce financial pressures in their families by lowering their hopes and expectations at school:

> I don't like asking for money to go on school trips because, sometimes I feel, like, we struggling to come up with the money to go on school trips.

A further disadvantage identified by some children was the cost of everyday items for school, like books and equipment. Karen was concerned that she would not have the right books for her GCSE courses. This was particularly problematic when teachers indicated that these were essential equipment for doing well on the course. Here Karen explains her dilemma; unable to expose herself to her teachers and afraid to put pressure on her mother, she waits and hopes:

When we went to school and teachers would say that we needed this and it would cost so much money. Well, I'd sit there and think – well, hang on – have we got enough for that? But I didn't want to say anything to the teachers because then I'd feel embarrassed. So I kept it to myself really and then just waited until mum would give me some money and I'd put some of it away and then she'd give me the rest for it.

Children spend a considerable part of their lives at school and the quality of their school experience can have a substantial impact on both their childhoods and potentially their future well-being as adults.

Negotiating poverty and exclusion

How do children mediate and negotiate these experiences of poverty and exclusion? Without sufficient money to go into town with friends or take part in activities, children find themselves caught by their circumstances. Poverty and disadvantage place considerable constraints on children's capacity for autonomous action and their ability to negotiate and resolve their social dilemmas.

Previous research has shown that children are very protective of their parents and this can take many forms, including self-denial of need and the moderation of demands. For some children, this can mean self-exclusion from activities – by not pursuing opportunities or failing to draw attention to activities perceived by them as too costly – in a bid to alleviate pressures within the home (Ridge, 2002). These children are active social agents and they employ a range of strategies to try to mediate or mitigate their circumstances. One way in which children can gain some measure of control over their circumstances is to generate alternative ways of gaining access to economic resources that can be used to enable them to participate more fully with their peers. Taking on part-time employment is one example, providing an opportunity for a measure of freedom and independence.

Income from paid employment can release children, to some degree, from the economic constraints of their family environment and render them economic agents in their own right. For the younger children under the legal age for employment, this strategy is not so easily available, although previous research with low-income children has shown that many of them are working under the legal age requirement (Daly and Leonard, 2002; Ridge, 2002). Children in the study who were too young to work strained towards employment as a potential way out of their social predicament. Alfie is 12 years old and feels excluded from the opportunities and activities of other children of his age. He is acutely aware that his friends have been meeting and sharing experiences from which he has been excluded. Although he did not work at the time of the interview, he was very keen to do so. His reasons were clear:

> Then I'll be able to go skating every week, I'll be able to go swimming with my friends. I'll be able to do things like that.

Peter is 11 years old and lives in a rural area where he is heavily reliant on buses for transport. His mother does not have a car and his school draws from a wide catchment area. This means that his opportunities to meet up with friends and take part in their everyday out-of-school activities are heavily compromised. For Peter, autonomous income from employment holds out the promise of much greater inclusion and connection with his friends:

> Well, I would be able to probably get my own bus fare and stuff so I'd be able to get out more and I'd be able to spend, like, nights out with my friends, cinema and stuff.

Although a high percentage of children and young people in the UK work, the situation of children on a low income is less clear (Mizen et al, 2001). There is some evidence that when children in poorer families do work they may take on more jobs and work for longer hours than their more affluent counterparts (Middleton et al, 1997). Therefore, although employment empowers children and allows them to gain a degree of inclusion and participation that they would not otherwise have, it is not without risk, and there is considerable tension between children's employment and the expectations and requirements of schoolwork. Children themselves are not unaware of these tensions and often have difficult choices to make between their present social well-being, their academic performance and, by extension, their future economic well-being (Ridge, 2002).

What do children's accounts tell us?

In their accounts of their lives before their mothers were working, the children in the study present a very similar profile of social and economic disadvantage and exclusion to that revealed in previous research with children living in Income Support households (Ridge, 2002). The issues and concerns they raise reveal the social and economic pressures that children experience on an everyday basis among their peers. Central to these experiences is the sustained challenge that poverty makes on children's capacity for social participation and inclusion. A key aspect of participation in children's lives is their ability to participate effectively and enrichingly in the activities and opportunities that are available to other, more affluent children. It is clear that barriers to participation are occurring at all levels of children's lives, including the individual, the social and, in the case of schooling, the structural and institutional.

Children in the Families, Work and Care Study came from families where the mothers had moved from Income Support into low-paid employment. Findings from the study show that for those children whose mothers had found stable employment, the family's increased income – bolstered by state support in the form of Tax Credits[5] – had resulted in an overall improvement in their lives[6]. However, for other children in the study, the experience was less positive, especially for those whose mothers found it difficult to work for reasons including insecure labour markets, ill health and problems with childcare (Millar, forthcoming). Of the 61 children in the study at the first stage of interview, 11 were living in families that had already dropped back out of the labour market and returned to Income Support. These children are likely to be especially vulnerable to further poverty, as research has shown that repeated transitions between benefits and employment can result in a high risk of poverty (Adelman et al, 2003).

Implications for government policies

Current policies directed at alleviating child poverty focus in general on three main areas: support for children, primarily through the education system, but also through greatly enhanced provision of services for children in their early years; support for parents, mainly directed at making work pay, childcare and parenting initiatives; and changes in fiscal support for children and their families through the tax and benefit system (DSS, 1999). However, anti-poverty measures to improve income have been firmly wedded to the welfare-to-work model, especially for lone mothers. To address the needs children identify here, a far more radical child-centred approach is needed. As Bradshaw (2002) argues, many poor children do not live in families where the parents work, or where employment is an option or a possibility. The experiences reported here relate, in general, to children's lives before their mothers were working when they were living in households receiving Income Support. Clearly, increasing financial support for children by raising Income Support levels is a fundamentally necessary step towards improving children's lives. Income Support is the safety-net provision for children and their families and plays a significant role in supporting the poorest children. However, current levels of Income Support are lower than the poverty line (Dornan, 2005). Although the government has increased child premiums in Income Support through the introduction of Child Tax Credits, it has not increased adult premiums, so families receiving Income Support are still living on low incomes overall. To truly benefit children, an adequate level of income is needed to support parents as well as their children.

Alongside increased financial support for the lowest-income families, it is necessary to develop a range of policy measures that would respond directly and meaningfully to children's expressed needs. Central to this must be measures to facilitate children's participation and inclusion within their neighbourhoods, including improved and accessible leisure services, increased concessions and free leisure cards. Transport can be addressed through the use of imaginative solutions such as the free transport for under-16s initiative in London.

The current Labour government has shown a commitment to listen to children and increase the overall participation of children in policy matters (CYPU 2001; Hallett and Prout, 2003). However, building participation and developing policies and practices that respond to children's concerns meaningfully presents a challenge (Sinclair, 2004; Tisdall and Davis, 2004), not least because children often identify issues and concerns that adults may not recognise as significant (Hill, 1999). This can be particularly problematic for low-income children, who are often the subjects of policy intervention but rarely involved in the identification or formulation of policies directed at their needs.

Education has become a key area of intervention in disadvantaged children's lives, and low-income children are seen as particularly at risk of 'failing' at school (Ermisch et al, 2001). As a result, children who are poor are all too easily conceptualised as 'poor' future adults, and policies directed towards the improvement of children's academic performances at school are informed by a model of children as future citizens and workers – there is considerably less attention paid to the quality of social inclusion and participation that poor children are experiencing in childhood.

Well-being at school is being compromised by inequitable education experiences. Despite acknowledging that poor children are missing out on school opportunities and learning experiences, there has been a marked absence of policies that could encourage equity and inclusion in schools (DfEE, 2001). Instead, policies are aimed at improving academic results, raising literacy and numeracy standards, and reducing the incidence of school exclusions and truancy (DSS, 1999). These measures – welcome though they are – do not address the issues and concerns identified by low-income children, here and elsewhere, about social inclusion and adequate participation in school life. When Tisdall and Davis (2004) traced the influence of children's and young people's contributions to developing policies for schooling in Scotland, they found that even when children identified social aspects of schooling to be equally as important and in need of support as academic learning, the Scottish Executive did not address these needs in its policy response.

Participation is a fundamental requirement for satisfactory social inclusion, and constraints on children's capacity to participate meaningfully with their peers leave them intensely vulnerable to marginalisation and social exclusion. The levels of economic and social support provided for children have a critical impact on their capacity to 'fit in' and 'join in' with their peers at home and at school. Creative solutions in service delivery[7] are needed to respond to the concerns expressed by children. Policy makers and practitioners need to ensure that adequate, effective and affordable participation becomes a guiding principle for anti-poverty policies and practices.

Notes
[1] Ongoing research study by T. Ridge and J. Millar, Centre for Analysis of Social Policy, University of Bath. ESRC funding Award No (RES-000-23-1079).

[2] Child-centred research requires an informed, considered and ethical approach at every stage of the research process (Alderson, 1995). To protect confidentiality, children's names are replaced by pseudonyms.

[3] Some children who were 14 when the sample was drawn were 15 at the time of interview.

[4] The sample was drawn from Inland Revenue records and we [T. Ridge and J. Millar] are very grateful for their help in this.

[5] Tax Credits provide a higher standard of support to families with children whose parent(s) are in work than is available for non-working families with children who are receiving Income Support.

[6] These findings are based on interviews carried out during the first year following the mother's move into employment. This is a longitudinal study and future interviews and analysis will examine the sustainability of employment and improved child well-being.

[7] For example, swipe cards for school meals that do not single out children who are receiving free school meals from other children.

References

Adelman, L., Middleton, S. and Ashworth, K. (2003) *Britain's Poorest Children: Severe and Persistent Poverty and Social Exclusion*, London, Save the Children.

Alderson, P. (1995) *Listening to Children: Children, Ethics and Social Research*, Ilford: Barnardo's.

Backett-Milburn, K., Cunningham-Burley, S. and Davis, J. (2003) 'Contrasting lives, contrasting views? Understandings of health inequalities from children in differing social circumstances', *Social Science & Medicine*, vol 57, no 4, pp 613-23.

Bradshaw, J. (2002) 'Child poverty and child outcomes', *Children & Society*, vol 16, issue 2, pp 131-140.

Christensen, P. and James, A. (2000) 'Introduction: researching children and childhood: cultures of communication', in P. Christensen and A. James (eds) *Research with Children: Perspectives and Practices*, London: Routledge Falmer, pp 1-9.

CYPU (Children and Young People's Unit) (2001) *Learning to Listen: Core Principles for the Involvement of Children and Young People*, London: Department for Education and Employment.

Daly, M. and Leonard, M. (2002) *Against all Odds: Family Life on a Low Income in Ireland*, Dublin: Institute of Public Administration.

Davis, H. and Bourhill, M. (1997) '"Crisis": the demonization of children and young people', in P. Scraton (ed) *'Childhood' in 'Crisis'?*, London: UCL Press Ltd.

Davis, J. and Ridge, T. (1997) *Same Scenery, Different Lifestyle: Rural Children on a Low Income*, London: The Children's Society.

DfEE (Department for Education and Employment) (2001) *Schools Building on Success, Raising Standards, Promoting Diversity, Achieving Results*, Norwich: The Stationery Office.

Dornan, P. (2005) 'Halving child poverty: a truly historic third term?', *Poverty*, 121, pp 17-19.

DSS (Department of Social Security) (1999) *Opportunity for All: Tackling Poverty and Social Exclusion*, Cm 4445, London: The Stationery Office.

Ermisch, J., Francescanii, M. and Pevalin, D. (2001) *Outcomes for Children of Poverty*, Department for Work and Pensions Research Report No 158, Leeds: Corporate Document Services.

Flaherty, J., Veit-Wilson, J. and Dornan, P. (2004) *Poverty: The Facts*, London: Child Poverty Action Group.

Ghate, D. and Hazel, N. (2002) *Parenting in Poor Environments*, Jessica Kingsley: London.

Gunter, B. and Furnham, A. (1998) *Children as Consumers*, London: Routledge.

Hallett, C. and Prout, A. (2003) *Hearing the Voices of Children: Social Policy for a New Century*, London: Routledge Falmer.

Hengst, H. (2001) 'Rethinking the liquidation of childhood', in M. Du Bois-Reymond, H. Sunker and H. Hermann Kruger (eds) *Childhood in Europe: Approaches, Trends and Findings*, New York, NY: Peter Lang.

Hill, M. (1999) 'What's the problem? Who can help? The perspectives of children and young people on their well-being and on helping professionals', *Journal of Social Work Practice*, vol 13, no 2, pp 135-45.

James, A. and Prout, A. (1997) *Constructing and Reconstructing Childhood: Contemporary Issues in the Sociological Study of Childhood*, London: Falmer Press.

James, A., Jenks, C. and Prout, A. (1998) *Theorizing Childhood*, Cambridge: Polity Press.

Lee, N. (2001) *Childhood and Society: Growing up in an Age of Uncertainty*, Buckingham: Open University Press.

Matthews, H. and Limb, M. (2000) *Exploring the 'Fourth Environment': Young People's Use of Place and Views on Their Environment*, ESRC Children 5-16 Research Briefing, Swindon: Economic and Social Research Council.

Middleton, S., Ashworth, K. and Walker, R. (1994) *Family Fortunes*, London: Child Poverty Action Group.

Middleton, S., Ashworth, K. and Braithwaite, I. (1997) *Small Fortunes*, York: Joseph Rowntree Foundation.

Miles, S. (2000) *Youth Lifestyles in a Changing World*, Buckingham: Open University Press.

Millar, J. (2006) 'Better-off in work? Work, security and welfare for lone mothers', in C. Glendinning and P. Kemp (eds) *Cash and Care*, Bristol: The Policy Press, pp 171-85.

Mizen, P., Pole, C. and Bolton, A. (eds) (2001) 'Why be a school age worker?', in P. Mizen, C. Pole and A. Bolton (eds) *Hidden Hands: International Perspectives on Children's Work and Labour*, London: Routledge Falmer, pp 37-54.

Morrow, V. (2001) 'Young people's explanations and experiences of social exclusion: retrieving Bourdieu's concept of social capital', *International Journal of Sociology and Social Policy*, vol 12, no 4, pp 37-63.

Pahl, R. (2000) *On Friendship*, Cambridge: Polity Press.

Pratt, S. and George, R. (2005) 'Transferring friendship: girls' and boys' friendships in the transition from primary to secondary school', *Children & Society*, vol 19, no 1, pp 16-25.

Ridge, T. (forthcoming) 'Negotiating childhood poverty: children's subjective experiences of life on a low income', in J. Qvortrup and H, Wintersberger (eds) *Children's Economic and Social Welfare Child Welfare*, EU Cost Action 19, Odense: University Press of Southern Denmark.

Ridge, T. (2002) *Childhood Poverty and Social Exclusion: From a Child's Perspective*, Bristol: The Policy Press.

Ridge, T. and Millar, J. (2000) 'Excluding children: autonomy, friendship and the experience of the care system', *Social Policy & Administration*, vol 34, no 2, pp 160-75.

Schor, J. (2004) *Born to Buy: The Commercialized Child and the New Consumer Culture*, New York, NY: Simon & Schuster.

Scraton, P. (1997) 'Whose "childhood"? What "crisis"?', in P. Scraton (ed) *'Childhood' in 'Crisis'?*, London: UCL Press Ltd.

Shropshire, J. and Middleton, S. (1999) *Small Expectations. Learning to be Poor?*, York: Joseph Rowntree Foundation.

Sinclair, R. (2004) 'Participation in practice: making it meaningful, effective and sustainable', *Children & Society*, vol 18, no 2, pp 106-18.

Tanner, E., Bennett, F., Churchill, H., Ferres, G., Tanner, S. and Wright, S. (2003) *The Costs of Education: A Local Study*, London: Child Poverty Action Group.

Tisdall, K. and Davis, J. (2004) 'Making a difference? Bringing children's and young people's views into policy-making', *Children & Society*, vol 18, no 2, pp 131-42.

Willis, P., Jones, S., Cannan, J. and Hurd, G. (1990) *Common Culture: Symbolic Work at Play in the Everyday Cultures of the Young*, Milton Keynes: Open University Press.

THREE

Children's perspectives on social exclusion and resilience in disadvantaged urban communities

Malcolm Hill, Katrina Turner, Moira Walker, Anne Stafford and Peter Seaman

Social exclusion and poverty: children's agency and perspectives

For politicians, campaigners and academics alike, the conjunction of the words 'children' and 'poverty' (or social exclusion) tends to be associated with a discourse of victimhood. There is a plethora of evidence about the harm caused to children who grow up in poverty in the UK, let alone worldwide (Bradshaw and Mayhew, 2005). It is undoubtedly important that poverty should be tackled, because of the effects on children's current well-being, as well as their future life chances. Children brought up in poverty tend to have poorer than average health and educational achievements. They are less likely to receive regular pocket money, go on school trips and holidays, or to be able to afford adequate clothing (Middleton et al, 1995; Bradshaw, 2002).

Until recently, though, little has been heard from children themselves. Perspectives that emphasise children's agency stress the importance of understanding their viewpoints, recognising that children are not passive in the face of poverty or indeed any other situation (Ridge, 2002). This viewpoint does not dissociate itself from the idea that poverty is wrong and harmful in its effects, but leads to a more subtle understanding of its diverse implications, which include differentiated responses.

ildren's resilience

Within this context, the concept of resilience has gained currency. This was a guiding concept for recent pieces of work by the authors and colleagues that form the basis for this chapter. These comprised two linked studies on parenting and children's resilience in disadvantaged communities (Seaman et al, 2006) and a literature review on resilience (Hill et al, 2006).

In academic circles, the idea of resilience has become increasingly popular in reaction to a previous literature that emphasised the negative consequences of a range of difficulties or risk factors including poverty, family disruption and abuse. Without minimising the ill effects of such childhood disadvantages, proponents of resilience observed that some children did well despite such early experiences (Rutter, 1985; Fonagy et al, 1994). They also drew out the practical implication that, as well as reducing risk factors in children's lives, a helpful strategy to promote children's well-being would be to enhance those features of their lives that enabled them to overcome difficulties (Gilligan, 1997; Luthar, 2006).

Resilience was initially framed largely in terms of discrete *factors*, which statistically were associated with good outcomes for children who had experienced adversity in their early years. Many factors were identified, though these can be classified as pertaining to three main levels (Olsson et al, 2003):

- the individual, for example, intelligence, self-belief, problem-solving skills, high self-esteem;
- the family, for example, warm attachments, harmony, consistency;
- the local environment, for example, friendships, good school experiences.

Little is known about the precise processes and mechanisms that contribute to resilience, though there is a large separate literature on *coping*, for instance distinguishing coping styles that are avoidant, focus on problem solving or concentrate on dealing with the emotional impact of stress (Stein et al, 2000). A key coping strategy within resilience approaches involves reframing, that is, altering perceptions in a positive direction by seeing adversity as a challenge and opportunity (Walsh, 1998; Newman, 2004).

Ungar (2004) criticised mainstream resilience thinking for neglecting the viewpoints of young people. The present chapter makes a contribution to rectifying that situation. This fits with current thinking within the social studies of childhood, which emphasises children's agency, both in terms of their active role in creating their social worlds and the value of their own perspectives on their lives (James and Prout, 1998; Hill et al, 2004). On the other hand, Valentine (2004) cautions that, although children are indeed experts on their local environment, their perceptions can be affected by risk-taking tendencies and a sense of invulnerability, which may distort their understanding of certain dangers.

The present study

The study of children's resilience in disadvantaged communities aimed to understand children's views on the positives and negatives, opportunities and threats in their local areas and how they responded to these (Turner et al, forthcoming). Thus the main focus was on environmental poverty, though many of the children also experienced financial poverty, since the two tend to go together (Ghate and Hazel, 2002), but some only experience one or the other. A parallel study of parents took place to which brief reference will also be made (Seaman et al, 2006).

The study was primarily qualitative, since the intention was to identify resilience processes rather than factors. Sixty individual interviews and 16 discussion groups were held with eight- to 14-year-olds living in four areas in the West of Scotland identified as deprived according to indicators such as high rates of free school meals and adult unemployment. These areas were chosen to give a spread of urban environment: inner city, outer estate, new town and industrial town. Access to the sample was gained through schools. In addition to the interviews and discussions, 259 questionnaires were completed in class by children from the relevant age groups in the study schools. It was not possible to consider inter-ethnic differences, since almost everyone in the study was white, reflecting the ethnic composition of the areas in the study.

Experiences of exclusion

The interviews produced evidence of exclusion, taking three main forms – material limitations, paucity of social capital and territorial restrictions. Questions about income and expenditure were covered more fully in the parents' interviews where many parental responses highlighted the problems of managing on low income (cf. Middleton et al, 1995; Bradshaw and Mayhew, 2005):

> If they do go out, it costs money. You've got the sports centre or the fun pool ... it's alright people saying 'it's only a fiver or a tenner', it's a lot of money if you don't work. (Mother)

> So they know that they have to go without chocolate biscuits and all the wee treats. (Mother)

In one sense, most of the children in the study had considerable social capital in that they felt supported and safeguarded by close social networks (parents, friends and parents' friends). Such trust is an important component of social capital (Portes, 1998; Putnam, 2000). However, another element that is particularly important for life chances is linkage to people who can assist with educational and job opportunities (Pavis et al, 2000). In this respect, the interviews with children (and parents) indicated that many lacked contacts that would assist them in fulfilling their aspirations. For instance, some of the children said they wanted to pursue professional careers, such as the law and medicine, but their knowledge of what this entailed appeared unrelated to personal exposure, other than through TV programmes. They lacked individuals in their networks who could act as role models, provide information about the requirements for such jobs or indeed facilitate access to suitable preparatory work.

The third form of exclusion – territorial restrictions – was in fact the most prominent in children's accounts. Their activities and movements were restricted geographically by perceived threats to their safety or comfort, so that certain spaces were to be avoided. Many of the children spoke about parts of their local neighbourhoods they saw as dangerous. For the most part, the risks they perceived in their local environment related to human behaviour rather than the built environment, though traffic was a concern, especially for younger children. The young people described their fears and anxieties about entering spaces (buildings, streets or park) that were regularly occupied by adults or teenagers whom the children regarded as aggressive or strange. They quite often attributed this to drug misuse or drunkenness. One group described how it was frequently chased by drunken adults while visiting the town centre.

Another kind of 'no-go' area resulted from the actions of territorial gangs of young people. In the questionnaire survey, gangs yielded the highest response to a set of questions about negative aspects of the local environment (69%), compared with, for instance, bad housing (14%), traffic (32%) and having nothing to do (63%). Such gangs have been a long-standing feature of certain deprived urban areas in the US, UK and elsewhere (Miller, 1980; McFadden, 2005). In all four study areas, children and young people spoke about modifying their activities and movements to take account of their fears and knowledge of local gangs. They indicated that the gangs had a persisting identity. Some parents recalled that gangs with the same name or location had existed when they were young, while one boy said he expected to join the local gang as his father and older brother had both been members. The children were very aware that the gangs sought to exercise power over the territory they lived and operated in, so that outsiders were at best not welcome and at worst attacked if they entered the territory. Children described the borders between different zones, such as a road separating different housing schemes or a bridge over a motorway (cf. Sibley, 1995). If they crossed the border into an area they did not belong to, they risked being attacked:

> If I am going to another area obviously I watch myself because there is young lassies oot there and boys that think anybody from another scheme is a total outsider.... gangs going up and gawn 'You're no fae here', 'So whit ye dae'ing here?' and then they start fighting. (14-year-old-girl)

> It is like a territory kind of thing, if you cross over, you get a doing. (11-year-old boy)

Some interviewees knew individuals who had been stabbed and a few said they had known, or knew of, individuals who had died in gang fights.

Besides territories of residence, gangs or groups of young people were sometimes seen as controlling certain public spaces at particular times, especially after dark. This could apply to a shopping centre, a community centre or club, where only members of the 'in' group felt safe when that group was present. One focus group described being afraid to attend a youth club dominated by a gang they did not belong to, while another said their shopping centre was unsafe at nights because of the presence of a group of 'Neds'.

Another type of exclusion from children's viewpoints took the form of adults who had or took on a role as gatekeepers of private or public property. Children described adult neighbours who shouted at them for making a noise, walking on the grass, playing games or seeking to retrieve a football. This highlights how places that children regard as offering opportunities are treated by adults as sites of control (Olwig and Gullov, 2003).

Individuals engaging with hazards and threats

Children described a number of strategies and mechanisms they deployed to deal with local risks, rooted in their understandings of the interaction between person, place and time that constituted perceived dangers. First, we present the methods used by individuals, although some entailed actual or potential assistance from others. Then we consider collaborative alliances whereby children cooperated with peers and parents in order to gain security from their company or availability to assist if difficulties arose.

A common approach, especially by younger children, was to insulate themselves from perceived threats by avoidance or protected passage through risky areas. This was a positive form of self-protection, but also limited their freedom. Others took a more detached or combative stance.

Avoidance

Children of all ages avoided areas that were littered and vandalised, and described how they felt uneasy in areas that were poorly lit or not located near to houses:

> I don't go to scary streets. (10-year-old boy)

A number of interviewees said they avoided areas where they expected to encounter a gang for fear of being attacked. It was claimed that a gang might pick on anyone they did not recognise. In one of the study areas, young people were afraid to enter the town centre at night, as they believed a gang there would attack anyone. One group provided a vivid account of an assault involving baseball bats. Children reported avoidance of people they saw as threatening. The younger interviewees also avoided main roads, strangers and adults who acted strangely.

Besides preventive evasion of dangers, a reactive variant was to 'run away' as soon as there was sign of trouble or fighting, whether or not this was in a place normally seen as safe or not. It was quite common for children to refer to running away or being chased, in relation to 'scary' adults, gangs or other threats like big dogs. Some younger ones said they had run away from adults they suspected were up to no good, for example, offering sweets.

Avoidance techniques were not simply a fearful response to major threats and exclusionary practices in their localities, but involved the development, sharing and deployment of detailed knowledge of the neighbourhoods the children lived in and the precise locations of hazards to their safety or well-being. Many gave a highly differentiated or time-sensitive account of places they frequented. An eight-year-old described how he had avoided a group of drunken teenagers on his way home from school by skirting a bush and taking a short cut that enabled him to get by without being seen.

The children's local intelligence had a temporal as well as spatial dimension. They knew that threatening adults and aggressive people of any age tended to be in certain localities at particular times of the day, week or year. Although some risky places were seen as permanent no-go areas, others were frequented except at high-risk times (for example, late at night). Children recognised that gang fights mostly took place at weekends, often fuelled by alcoholic drinking, and so adapted their plans accordingly.

The avoidance approach was an understandable strategy for keeping safe, but it not only restricted liberty of movement and activity in a general sense, but also meant that young people could not access recreational or other resources in the avoided areas. This limited their ability to meet their immediate needs and wants, as well as opportunities to develop skills and knowledge that could enhance their futures (through sports or drama, for instance). The exclusions affected their current well-being and their future becoming. This illustrates how a 'resilient' response to certain kinds of adversity may have drawbacks as well as benefits.

Identifying safe places and times

The corollary of avoiding certain locations was that children preferred to stay in familiar, trusted locations. Many children spoke of locations they felt were safe because of familiarity and the presence of trusted adults:

Adults watch over you and things. (10-year-old girl)

Younger children described how they played only in their own garden and street, while older participants described how they remained in their own housing scheme or only visited other areas where they knew people A few mentioned hiding (in bushes, for example) when seeing gangs. Older children chose to visit shopping centres or sports facilities at times they believed drunken adults or aggressive teenagers were unlikely to be there. This is an example of what Harden and colleagues (2000) refer to as children's reflexive monitoring of threats.

Keeping a low profile

Risky people and places could not always be evaded. A strategy adopted when in the immediate presence of a threat was to merge with the background in order not to draw attention to oneself. Adopting a neutral appearance and avoiding eye contact were described as protective mechanisms when passing gangs or aggressive individuals in the street.

> I have learned to keep my head down, so I don't really get picked on 'cause I am just a person walking and I don't dress differently. I just dress in my school uniform. (12-year-old boy)

> You just like walk past them, don't even look them, you don't look back if they say anything. [Then they] usually they leave you alone. (11-year-old boy)

Others ingeniously pretended to be on their mobile phone when walking past people who gave them cause for concern.

Of particular importance in the West of Scotland context with its history of sectarianism associated with loyalty to particular football clubs was to hide being a fan at times when tensions between supporters could be incendiary. Young people reported not wearing their football strips out of doors following a controversial game between Celtic and Rangers.

A common response to bullying was to ignore the perpetrator. Some children argued that this usually led the person to desist, whereas they thought that resisting or informing parents or teachers could lead to revenge attacks:

> I tried to ignore it because to retaliate they would all jump on me.... If I've been spat on, I'll go home and get washed but nothing really, you just have to accept it. (14-year-old girl)

Creating safe passage

Exposure to threats was greatest when walking alone, so motor vehicles or company were seen as offering protected transit through unsafe areas. A number of young people said they preferred to travel for leisure purposes by public transport or even taxis rather than walk, in order to avoid threatening situations. This is another example of an ambivalent resilient mechanism, since this helped cope with risk, but restricted choice and entailed financial costs.

Going to or through a risky place was made safer if a journey was made with others. One means of arranging this was to ask parents or friends' parents to go along (this was also a favoured strategy by parents, who might insist on it). Children of all ages told of how their parents would provide lifts or accompany them to places, which they usually appreciated, though sometimes this 'dependence' entailed a loss of face among peers. One 14-year-old girl said she asked her father to collect her rather than catch a bus in a place where there was a group of 'Neds'. As children grew older, they were less willing to be seen in public with parents, so they relied more on friends or, less often, older siblings.

Use of mobile phones meant that children could move about with a protective person available though not physically present. This has dramatically altered the capacity of children to stay in touch with significant others at a distance and provided a sense of security to many. They informed parents and friends of their whereabouts and had the capacity to obtain help immediately if needed:

> I take my mobile just in case when I go to the shop and if I don't come back my mum will just come on my phone and ask where I am. (Eight-year-old girl)

> If I'm going about, take my mobile wi' me and that. (11-year-old girl)

Detachment and retaliation

Several older respondents (aged 12-14) did not see aggression as something scary to be avoided, but had come to see it as a matter of interest or even amusement, for which they were a detached audience. Some said they would stop and watch fights, so long as they could remain uninvolved. One young woman described regular drunken adult behaviour and fights at two local pubs as 'a good laugh'.

With adult threats, the difference in power meant that challenging aggression directly was not usually an option. Similarly, an individual facing a gang would normally be foolish to take them on, though there might be no choice. One young man had tried running away when a group attacked him but they caught him up so he then fought back. While some also eschewed retaliation in the face of peer aggression, quite a few males and females said this was their preferred response, particularly if this was on a one-to one basis. Several described instances of doing so:

> He was annoying me and shoving me about and all that and then I just turned round and I hit him. (Young person)

Some argued that confronting an aggressor was necessary to prevent bullying recurring and it was also a way of dealing with their own fears.

Joining in

Some young people, particularly but not exclusively boys, indicated that the safest or indeed 'natural' response to gang activity was to join the local gang. They conveyed a sense that all their friends were or would become members and that 'if you don't do it then you get slagged' (11-year-old boy). The resilience literature includes opposite viewpoints on the success of this strategy, which in turn reflect different criteria (children's future interests, as perceived by adults, or children's autonomy). Luthar and Burack (2000) observed that some young people value competencies that bring success in the context of their current relationships and activities (such as gang membership, crime), but these may be unhelpful as regards their social inclusion and their future prospects. On the other hand, it has been argued that the resilience literature usually disregards or devalues the aspirations of young people seeking ways to survive in adversity, which may include 'antisocial' behaviour that provides status and meaning (Ungar, 2004).

Peers as threats and supports

It has been noted already that peer gangs were a major threat to children's sense of security while peer friendships offered safety and supports. It is well known that for children and young people at all ages peers are normally central to their social worlds (Borland et al, 1998). Peers provide a wide range of emotional and social support and are also major sources of knowledge and understanding, but there is also a tendency for adults to see peer influences as negative and to demonise peer associations. This was true of many parents' accounts in the parallel study. While the parents made little mention of children's peers as sources of support and safety, these were prominent in children's own accounts. Moreover, on a fixed-choice question on the children's questionnaires with 12 options for what made the local area good to live in, the highest support was for having 'friends nearby' (72%), compared with 27% for having plenty to do, 34% for being safe and 48% for good schools. Among answers to a question about what they did to keep themselves safe, by far the most common response, given by about 80% of the children, was to be with friends. The next most common response (by just over half the sample) was to take a mobile phone.

Many children said they felt safe going around with peers. As one 10-year-old boy said, the best way to keep safe was to 'travel in groups'. The children and young people explained that gangs were less likely to attack someone who was in a group, and that friends could offer support or run for help if something happened:

> There are less likely to attack you because there are more of you and you could beat them up. (11-year-old boy)

> If you've got all your pals with you naebody'll touch you. But if you're yirself ... they ca' you an item and you'll get a doing. (12-year-old boy)

However, the safety associated with going around in a group had to be weighed against the fact that it might be viewed unfavourably:

> I don't hang about with a big gang, maybe one or two people because if you are in a gang, other people think you want trouble. (13-year-old girl)

Thus group association could become a risk in itself, since a group of friends congregating for company and safety could be seen by others of the same age as a threatening gang or by adults as a set of trouble-makers – a perception that media and political comments in the context of antisocial behaviour may serve to reinforce.

Some described how friends would accompany each other home at night and use phone contact and text messages to 'look out for each other' or make sure friends had reached destinations safely. In one extreme example, a 12-year-old boy's parents had been attacked in their own home. The boy reported that in the following period he would allay his own safety fears by staying at a friend's or having friends stay over.

These were preventive actions, but peers also came to assistance when trouble actually happened. Even those as young as eight would go to help each other and this was not confined to friends. In the illustration below, the child attacked was a stranger and yet the respondent had acted as a good Samaritan:

> There's people around the corner and they were getting bullied so I went over to them. At the time I didn't know them and I said what's wrong and they went 'people are bullying me' and then she said they were calling her stuff like that wasn't nice ... I went back home and I told my mum and my mum took her back in the house and they discussed it. And I was sitting beside the girl asking her questions so I was making her feel better and make her cheer up. (Eight-year-old girl)

It was also the case that many of the actions taken by young people were affected in a major way by how they expected this to be seen by their peers. Associated with this was a desire not to be seen as weak or dependent on adults. Examples included putting up with bullying rather than complaining to an adult and avoiding being seen with parents even if this might be safer.

Alliance with parents and siblings

There was evidence from both the children themselves and parents in the parallel study of a fair degree of consensus and alliance over such matters as keeping safe and out of trouble. In the main, the children accepted parents' reasons for concerns about their well-being and for having rules and sanctions. Young people were able to give reasons for the occasions they had been grounded and indicate it was a just response:

> Aye, I think it is fair because if I'm given a certain time to be in and I'm no' then that's me breaking a rule. (14-year-old boy)

An interesting characteristic of the young people's data was the high degree to which they felt cared for by parents applying safety rules, such as the requirement to let parents know where they were and agreement to be back by a certain time. Respondents of all ages reported always telling a parent where they were going and younger children revealed it reassured them that someone would know if they were to go missing. Two sisters (aged 11 and 14) described taking a visit to the city centre and asking their father to call regularly on their mobile to check they were all right. Those who had been bullied or approached by strangers had found it helpful to discuss with their parents their experiences and the fear of being bullied or approached again. Younger children often described telling a parent when they were afraid, worried or unhappy, for the most part feeling that this had helped sort things out. Understandably, children aged 8 to 10 were more likely to confide in parents, because as one put it:

> Your mum and dad are the people who love you the most, so they are the best ones to go to talk if you are feeling unhappy about something or if your friends have called you a name. (10-year-old girl)

This was true for some older children too, but others explained that they would not discuss worries with parents, as it was embarrassing or they felt parents would react in an angry, over-protective or intrusive way. In such cases, quite often an aunt, uncle or sibling might be preferred as a confidant. On the other hand, one 14-year-old girl believed that through being open with her parents she gained more trust and autonomy.

Young people's awareness of the risks in their neighbourhoods usually led them to value the support of parents in recognising the risky nature of play and leisure time. This did not stop some deviating from parental expectations (cf. Solomon et al, 2002). There were many examples in both studies of children seeking to assert autonomy, for example by switching off mobile phones so parents could not make contact or, when grounded, behaving in a manner at home that interfered with what parents wanted to do. In the questionnaires, nearly half indicated that parents frequently did not know what they were doing, although they more often knew where they were.

Quite often older siblings were important as sources of security or support. A number of young people said they felt safer going into risky areas with an older brother or sister. They were also valued as confidants as they were more experienced ('been through the, like, whole adolescent stage': 14-year-old girl).

The role of community-based services

Young people spoke positively about sports facilities and clubs in their areas. These formal and supervised spaces, mostly indoors, often compensated for a perceived absence of safe outdoor public spaces. Besides local government recreational facilities, the children attended clubs run by local people. These normally took place in low-cost premises such as schools and community halls, so that the entrance costs were minimal (25 or 50 pence a time) and affordable by children in families with low income.

Children pointed out that involvement with recreational and social organisations helped keep them safe and avoid getting into trouble:

> 'cos if we were just hanging about and, like, someone started trying to fight us an' all that, it keeps us away from fights because we would be in here. (12-year-old boy)

> My fitba team keeps me aff the streets! (14-year-old boy)

Aspirations, social capital and social exclusion

The resilience literature has highlighted the important role played by sense of purpose and educational success in helping overcome disadvantage (Hill et al, 2006). In the present study, the children were asked what made them feel good or confident. The main replies were about:

- friends, for reassurance and support;
- fun experiences, such as being at a club or listening to music;
- receiving money or gifts;
- receiving praise;
- doing well at school.

Respondents' prescriptions for doing well in the future included working hard at school, doing part-time work now, getting use to handling money, and engaging in sports and hobbies that might lead to jobs. One young woman gave a sophisticated account of the value of moving beyond existing social networks to build up contacts and skills:

Meeting different people, like people you wouldn't usually talk to. So it is always improving, like, your social skills. (14-year-old girl)

Just under half the young people who completed questionnaires said they hoped to go to university, although, in view of their backgrounds, it is unlikely that such a proportion will achieve their ambition. Most of them hoped or expected to go into non-professional jobs, like beautician, dancer, actor, driver, joiner, footballer, fireman or lab technician, though a significant minority did want to be teachers, lawyers, vets and so on.

In relation to certain trades like hairdressing or bricklaying, children described in considerable detail what this would involve, while most of those who mentioned professional career aspirations were much more vague about what this entailed or how they might achieve it. Several gave lack of employment opportunities nearby as the reasons they expected to move elsewhere once they were adults.

Conclusion

The young people in this study all lived in disadvantaged areas, often in low-income households. On the whole, they were happy with the places they lived in, largely on account of the familiar adults and peers around them. They also had a range of concerns, mainly centring on threatening individuals or groups living locally, though also sometimes about their family or school. The proximity and direct experience of violence was central to worries voiced by the majority of young people. This had major implications not only for their safety and exclusion from certain areas, associations and activities, but also for their long-term prospects.

For the most part, the children and young people did not simply accept threats to their safety or happiness but took active steps to protect themselves and overcome difficulties, sometimes alone but more often in alliance, especially with peers and parents. Whereas much of the resilience literature has identified discrete *factors,* many of which are beyond the control of the individual or have already happened, the children and young people in this study identified *processes and mechanisms* that almost any child can use; they are learnable.

The children demonstrated a detailed and highly differentiated understanding of the people and places surrounding them. They were, of course, not infallible and some had been victims of assaults or had had frightening experiences. However, mostly they had found ways of negotiating through and round threatening people. This entailed use of individual or shared knowledge, for example, about which places to avoid or what times certain spaces were safe. Many parents favoured the use of formal leisure facilities and activities as a means of keeping their children safe as well as active and learning. Most children valued these too.

The children (and their parents) had adopted differentiated strategies and tactics to manage the threats in their local environments. Sharing knowledge about these could increase the capacity of young people to survive and counter these threats to their well-being. However, this is, of course, to deal with the symptoms rather than the root problems. It is important also to help integrate socially excluded families and individuals into safety-enhancing informal networks where they can learn of safe activities for young people and develop reciprocal arrangements with other parents. Ensuring safe and low-cost access to organised activities is another prime means of preventing children from becoming the victims or perpetrators of antisocial behaviour and bullying. A long-term strategy also needs to tackle long-standing deficiencies in the local environment and opportunities, whose socioeconomic antecedents require tackling in ways that include local people, adults and children. A combination of national and local policies is required that build on the strengths exhibited by people in this study while also tackling both the causes and symptoms of aggression by certain adults and young people under the influence of alcohol, drugs and gang culture (Henderson 1999; Holman 2001).

References

Borland, M., Laybourn, A., Hill, M. and Brown, J. (1998) *Middle Childhood*, London: Jessica Kingsley.

Bradshaw, J. (2002) *The Well-being of Children in the UK*, London: Save the Children.

Bradshaw, J. and Mayhew, E. (2005) *The Well-being of Children in the UK* (2nd edn), London: Save the Children.

Fonagy, P., Steele, P., Steele, H., Higgitt, A. and Target, M. (1994) 'The theory and practice of resilience', *Journal of Child Psychology and Psychiatry*, vol 35, no 2, pp 231-57.

Ghate, D. and Hazel, N. (2002) *Parenting in Poor Environments*, London: Jessica Kingsley.

Gilligan, R. (1997) 'Beyond permanence: the importance of resilience in child placement practice and planning', *Adoption & Fostering*, vol 21, no 1, pp 12-20.

Harden, J., Backett-Milburn, K., Scott, S. and Jackson, S. (2000) 'Scary faces, scary places', *Health Education Journal*, vol 59, no 1, pp 12–22.

Henderson, P. (1999) 'Community work with children', in M. Hill (ed) *Effective Ways of Working with Children and Families*, London: Jessica Kingsley, pp 92–105.

Hill, M., Davis, J., Prout, A. and Tisdall, K. (2004) 'Moving the participation agenda forward', *Children & Society*, vol 18, no 2, pp 77–96.

Hill, M., Stafford, A., Seaman, P., Ross, N. and Daniel, B. (2006) *Parenting and Resilience*, London, National Children's Bureau.

Holman, B. (2001) 'Neighbourhood projects and preventing delinquency', *Youth Welfare*, vol 1, no 1, pp 45–52.

James, A. and Prout, A. (1998) *Constructing and Reconstructing Childhood*, London: Falmer Press.

Luthar, S.S. (2006) 'Resilience in development: a synthesis of research across five decades', in D. Cicchetti and D.J. Cohen (eds) *Developmental Psychopathology: Risk, disorder, and adaptation, vol 3*, New York, NY: Wiley.

Luthar, S.S. and Burack, J.A. (2000) 'Adolescent wellness: in the eye of the beholder?', in D. Cichhetti, J. Rapoport, I. Sandler and R. Weisenberg (eds) *The Promotion of Wellness in Children and Adolescents*, Washington DC: Child Welfare League of America.

McFadden, J. (2005) 'Gang together to beat the violence', *The Herald* (Glasgow), 29 March.

Middleton, S., Ashworth, K. and Walker, R. (1995) *Family Fortunes*, London: Child Poverty Action Group.

Miller, W.B. (1980) 'Gangs, groups and serious youth crime', in D. Shichor and D. Kelly (eds) *Critical Issues in Juvenile Delinquency*, Lexington, MD: Lexington Books.

Newman, T. (2004) *What Works in Building Resilience?*, Ilford: Barnardo's.

Olsson, C.A., Bond, L., Burns, J.M., Vella-Brodrick, D.A. and Sawyer, S.M. (2003) 'Adolescent resilience: a concept analysis', *Journal of Adolescence*, vol 26, no 1, pp 1–11.

Olwig, K.F. and Gullov, E. (2003) *Children's Places*, London: Routledge.

Pavis, S., Platt, S. and Hubbard, G. (2000) *Young People in Rural Scotland: Pathways to Social Inclusion and Exclusion*, York: Joseph Rowntree Foundation and York Publishing Services.

Portes, A. (1988) 'Social capital: it's origins and applications on modern sociology', *American Review of Sociology*, vol 24, pp 1–24.

Putnam, R.D. (2000) *Bowling Alone*, New York, NY: Simon & Schuster.

Ridge, T. (2002) *Childhood Poverty and Social Exclusion*, Bristol: The Policy Press.

Rutter, M. (1985) 'Resilience in the face of adversity', *British Journal of Psychiatry*, vol 147, pp 598-611.

Seaman, P., Turner, K., Hill, M., Walker, M. and Stafford, A. (2006) *Parenting and Children's Resilience in Disadvantaged Communities*, York: Joseph Rowntree Foundation.

Sibley, D. (1995) *Geographies of Exclusion*, London: Routledge.

Solomon, Y., Warin, J., Lewis, C. and Langford, W. (2002) 'Intimate talk between parents and their teenage children', *Sociology*, vol 36, no 4, pp 965-83.

Stein, H., Fonagy, P., Ferguson, K.S. and Wisman, M. (2000) 'Lives through time: an ideographic approach to the study of resilience', *Bulletin of the Menninger Clinic*, vol 64, no 2, pp 281-96.

Turner, K., Hill, M., Walker, M. and Stafford, A. (forthcoming) 'How children from disadvantaged areas keep safe', *Health Education*.

Ungar, M. (2004) *Nurturing Hidden Resilience in Troubled Youth*, Toronto: University of Toronto Press.

Valentine, G. (2004) *Public Spaces and the C. lture of Childhood*, Aldershot: Ashgate.

Walsh, F. (1998) *Strengthening Family Resilience*, New York, NY: Guilford Press.

FOUR

Children and the local economy: another way to achieve social inclusion

Rosie Edwards

Here is an opportunity to view the world differently. This chapter sets three challenges to those seeking to tackle child poverty and social exclusion. The first is that the local economy can have an impact on child poverty. The second is that an asset- and solution-based focus on child poverty can have a more positive and sustainable impact. The third is that children and young people should be seen as positive agents for change in their communities, who can also have an impact on both child poverty and social inclusion. I shall start with the perceived picture as it stands, and mention briefly some recent challenges to that picture. The chapter then explores in more detail the way in which children and young people currently feature in moves to tackle child poverty and social exclusion. It goes on to ask how different that might look from an asset-based, child- or young person-led approach that focuses on the local economy. The chapter finishes with some suggestions for how to take this approach forward and a challenge to existing policies.

Since the early 1990s, successive governments have instigated a series of initiatives designed to promote the social and economic regeneration of communities across the UK. While all have favoured Area Based Initiatives at local level to promote social and economic inclusion in addition to taxation and labour market measures, there have been continuing reports of dissatisfaction with their results, both in terms of jobs and services created, sustainability and whether they were targeting the most excluded groups (Bramley et al, 1998; Howarth et al, 2001).

Since 1997, a series of government initiatives has focused on children and young people as part of a commitment to end child poverty by 2020 (DSS, 1999; HM Treasury, 2001). The context for these initiatives has been a strong national economy:

> The long term funding we announce today for Britain's
> public services is possible because the bills of economic
> failure in unemployment and debt have been radically
> reduced; the state of our public finances is strong; and despite
> uncertainties in the global economy, inflation is under
> control, interest rates have been low and stable, and
> unemployment and growth continue to rise. (Gordon
> Brown, Chancellor's Commons statement on the 2002
> Comprehensive Spending Review, *Guardian*, 16 July 2002)

The economic impact of policies on children tends to focus on the
macro-level debate about measures to bring children out of poverty
(Hills, 1999; Piachaud and Sutherland, 2000). Nor do current policies
encourage us to think how the social and economic inclusion agenda
might be advanced if children and young people were viewed as an
asset to their community, and an integral part of its regeneration.

There are, however, recent challenges to the view of marginalised
communities as recipients of the results of national policies.

In *Claiming the Health Dividend* (Coote (ed), 2002), a number of
writers suggest that the National Health Service (NHS) and health of
the community could benefit from better use of NHS resources to
regenerate local economies, to provide greater training, to promote
employment and to encourage business start-up opportunities for local
people. Coote and colleagues suggest that a gap in national economic
policy stems from its focus on international trade and markets, where
an increase in private wealth is a prerequisite to increased public
spending. The report develops the idea that local people are an asset to
their communities, and that by strengthening their facilities, skills and
resources, the wider economy in run-down communities is improved.

Kretzman and McKnight (1993) challenge the needs-led view of
communities, most graphically by overturning the traditional
representation of communities as 'needy' and representing them in a
positive way through their institutions, associations, groups and
individuals. They assert that by first mapping and then mobilising
assets of all types within the community, communities can create
substantive and sustainable change. They term this approach 'asset-
based community development' (Kretzman and McKnight, 1993).

Can Do Citizens (Pike, 2003) illustrates how local people in
marginalised communities have a range of assets and skills, that both
can be and should be the basis of generating positive change in their
communities. It challenges the idea that communities under pressure
are poor in social capital and distinguishes between bonding capital

(seen as strong), and bridging and linking social capital (with other networks and institutions), which are weak, but can be developed using an asset-based approach to community development.

Where do children feature in this world?

There is a gap between wanting to tackle child poverty and understanding the impact of child poverty from a child's point of view. This reduces governments' ability to deal with child poverty. Qvortrup (1997) pointed out that since children are largely seen in relation to their parents and both statistics and research focus on adults or on parents, children are effectively invisible:'… children as a separate social entity hardly appear in our statistical and research documentation' (Qvortrup, 1997, p 89). This invisibility has its roots partly in our attitudes to community, but also in the increasing competition for resources, linked to the growing elderly population worldwide.

Children are thus seen as a silent presence dependent on parents and carers for their social and economic status, and either a contributor to or a cause of poverty.

Authors such as Willmott (1986) and Abrams (1978, 1980) consider the nature of community in the UK. They explore in detail the nature of the adult community and the strands that enable ties at the community level. However, references to children in their work mainly concentrates on how activities such as childcare, babysitting and friendship are required to be carried out by adults for strong communities to be sustained (Willmott, 1986) and how values such as reciprocity underpin community networks focused entirely on the perceptions of adults (Abrams, 1978, 1980). It is easy to see how communities faced with an increasing elderly population, policies to support older people or those with mental health problems or disabilities in the community, and a decline in traditional sources of employment, resulting in an increase in early retirement and unemployment, might choose to focus on those issues (Kramer, 1990) and hence the concerns of the adult community (Qvortrup, 1997).

Over two generations, negative stereotypes of young people, rather than children and young peoples' issues, have made the headlines. Two significant documents from the early 1980s highlight how young people are often falsely perceived by agencies as a problem in the analysis of the social and economic problems related to unemployment and civil unrest, particularly as they affect young people in black and minority ethnic (BME) communities (Scarman, 1981; Sheppard, 1983). Both Lord Scarman and Lord Sheppard identified the distance and detachment that had developed over the previous generation between young people in inner-city communities and those making decisions about their lives. A study from the mid-1990s identifies the structural economic decline in communities such as Moss Side and Hulme in Manchester as dating back to the early 1980s (Russell, 1995). A cycle of decline affected children and young people not only in terms of job prospects, but also in terms of social and environmental quality of life, as well as the impact of family poverty. However, the national policy focus on child poverty does not return in the UK until Tony Blair's Beveridge Lecture in 1999. Current UK experience and understanding of poverty and social exclusion still focuses largely on an adult-centred world and sees young people primarily as a problem or threat (Ridge, 2002).

There has, however, been a strong lead from practitioners and researchers considering the role of children and young people in community development and anti-poverty work from the mid-1990s, rooted in explorations of children's rights and participation and community development across the world (Craig, 2001). It is important to understand the explicit link between community development, participation and anti-poverty work in order to appreciate the way in which the concept of the ladder of participation (Arnstein, 1969) and the subsequent exploration of a children's ladder of participation (Hart, 1997) opened up the theory and practice of children's participation. In the UK, the implementation of the 1989 Children Act and the adoption of the United Nations Convention on the Rights of the Child played a key role in raising the profile of the debate about the participation and rights of the child, along with a growing range of studies and international learning from academic and practice sources focusing on the child rather than the parent (Henderson; 1995; Davis and Ridge, 1997; James and Prout, 1997).

It is now possible to observe a pattern whereby concepts developed in relation to an adult world are closely followed by reflection on the relevance or meaning of these concepts in the world of children and young people. Most recently this has been seen in the development and exploration of two concepts: first, social capital (Putnam, 1993), as a way of understanding the value and workings of the networks and informal systems in communities and the subsequent consideration of whether the concept is meaningful for children (Jack and Jordan, 1999; Morrow, 1999); and second, capacity building (Skinner, 1997; Taylor, 2000), which has used the same terminology in relation to activity with children and young people (Finn and Checkoway, 1998; Wilkinson et al, 1999).

Recent UK studies have considered the impact of poverty from a child's viewpoint and reflect on issues such as pocket money, transport, play and leisure (Willow, 2001; Ridge, 2002). In the UK, Youth Banks offer an opportunity for young people to make decisions about resources for youth-led community projects. There seems to be more focus on altruism and civic participation than on the anti-poverty aspect (NYA, 2001; PWNE, 2005; www.youthbank.org.uk).

Some initiatives developed through the government's Children's Fund programme, such as Investors in Children in the north-east and Children Can Do in the south-east of England, have taken an anti-poverty and asset-based approach, but overall they are in a minority. The programme originated as part of government's policy to eradicate child poverty, but is described in terms of prevention, participation and partnership (DfES, 2001).

There seem to be clearer examples in international experience where children have been more proactively involved in issues that have an economic impact on their communities. Studies cover a range of issues from research in Australia on the impact of involving young people in neighbourhood change by seeking their views on meeting places and traffic flow, to a project in Zimbabwe showing the impact of children's involvement on family networks, work and health if children are given the opportunity to consider the interplay between them (McIver, 2001; Percy Smith and Malone, 2001).

One powerful study demonstrates the impact of current international trade policies on child health and makes the links between policy, strategy, implementation and results (Hilary, 2001). It makes a link between the pressure on developing countries to accept cheaper imports, and the effect this has on local farming and jobs, and, in turn, on the affordability of education and the incidence of illness and malnutrition. At the local level, a study sponsored by the same organisation shows how children's identification of problems or their problem-solving approach can lead to better outcomes for the local community (Nurick and Johnson, 2001).

Hasler (1995) comments that 'children are a significant part of community life' (p 171) and goes on to identify the complex dynamics of power that challenge any attempt to promote local participation and indeed the involvement of children and young people. Many authors have written of the fear and vulnerability experienced in poor communities that experience exclusion (Sheppard, 1983; Russell, 1995; Ridge, 2002).

All refer to the experience of children and young people in BME communities, on the one hand receiving the poorest services and the fewest opportunities and on the other hand labelled as being at fault for the quality of life in the community.

A common misconception among employers is that black and minority ethnic communities suffer high rates of unemployment because they have low skill levels. In fact these communities suffer disproportionate levels of unemployment despite equal or sometimes above average attainment. (Bishop et al, 2002)

Children and young people growing up in poor communities experience discrimination and struggle to feel included in everyday activities. Tess Ridge's study (2002) shows the tension between the lack of confidence that results and the hopes and aspirations of young people:

> 'To have like something to do around the village.… Like putting in a few places where we could go, parks that are more advanced for our age.' (Ridge, 2002, quoting Shamus [12 yrs], p 107)

> 'Because I would be able to get things myself, I feel like there is something in me waiting to come out when I've got the money to do it.' (Ridge, 2002, quoting Lisa [15 yrs], p 108)

While government has developed an analysis of poverty and social exclusion that places economic causes at the centre (Bramley et al, 1998; SEU, 2000, 2001) and has taken great care to consider the dynamics of child poverty and social exclusion (HM Treasury, 2001), new policies do not seem to take a child-centred approach (Ridge, 2002). Equally, there is no clear analysis of how to address issues of poverty and social exclusion in the local economy, either for adults or children.

What would a child-centred approach to the local economy look like?

Russell (1995) describes how in the communities of Hulme and Moss Side money 'washes in and out of the area' (p 143). He identifies the damaging cycle of drugs, crime and alternative local economy and raises the question of how community life might be different if jobs and resources were retained and controlled within the community with the positive involvement of young people.

Claiming the Health Dividend (Coote, 2002) is wide reaching in its recommendations for the NHS and the local economy, covering jobs, buildings, transport, energy, education and health, but what would these proposals mean if they were approached from the perspective of outcomes for children, and of children's views and involvement?

The employment proposals in the report suggest prioritising the training and employment of local people, supporting this through access courses, mentoring and school hospital links. The report highlights issues such as underestimating local people, and the need for a strategic approach that thinks through where there might be opportunities for local people at any stage.

From the perspective of outcomes for children, there would be positive outcomes in terms of training and jobs for parents and education and training paths for children as they get older. Employment of local people would enhance the understanding of the needs of the local community, whether in terms of cultural diversity, particular health issues or self-esteem. Local apprenticeships for young people could be a specific way of ensuring continuity. The increased staffing levels in hospitals and health services would provide a better service for children and young people (The Children's Society, 1999).

These same principles could be transferred to other local employment sectors where services are under similar pressure (such as education (Russell, 1995)). The importance of getting on well at school has been commented on by children and young people (Ridge, 2002). The likely connection between social exclusion and a poor relationship to school and teachers has also been raised by young people themselves (Morrow, 1999). This suggests that solutions to social exclusion will come from young people having opportunities to develop greater roles in a range of local services. This analysis combines the idea that social inclusion is fostered by people who experience greater economic/employment opportunities with the notion that inclusion requires the fostering of positive social relationships.

What impact does this model have on the place of children in the local economy?

Claiming the Health Dividend (Coote, 2002) goes beyond the recent approach to regeneration leading to a range of benefits for people living and working in a community, because it describes a holistic means of investing in the local economy. The following examples illustrate the positive changes that could result if children and young people were invited to consider local services from their perspective. Their influence could range from improved locations and content of local services to direct shaping and management of services.

The impact of economic multipliers has been referred to previously (Russell, 1995). Whereas experience for many children in their local community is of boarded-up shops and derelict buildings, a local purchasing policy could have a positive effect on key local suppliers of services (The Children's Society, 2001a). Local purchasing policies in the health service could result in more relevant and better-used child health services. A local purchasing policy could be replicated in other local services such as education, leading to wider use of local school facilities, investment in local businesses and development of new young person-led services.

The standard and nature of childcare facilities is of interest to children as much as to adults (Williams, 1999). While better childcare facilities can mean employment or training opportunities for parents, for children they can mean quality facilities that improve their social networks and provide opportunities for play. Whereas the National Childcare Strategy has a strong focus on welfare to work for parents, the Kings Fund report (Coote et al, 2002) acknowledges both the needs and interests of children, which parents and providers need to take into account in terms of quality, location and time spent there. Interviews with children reflect the importance of family relationships, which childcare provision and employment need to be able to enhance (Roker, 1998; Ridge, 2002).

In both rural and urban areas, travel and lack of transport are major issues for children living in poor communities, and they present clear ideas about ways to improve services. These range from mobile services, to changes in transport routes, times and running of services (Davis and Ridge, 1997; Wilkinson et al, 1999; Percy Smith and Malone, 2001). Nevertheless, studies of rural areas show that the equation is not simple. Transport schemes that work well in cities, such as the promotion of buses over use of the private car, may take longer to develop in rural settings. Indeed, in a submission to the DETR in 2000, children and young people from the West Country described the isolating impact on leisure, education and travel opportunities of living in Cornwall and the Scilly Isles (The Children's Society, 2000a). They raised fundamental questions about whether as a society we are prepared to redress the balance between urban and rural living in the way we allocate services, and, if so, how.

Changes in energy sources and use have a complex relationship with global impact, but children in a range of communities around the world have identified the importance of environmental issues on their lives (Nurick and Johnson, 2001; Willow, 2001). Some projects in Kenya and India have enabled children to address issues such as lighting and tree felling, using the strength of children's clubs to stake a place in community decision making (Hart et al, 2004).

Design of buildings and surrounding space has been a key theme for practitioners and researchers exploring the impact of the built environment and changing opportunities for children's participation (Adams and Ingham, 1998). The development of the Single Regeneration Budget has provided opportunities to enhance local training and employment for young people and parents at the same time as opening up participation channels for children. However, it should be noted that these have seldom been systematically taken up and there are few examples that replicate the 'Smarties' ecological timber framed building in East Kent that enabled parents, architects, children and young people to collaborate on design construction (Edwards, 2002).

Further considerations from practice and recent experience:

The framework developed in *Claiming the Health Dividend* (Coote, 2002) provides a holistic approach to both the community and the local economy from the perspective and the needs of people locally. It shows that a coordinated and national strategic approach to local economic development could be more child-centred, but targets, monitoring and evaluation need to be built in to enable the benefits to children to be tracked and evidenced.

For example, the underpinning issue for Coote's report was that 'a virtuous circle' would guarantee improvements to health. However, research sponsored by the Department of the Environment, Transport and the Regions demonstrated that public expenditure processes aimed at prioritising poor communities did not necessarily have an impact on poverty and social exclusion (Bramley et al, 1998). The recent Health Impact Assessment reports on children's health have resulted in the development of a Children National Service Framework, not only to develop children's health services, but also to strengthen the systems for measurement (DH/DfES, 2004).

Action research with children in communities has shown that there are further aspects of community life where children and the local economy can benefit from service development. Young people and workers at The Children's Society's Advice Development Project in Maltby, South Yorkshire produced a CD Rom that suggested that advice services were often inaccessible in terms of premises and opening times, and that staff were not used to advising young people. These findings led to the development of a model for community education with young people, Advice Made Easy; a system for liaison with advice agencies designed to improve services; and a system for young people to become volunteers initially and then train as advice workers (The Children's Society, 2000b). In Ramsgate, Kent, the difficulties of recruiting trained staff to youth work and community development posts led the Thanet Community Development Project to develop a capacity-building project to encourage young people and parents to train for youth and community development work. The project used the Priority Search action research approach to identify barriers to learning and then address these with partners. It also enabled the development of a pilot course based on Open College Network accredited training and tested/evaluated by local people. The course encourages local young people and parents to take up training on how they can support local children and young people to shape their community. The course also enables these participants to encourage others through a 'training for trainers' approach (The Children's Society, 2001b).

Can do Citizens outlines an all-encompassing approach to recognising local people's assets, and ensuring that they are used for the benefit of local people: examples range from young people campaigning to save sports and leisure assets to individuals developing projects in their communities (Pike, 2003). Matthew Pike shows that if service providers view local people as able to provide services, resources and skills that help the development of the local economy, then the relationship between them changes from giver and supplicant to be replaced by an exchange or reciprocal relationship. The result is an increase in the assets held in the local community, an increase in civic engagement and improvements in local services and quality of life. This summarises the Community Service Agreement which provides a mechanism for creating a way forward that involves all ages and can work within local planning and service development systems (Pike, 2004).

Despite these approaches, studies of the local community and economy often ignore recent developments within childhood studies. For example, some researchers have investigated whether the spending power of children and young people is a key way of keeping resources in the local economy. Others have explored the importance of pocket money and found that children see it as an important part of their self-esteem, perceive it to enable independence and believe it helps them to maintain friendship networks (Roker, 1998; Ridge, 2002). However, until there is more research into initiatives such as the development of credit unions in primary schools and the involvement of children in priority setting for local expenditure and until such approaches become a regular part of local economic development, we will be unable to fully understand the extent to which the involvement of children and young people will impact on community economic development and the retaining and development of resources in local communities.

In addition to such research, we need to act more effectively on the type of information we already have. For example, despite the fact that initiatives such as the Liverpool 8 Children's Research Group presented a coherent case for involving children in environmental planning as far back as 1992 (Adams and Ingham, 1998), 10 years later a city council report stated that 'there needs to be a fundamental change from consulting with children to children's participation in decision making' (Donnelly, 2003, p 3).

There are also dilemmas in relation to children's spending power (Wampler, 2000). Many economies in developing countries rely on the employment of children, and the exploitation of child labour has become a major issue (Hilary, 2001). Riggio places the economic issues in the context of children's rights and highlights the benefits that programmes involving children in decision making can offer in terms of education, economic development and citizenship (Riggio, 2002).

Children also place great value on community space for leisure, play and socialising (Adams and Ingham, 1998; Percy Smith and Malone, 2001). Children prioritise peer, family and community relationships alongside the need for quality leisure, shopping, transport and learning services in their neighbourhoods (Davis and Ridge, 1997; Roker, 1998; Willow, 2001; Ridge, 2002).

It has been observed elsewhere that outside space has particular meaning for children (Henderson, 1989), but more recent consideration of children's networks and experience at neighbourhood level indicates that their concepts of community, relationships and space are complex (Morrow, 1999). This raises questions on how local service providers engage with a diversity of childhoods. The lack of civic participation clearly limits children's impact in their community (Morrow, 1999; Ridge, 2002). It raises the question of how we can promote social inclusion for children if we do not consider their participation in community life as a systematic necessity and a right.

Shaping the local economy with and for children from the grass roots

Community development provides a framework for building capacity not only within communities where people feel marginalised, but also with agencies and organisations that hold the power to assist or block developments (Craig, 2001). However, it also offers children and adults the opportunity to shape both community and economy. They can do this not only through their planning, activities, advice, initiatives and local partnerships, but also by making their assets and skills available as part of this development process. Service providers can reciprocate by bringing their resources to that process (Kretzman and McKnight, 1993; Pike, 2004).

In recent years, government has begun to grasp the nettle of consultation with children and young people (CYPU, 2001). However, until government at all levels sets a framework for the participation of children and young people in service development and in the development of the local community and economy, progress will be slow.

There is already international experience we can draw on. The asset-based approach to communities, offered by Kretzman and McKnight (1993), provides the basis of a framework that relates easily to the holistic approach to community and local economy offered by Coote (2002). Young people have also suggested a framework that focuses on breaking down the bricks in a wall of exclusion and developing the building blocks for inclusion through opportunities and resources (Edwards and Percy Smith, 2004).

In developing any framework that identifies benefits for adults, it is critical to establish at the same time the benefits and outcomes for children and ensure that monitoring and evaluation includes children systematically. The experience of programmes involving children and young people in participatory budgeting and other forms of decision making over resources indicates not only that this is possible, but also that there is substantial success to draw on that demonstrates economic as well as citizenship benefits (Riggio, 2002). The targets set in any community to achieve positive change need to arise from experience of the chain reaction, where investment in children and their communities starts from asking rather than telling children and young people, improves services and benefits to children and across the community as a whole, and increases a sense of both social inclusion and community pride.

References

Abrams, P. (1978) 'Community care: some research problems and priorities', in J. Barnes and N. Connolly (eds) *Social Care Research*, London: Bedford Square Press for Policy Studies Institute.

Abrams, P. (1980) 'Social change, social networks and neighbourhood care', *Social Work Service*, vol 22, issue 1, pp 12-23.

Adams, E. and Ingham, S. (1998) *Changing Places*, London: The Children's Society.

Arnstein, S. (1969) 'A ladder of citizen participation', *Journal of the American Planning Association*, vol 35, issue 2, pp 216-44.

Bishop, H., Cameron, M. and Edmans, T. (2002) 'Employment', in A. Coote (ed) *Claiming the health dividend: unlocking the benefits of NHS spending*, London: King's Fund, pp 19-27.

Bramley, G., Lancester, S., Lomax, D., McIntosh, S. and Russell, J. (1998) *Where Does Public Spending Go*, London: Department of the Environment, Transport and the Regions.

Brown, G. (1992) 'Chancellors Commons Statement on the 2002 Comprehensive Spending Review,' *The Guardian*, 16 July.

CYPU (Children and Young People's Unit) (2001) *Building a Strategy for Children and Young People*, London: CYPU.

Coote, A. (2002) *Claiming the Health Dividend*, London: King's Fund.

Craig, G. (2001) 'Community development with children', in D. McNeish, T. Newman and H. Roberts (eds) *What Works? Effective Social Care Services for Children and Families*, Buckingham: Open University Press.

Davis, J. and Ridge, T. (1997) *Same Scenery, Different Lifestyle*, London: The Children's Society.

DfES (Department for Education and Skills) (2001) 'Developing preventative practices: the experience of children and young people and their families in the Childrens Fund', Brief RB 735, London: DfES.

DH (Department of Health)/DfES (2004) *National Service Framework for Children, Young People and Maternity*, London: DH/DfES.

Donnelly, E. (2003) *Consulting Children and Young People in Liverpool*, Liverpool: Liverpool City Council.

DSS (Department of Social Security) (1999) *Opportunity For All*, London: DSS.

Edwards, R. (ed) (2002) *Anti-Poverty Toolkit*, London: The Children's Society.

Edwards, R. and Percy Smith, B. (2004) *Young People, Homelessness and Social Inclusion in Youth Policy*, Leicester: National Youth Agency.

Finn, J.L. and Checkoway, B. (1998) 'Young people as competent community builders: a challenge to social work', *Social Work*, vol 43, no 4, pp 335-45.

Hart, J., Newman, J., Ackermann, L. and Feeny, T. (2004) *Understanding and Evaluating Children's Participation in Development*, London: Plan UK and Plan International Ltd.

Hart, R. (1997) *Children's Participation: The Theory and Practice of Involving Young Citizens in Community Development and Environmental Care*, Florence: UNICEF/Earthscan.

Hasler, J. (1995) 'Belonging and becoming', in P. Henderson (ed) *Children in Communities*, London: Pluto Press, pp 169-82.

Henderson, P. (ed) (1989) *Working with Communities*, London: The Children's Society.

Henderson, P. (ed) (1995) *Children and Communities*, London: Pluto Press.

HM Treasury (2001) *Tackling Child Poverty: Pre-Budget Report*, London: HM Treasury.

Hilary, J. (2001) *The Wrong Model*, London: Save the Children.

Hills, J. (1999) *Persistent Poverty and Lifetime Inequality: The Evidence*, Case Paper 5, London: London School of Economics.

Howarth, C., Kenway, P. and Palmer, G. (2001) *Responsibility for All: A National Strategy for Social Inclusion*, London; New Policy Institute and the Fabian Society.

Jack, G. and Jordan, B. (1999) 'Social capital and child welfare', *Children & Society*, vol 13, no 4, pp 242-56.

James, A. and Prout, A. (eds) (1997) *Constructing and Reconstructuring Childhood*, London: Falmer Press.

Kramer, R. (1990) 'Voluntary organisations in the welfare state: on the threshold of the 1990s', Working Paper 8, The Centre for Voluntary Organisations, London: London School of Economics.

Kretzman, J. and McKnight, J. (1993) *Building Communities from the Inside Out: A Path Towards Finding and Mobilising a Community's Assets*, Evanston, IL: Institute for Policy Research.

McIver, C. (2001) *Do Not Look Down On Us: Child Researchers Investigate Informal Settlements in Zimbabwe*, Participatory Learning and Action Notes, October, London: International Institute for Environment and Development.

Morrow, V. (1999) *Searching for Social Capital in Children's Accounts of Neighbourhood and Network*, London: Gender Institute, London School of Economics.

Nurick, R. and Johnson, V. (2001) *Putting Children's Rights and Participatory Monitoring and Evaluation into Practice*, IIED Participatory Learning and Action Notes, London: International Institute for Environment and Development.

NYA (National Youth Agency) (2001) *Policy Update: October*, Leicester: National Youth Agency.

Percy Smith, B. and Malone, C. (2001) *Making Children's Participation in Neighbourhood Settings Relevant to the Everyday Lives of Young People*, IIED Participatory Learning and Action Notes, London: International Institute for Environment and Development.

PNW (Participation Workers Network) (2005) *They Help You Get Respect*, London: Carnegie Young People's Initiative.

Piachaud, D. and Sutherland, H. (2000) *How Effective is the British Government's Attempt to Reduce Child Poverty*, CASE Paper 38, London: London School of Economics.

Pike, M. (2003) *Can Do Citizens*, London: Scarman Trust.

Pike, M. (2004) *Community Service Agreements*, London: Scarman Trust.

Putnam, R. (1993) 'The prosperous community: social capital and public life', *The American Prospect*, vol 4, no 13, pp 1–12.

Qvortrup, J. (1997) 'A voice for children in statistical and social accounting', in A. James and A. Prout (eds) *Constructing and Reconstructing Childhood*, London: Falmer Press, pp 85–106.

Ridge, T. (2002) *Childhood Poverty and Social Exclusion*, Bristol: The Policy Press.

Riggio, E. (2002) 'Child friendly cities', *Environment and Urbanization*, vol 14, no 2, pp 45–53.

Roker, D. (1998) *Worth more than this*, London: The Children's Society.

Russell, D. (1995) 'The fear of our own children', in P. Henderson (ed) *Children and Communities*, London: Pluto Press, pp 139–56.

Scarman, Lord (1981) *A Report into the Disturbances in Brixton*, London: HMSO.

SEU (Social Exclusion Unit) (2000) *National Strategy for Neighbourhood Renewal: A Framework for Consultation*, London: SEU.

SEU (2001) *A New Commitment to Neighbourhood Renewal*, London: SEU.

Sheppard, D. (1983) *Bias to the Poor*, London: Hodder & Stoughton.

Skinner, S. (1997) *A Handbook of Community Capacity Building*, London: Community Development Foundation.

Taylor, M. (2000) 'Communities in the lead: power organisational capacity and social capital', *Urban Studies*, vol 37, no 5-6, pp 963–73.

The Children's Society (1999) *East London Project Report*, London: The Children's Society.

The Children's Society (2000a) *Submission to the DETR*, London: The Children's Society.

The Children's Society (2000b) *Advice Development Project, Advice Made Easy*, London: The Children's Society.

The Children's Society (2001a) *Partington Family Centre Project Report*, London: The Children's Society.

The Children's Society (2001b) *Thanet Community Development Project, An Evaluation of Capacity Building*, London: The Children's Society.

Wampler, B. (2000) *A Guide to Participatory Budgeting*, Brazil: Barra Mansa.

Wilkinson, M. with Craig, G. and Alcock, P. (1999) *Involving Young People in Anti Poverty Work*, London: The Children's Society and London Borough of Greenwich.

Williams, P. (1999) *An Evaluation of Thanet Child Care and Training Scheme*, London: The Children's Society.

Willmott, P. (1986) *Social Networks, Informal Care and Public Policy*, London: Policy Studies Institute.

Willow, C. (2001) *Bread is for Free*, London: Save the Children UK.

Part Two
Participation: politics and policy

Reconnecting and extending the research agenda on children's participation: mutual incentives and the participation chain

Alan Prout, Richard Simmons and Johnston Birchall

Introduction

During the past two decades, many societies have seen an accelerating movement towards the idea that children should participate in public affairs and have a voice in relation to decisions that affect them. Enshrined in Article 12 of the United Nations Convention on the Rights of the Child (UNCRC), this notion has gathered both general support and efforts at practical implementation. Indeed, it has become part of the rhetorical orthodoxy, even among those such as the current English government, which has been a generally unenthusiastic proponent of children's rights. For example, five years ago the Children and Young People's Unit (CYPU) was established to develop a 'joined-up policy' in this area and stated that:

> We want to hear the voices of young people, influencing and shaping local services; contributing to their local communities; feeling heard; feeling valued; being treated as responsible citizens. (CYPU, 2001, p 27)

The burden of our argument in this chapter is that research (and indeed wider discussions) of children's participation have, in the main, been too isolated from the debates about participation in general. That body of work, it is true, refers almost entirely to adult participation. Nevertheless, we believe there is much that those concerned with children's participation can learn from it.

An important *prima facie* case for linking the research literatures on adults' and children's participation comes from considering how they both form part of a larger pattern of social change. The emergence of children's voice is, in part, the product of a more general shift in institutional practice that has affected children and adults alike. It is a sociological commonplace to remark that we live in a period of rapid social change. Theorists such as Beck (1992) and Giddens (1990, 1991) argue that this has eroded and fragmented once taken-for-granted institutions and has led to a new sense of uncertainty and risk. A widespread response to (and subsequent cause of) this destabilisation has been the installation of techniques of reflexivity into institutional practice. Reflexivity, it is argued, is needed in order to create the more responsive and flexible institutions demanded by the conditions of late modernity. The rise in calls for participation and the summoning up of the voice of a multitude of actors is the result. Political parties poll voters and conduct focus groups. Citizens are consulted through local and national panels. Consumers are plugged into the elaborate circuits through which new products are devised, tested, produced and marketed. Patients are asked to evaluate their treatment experiences. And so, as one part of all this, children are also seen as having something valuable to tell the firms, service providers, courts and so on.

Public services and their governance are central to this debate, especially in countries with well-developed welfare states. In these countries, greater institutional reflexivity has been identified as a means of reconstructing public services and rebuilding eroded levels of support for them. Consequently, participation has moved much more into the foreground of public policy discussion. A desire to enhance the performance of key public services, perceived needs for new forms of accountability, and concerns over the legitimation of public authorities have all combined to help promote participatory ideas and strategies to a more central position. Participation gained its current prominence in the UK during the 1990s, at the height of the New Right agenda (Stoker, 1997). Enhanced user participation was widely promoted as a feature of administrative reform strategies – at least in rhetoric (Peters and Savoie, 1998; Pierre, 1998). More recently, this agenda has been developed by the New Labour government in the UK, in a range of initiatives that has seen participation emerge as a significant policy theme (Newman, 2001; Bochel and Bochel, 2004; Cabinet Office, 1999; DETR, 1998, 1999; DH, 1998, 2001; DTI, 2001; NCC, 2001, 2004). In response, service agencies have engaged in evaluating their own policy and practice, and there has been a move towards creating a range of alternative forms of user participation (such as consumer councils, panels and forums, and/or participation in agencies' governing structures) to supplement more traditional methods (Stewart, 1997; Lowndes et al, 2001a, 2001b). Together, these developments lead Beresford (2001, p 267) to assert that 'there has never been so much political and policy interest expressed in participation, across so many fields'. As a result, service users are being asked to participate more and more in the planning, provision and evaluation of services. The recent growth in calls for children's participation, such as that from the CYPU referred to above, can be seen as part of this development and drawing on the various rhetorics that it has generated.

The emergence of participation as a theme in public service governance has attracted a good deal of research attention. In this chapter, we focus on two linked theoretical frameworks that have emerged from this body of work and suggest that they can make a useful contribution to developing the research agenda on children's participation. These ideas are drawn from the work of Birchall and Simmons (2004; Simmons and Birchall, 2005), which are currently being followed up in new research (Simmons et al, 2006). The first of these, mutual incentives theory (MIT), concerns the motivations of people to participate. It focuses on whether their motivations are primarily individual or collective. The second, the concept of the participation chain, recognises that knowledge of people's motivations is not enough. It extends MIT by looking at how the different components that make up the process of participation are linked together. It therefore 'joins up' factors such as the resources for, mobilisation into and the dynamics of participation as well as what motivates people to take part.

Why people participate: rational choice or mutual incentives?

Although children's motivation to participate is a topic of great importance, identified by McNeish and Newman (2002) as one of four key elements to effective practice in developing children's participation (the others are addressing attitudinal barriers, creating participatory structures and processes, and achieving inclusive participation), it is has not been subject to a great deal of focused research. However, the motivation of adult public service users to participate has been investigated quite extensively and there is much to learn from this work. Primarily, research on why people take part in processes of collective participation, such as joining a user group or tenants' organisation, has been carried out in terms of incentives and attitudes. These are considered to be the 'internal', psychological mechanisms that explain why some potential participants make the decision to take part, while others do not.

Much of this literature is based on 'rational choice' theory (for an exposition of its different variants and critique of it see, for example, Scott, 2000). Like the notion of *homo economicus*, of which it is a version, this has an individualist orientation. It presupposes that people will behave in ways calculated to maximise their individual benefit. The theory, therefore, faces a problem in relation to collective action. This is because it predicts that most people will not participate in such action, of which some forms of participation are examples, to achieve common goals (Olson, 1965) but will instead 'free-ride' on the efforts of others, unless there are private payoffs (termed 'selective incentives') that they calculate to exceed the costs of participation. As the private payoffs from participation are usually considered to be low, rational choice theory creates a paradox: why, in spite of the cost/benefit calculation, do people nevertheless continue to participate?

For Finkel and colleagues (1989), narrow rational choice explanations predict excessive abstention, and are better at explaining why individuals do not participate than why they do. Similarly, Whiteley and Seyd (1992, pp 59-61) argue that there is a need to 'consider a wider array of incentives . . . where the individual "thinks" collectively rather than individually'. There have been various attempts to do this (for example, Muller and Opp, 1986, 1987; Finkel et al, 1989; Finkel and Muller, 1998). In perhaps the most sophisticated model to date, Whiteley and Seyd (1992, 1996, 1998; Whiteley et al, 1993) combine social-psychological and rational choice explanations in their General Incentives Model, which, alongside selective incentives, features such factors as collective incentives, expressive incentives, altruism and social norms. However, these models still work within a rational choice framework, although it seems to us that in doing so its basic assumptions are stretched up to and beyond breaking point in the effort to accommodate additional, more collectivist, dimensions.

An alternative is found in Birchall and Simmons' MIT, which moves beyond rational choice theory by, from the start and consistently, considering both collective as well as individual factors involved in participation. This approach makes very different assumptions about human nature from those of *homo economicus*, seeing it as both inherently individualistic and deeply collectivistic (for an exposition of some of the sources of this view see, for example, Ridley, 1996). It accomplishes this by combining two further general social-psychological theories of motivation (one individualist, the other collectivist) that are both broad in scope and detailed in their predictions. The first, developed from social exchange theory (Homans, 1961, 1974; Blau, 1964; Ekeh, 1974; Molm, 2000, 2003; Alford, 2002), assumes that people are motivated by individual rewards and punishments, and provides a set of generalisations about how these interact. The second, developed from social cooperation theory and, especially, games theory (Sorokin, 1954; Axelrod, 1984; Argyle, 1991; Vugt et al, 2000), sees human behaviour as inherently collective because collective strategies, in which immediate individual interests are deferred, can have distinct benefits in themselves. It suggests that participation can be motivated by three variables:

- shared goals: people express mutual needs that translate into common goals;
- shared values: people feel a duty to participate as an expression of common values;
- sense of community: people identify with and care about other people who either live in the same area or who are like them in some respect.

This theory suggests that the more each of these three variables is present, the more likely people will be to participate.

MIT and motives to participate

MIT, then, takes into account both individualistic and collectivistic incentives. The individualistic incentives are shown in Figure 5.1. This is an enhanced model of costs versus benefits, considering also the positive effects of habit and the negative effects of opportunity costs (whereby the individual calculates the cost of opportunities foregone) and satiation (whereby the oversupply of benefits reduces their subjectively perceived value).

In an empirical study of public service users' motivations to participate in forums such as tenants' organisations, self-help and service user consultative groups, based on the MIT approach, Birchall and Simmons (2004; Simmons and Birchall, 2005) sought to measure both individual and collective incentives[1]. They found that for most people neither the direct or opportunity costs of participation to an

Figure 5.1: Individualistic incentives

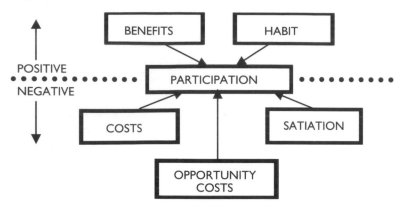

individual nor satiation appear to provide significant barriers to participation. In fact, the benefit most widely reported as becoming less valuable as participation continued was 'getting my own problems solved'. This backs up a key qualitative finding of the study that some participants move from a narrow focus on their own problems to a wider focus once they become more involved. The positive factors in Figure 5.1 are benefits and 'habit'. Benefits can be subdivided into 'external' material/tangible) and 'internal' (affective/expressive) (see Figure 5.2). External benefits were not widely reported to be influential. By comparison, more respondents considered internal benefits to be valuable. These findings tend to confirm those of Verba and colleagues (2000), that taking part makes activists feel good about themselves. As for habit, the study found that its effects are largely confined to a single participant type, 'habitual participants', which we will discuss below.

Participants' motivations appear – from these findings – to be clear-cut: the benefits outweigh the costs, and this makes participation more likely. However, such a conclusion would be premature. The primacy of individualistic incentives is called into question by a key finding from our research: around 80% of participants said they would still participate without any of the above benefits. While this seems contradictory, it implies that they might have collectivistic incentives that outweigh the individualistic ones. Indeed, when asked, 79% of participants overwhelmingly stated that they wanted to get benefits for the group as a whole rather than just for themselves as individuals. Next came those (19%) who said they wanted both. This indicates

Figure 5.2: Costs of participation

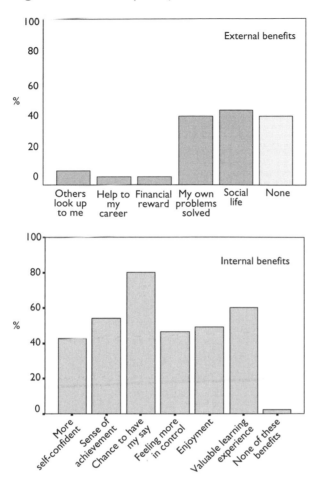

that the pursuit of individual benefits is often secondary to a wider set of concerns, which MIT terms collectivistic incentives (Figure 5.4).

The study found that participants have a strong sense of community, shared goals and, to a slightly lesser extent, shared values. Non-participants scored significantly less highly on each of these three measures (p < 0.01). These findings indicate that collectivistic motivations are the primary mechanism in the motivation of service users to participate. However, checks were still needed on whether the differences between participants and non-participants were a cause or an effect of participation. Several features of the data suggested a causal relationship. For example, it was significant that, when the length of time people had been involved in participation was examined, people

Figure 5.3: Benefits of participation

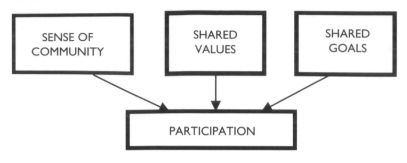

Figure 5.4: Collectivistic incentives

who had only been participating for a short time had higher collectivistic motivations than non-participants. Nevertheless, those who had been participating for longer were found to have increasingly heightened collective motivations. This suggests that, with continuing participation, people's collectivistic motivations are reinforced and their commitment to the group develops (see also Klandermans, 1997; Passy and Giugni, 2000).

Having established that, while individual incentives are not absent, it is collective incentives that play the most important role in motivations to participate, the study went on to measure collectivistic incentives among both participants and non-participants. Cluster analysis of data from a 30-dimension scale of collective motivations revealed that there seem to be different types of participant and non-participant. Five clusters of participants and three of non-participants emerged. Cluster membership was then cross-tabulated with participants' other responses to generate a more detailed picture of their characteristics. Among participants, we were able to characterise four different types of activist, and one less active participant type.

First, there were the 'campaigners'. These participants were very active and confident in their participation, taking the lead, joining committees and so on. As 'doers', they tended to seek change rather than defend the status quo. They also tended to be more interested in politics, and to have a negative view of the role of authorities. Campaigners exhibited very strong mutualistic motivations.

Second, there were the 'foot soldiers'. These were also quite committed and active, but were happier to contribute in less leading positions than the campaigners. They scored highly on sense of duty items and community identity, but low on social trust. Trust tended instead to be invested in the group, which was considered to know best how to improve services.

In contrast with the first two types, the third type, dubbed the 'scrutineers', tended to be thinkers rather than doers. They were not as active as either of the above clusters of participants, attending meetings very regularly but avoiding taking on wider responsibilities in the group. Scrutineers scored quite low on sense of duty items – they were clearly there on their own terms. They were therefore more likely to consider that the group was trying to take on too many problems or problems that were too difficult to solve. This could prevent them from becoming more active themselves, yet they were generally supportive of the group and its more active members.

Fourth, were the 'habitual participants'. These were guided particularly by internalised norms. Participation had become part of their regular programme of activities and was mature and stable, but they were not generally heavily involved in the core functions of the group.

Finally, there was one cluster of 'marginal participants', who were less active and usually of short standing with the group. These users were relatively uncommitted and inactive. Participants in this cluster were much less motivated, perceiving the costs to be higher and benefits lower. Their collectivistic motivations were almost at non-participant levels, which suggests that it would not take much for them to decide to stop.

There were also three groups of non-participants. First, there were those who were on the margins but had not yet chosen to participate. These users were generally positive about participation. While they did not perceive the costs of participation to be particularly high, they lacked strong enough motivations (benefits and collectivistic motivations) to come forward and get more involved. However, with the right encouragement, they might be persuaded. Second, there were those who felt alienated. These were likely to be more negative about participation, and to feel quite unconfident about coming forward to participate. Third, there was a minority who were simply apathetic. They did not have an opinion one way or another on participation – it was simply 'off their radar'.

The participation chain

The insights of MIT are important because they clarify the complex, dynamic mixture of individual and collective motives that lead people to participate. However, on their own they are not enough to explain what makes people participate and, especially, keep on participating. Individual and collective motivations therefore need to be linked to other aspects of the participation context if we are to provide a more rounded interpretation of why people, adults or children, take part. This leads us to propose just such a general model of motivations to participate, which we have termed the 'participation chain' (see Figure 5.5). As well as individual and collective motivations, the model includes resources, mobilisation and dynamics. We conceptualise these 'links in the chain' as non-sequential – they interact with each other together and separately.

Important resources are usually thought to include time, money, skills and confidence. Birchall and Simmons examined the effects of service users' personal resources in relation to their participation. Money did not show up as being important in our results, although this conflicts with other studies and may be an artefact of the sample, which was heavily skewed towards low incomes. Neither did time availability act as a persistent barrier. It was also found that time was influential in whether adult participants got started or not, but once people were involved it had little further effect. On proxy measures, non-participants showed up as tending to have less spare time than participants. However, among participants, there was little difference in the activity of those who had more or less of this resource. For participants, time appears to be a resource barrier that can be overcome.

Skills, however, were important, both in getting started and in supporting higher levels of participation. Similar effects were found for confidence. Participants reported much higher levels of confidence than non-participants. Among participants, confidence also had a strong correlation with the extent to which service users participate. However, the relationship between skills and confidence was not straightforward. Participants with qualifications reported feeling very confident about their ability to participate, but the correlation with another measure (regarding their confidence in personally making a difference to getting things done) was not significant. Previous experience did not correlate significantly with either indicator of confidence. However, participants who had received training were significantly more likely to report feeling more confident on both levels.

The analysis is also expanded to include the mobilisation of

Figure 5.5: The participation chain

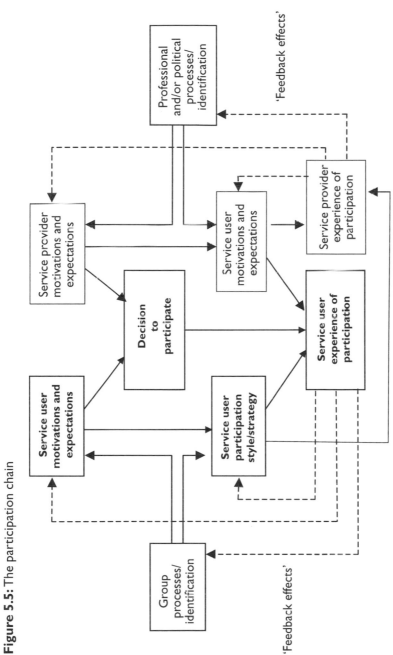

participants. In common with Lowndes and colleagues (1998, 2001b), the study found participants to be more strongly engaged by certain 'catalysing issues' than were non-participants. In relation to public services, these issues include negative relationships with authorities, a sense of relative deprivation, and a desire for change. Qualitative analysis also shows that opportunities to participate were evaluated positively by around 80% of participants when they first became aware of them. Conversely, around 70% of non-participants were more neutral or negative in their comments.

Positive evaluations of opportunities to participate, particularly in terms of their attractiveness, timeliness, relevance and expected effectiveness, therefore look to be important for mobilisation. Finally, 'active' recruitment (or being asked), as opposed to 'passive' recruitment (after reading written notices or making enquiries for themselves), was reported by around 80% of participants. Non-participants were significantly less likely to have been subjects of active recruitment (p < 0.05). Furthermore, qualitative analysis suggests that the connectedness of individuals to recruitment agents in their own social networks can influence the likelihood of recruitment. In short, it does not only matter that people get asked to participate; it matters who does the asking.

Finally, cultural and institutional factors often seem to affect attempts to foster and sustain (or sometimes block and frustrate) users' political participation. We can, therefore, consider a fourth set of factors, involving the dynamics of participation but often reflecting the cultural and institutional contexts that foster or frustrate participative initiatives. Here the literature (on adults) is also relatively well established. Key studies have looked at 'feedback effects' from participation (for example, Parry et al, 1992; Finkel and Muller, 1998). As the Department of the Environment, Transport and the Regions (DETR) observes (DETR, 1998), people often hold a positive view of their experience of participation, which may lead to the affirmation of participants' key motivations (for example, Snow et al, 1986; Snow and Oliver, 1993; Smith, 1994), and to the development over time of a commitment to

Figure 5.6: The dynamics of user participation

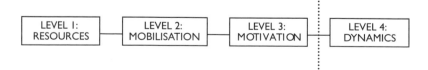

participate (for example, Andrews, 1991; Cress et al, 1997; Passy and Giugni, 2000). The role of the group must also be acknowledged in so far as it has a mediating role in structuring individuals' ongoing motivations and behaviour (for example, Baron et al, 1992) (see Figure 5.6).

In common with DETR (1998), Birchall and Simmons' qualitative findings showed that the majority of service users held a positive view of their participation experience: hence the development over time of a commitment to participate. Service users' perceptions of how difficult it would be to stop participating correlated significantly with both the level of their activity and the strength of their collectivistic motivations. The group constitutes another important aspect of the dynamics of participation. At the point where the initial decision to participate is made, users' knowledge of and relationships with the group tend to be quite abstract. Yet once they start to participate, the group can play an important role in the transformation of individuals' motivations over time. This may involve the promotion of collectivistic motivations to a primary position in people's 'motivational hierarchy'. If the experience of participation is positive (which may depend in part on positive perceptions of the structure, size, status and success of the group), the group may also help to develop greater commitment to participation. For example, participants may increasingly align their aims with those of the group ('shared goals'), or internalise group norms ('shared values').

Children's participation

There are few research studies of children's participation that systematically take into account the full range of factors assembled in MIT and the participation chain. One significant exception is Thomas's (2002) study of 'looked after' children and their participation in decision making at reviews and planning meetings. This setting is one that has an inevitable focus on the individual and is, therefore, somewhat different from participation processes intended for children as a group. Nevertheless, Thomas identifies a series of questions, in the main derived from his field material, that parallel those discussed above. These include the differences between participants and non-participants, the provision of opportunities to participate and why some children choose not to take them up, and different attitudes to involvement. While this research does not explicitly draw on concepts drawn from the recent literature on (largely adult) participation, except for Arnstein's (1969) notion of the ladder of participation and Hart's (1992) adaptation, the analysis suggests that this could be done.

However, the dearth of cross-referencing between research on adult and child participation does not mean that many common factors are not implicitly recognised in many different discussions of children's participation. They often are, especially by writers who synthesise the accumulated experience of the many different projects and initiatives across the UK and internationally (see, for example, Lansdown, 2001; Sinclair, 2004; Lansdown, Chapter Eight, this volume). All this suggests that there is a great deal of scope for deploying the MIT and the participation chain exactly because they draw on a wide range of factors found by research to be important and pull these together in a model that can generate a systematic set of research questions.

Starting with motivation and incentives to take part, it is clear that this has been recognised as a key issue in many discussions of children's participation. Children's participation is frequently promoted through claims that it brings benefits, generally seen as a mixture of individual ones (for example, improved self-esteem and assertiveness, feelings of empowerment, and access to information and skills) and collective ones (for example, services becoming more responsive to needs, improved decision making, the fulfilment of rights and legal responsibilities, enhanced democracy and promoting child protection) (see Sinclair, 2004). Thomas's (2002, p 170) study is an exception in its suggestion of a typology of different types of attitude among children to their (individual) participation in decision making: the 'assertive' (children have the right to be heard); the 'submissive' ('we don't need much say'); the 'reasonable' (children and adults should listen to each other); and the 'avoidant'. However, this deals with attitudes rather than patterns of actual participation and, to our knowledge, few studies have been undertaken to look systematically at children's motives for participation, how these are balanced between individual and collective benefits, whether these cluster into different types of participant, and how these change over time as experience of participation is gained[2].

In terms of resources for participation, there is some evidence from studies of adults to suggest that these are important in shaping which individuals become active and which do not. Verba and colleagues (2000, p 265) observe of adults that, '... participatory activities vary in their resource requirements and individuals vary in their resource endowments. Resource constraints are an important factor in determining who becomes active in what way'.

Research that examines the prior resource factors that differentiate individual children in terms of their participation is hard to find, although there is a keen appreciation by practitioners and policy makers of the need to broaden participation to include socially marginal children and those excluded in various ways, for example by class, gender race and disability. It is not uncommon for opinions generated in children's participative forums to be dismissed as those of a vocal, white, male, middle-class group. It is important to emphasise, as Lansdown (2001, p 14) does, that:

> Children, like adults are not a homogenous group ... what is important is that all the children who have a legitimate interest in a project are encouraged and enabled to participate and that weaker or more isolated children are not marginalized. There is a danger that the only children who get involved are the articulate, better off, able individuals who, while having a valid contribution to make, do not reflect the breadth of children's experience.

Studies of children's experiences of poverty (see Ridge, 2002 and Chapter Two, this volume), for example, suggest that poverty does restrict children's capacity to participate in activities that their better-off peers enjoy, so there may well be differences among children in this respect. As Lansdown (2001, p 15) notes, organisational thinking about children's participation needs to plan simple practicalities by, for example, providing travel costs, even local bus fares, in advance of any meetings. Similarly, careful thought needs to given to practices that do not exclude children because of gender, race and disability. In relation to time, studies such as that by Christensen (2002) suggest that children as well as adults are affected by a contemporary time squeeze. But how this affects different children and how it impacts on their capacity to take part in participative democracy is unknown.

It is significant that McNeish (1999, p 199), while considering barriers to participation, links motivation to skills development:

> *Motivating and supporting participants:* young people also require support, information and skills development in order for them to become active participants. Organisations need to consider what the incentives are for young people to become involved.

At a more general level, the issue of resources is reflected in many discussions of children's participation in a way related to the status of children in society. Children are simultaneously recognised as having enormous insight, energy and commitment to bring to participation and, at the same time, needing an infusion of resources to support it, especially resources for empowerment and developing new skills. For example, the report on an initiative to set up a Liverpool Children's Bureau (Liverpool CVS, The Children's Society and Save the Children, undated), which involved a high degree of children's participation, suggests that 'children have brilliant ideas' but also that long-term resources, especially support from adult workers, are needed to sustain their participation. Similarly, Larter's (1998, p 22) study of Youth Councils suggests that failure to involve children does not take into account their 'experiences or competence in making difficult decisions'. At the same time, Larter calls for training for young people in taking part in such initiatives.

This position is theoretically mirrored in the social studies of childhood (see, for example, James et al, 2000). On the one hand, children are seen as social actors, implying that children have knowledge, capacities and competencies developed through their everyday interactions with others that they can bring to participative activities. On the other hand, children are seen as a minority group: they are systematically excluded from access to many of the resources that many adults take for granted and are stereotyped as irrational, incompetent and deficient when compared to an idealised version of adults. Thomas (2002, p 169), for example, finds that that a belief pervasive among adults is that adults know best and children are not to be trusted to make really important decisions. This underlines that recognising existing skills and calling for the development of new ones is not contradictory, especially for groups that have been stigmatised or excluded. However, it must also be recognised that what is said of children is, in fact, said of many adult groups, such as tenants and disabled people. Children and adults alike bring many personal resources to the participation table but they can often be further empowered by training and skills development.

The participation chain pays particular attention to the creation and promotion of opportunities for participation, or 'facilitating conditions' as McAdam (1996) terms them, and these have been widely identified as an important factor (for example, Lowndes and Wilson, 1999; Maloney et al, 2000). Not surprisingly, this is a theme frequently raised in discussions of children's participation. Hill and colleagues (2004, p 84), for example, after recognising the many efforts of professionals and agencies to develop children's participation, go on to say:

> ... frequently children's views are not sought or, if sought, still disregarded within everyday institutions (for example, schools), local government settings (for example, social service departments) and national government processes (for example, in the drafting of Home Office legislation).... The refusal to accept that children and young people are competent witnesses to their own lives has confined them to a state of impotency, at the mercy of adults, some of whom, as history teaches us, cannot be relied upon.

Clearly, lack of opportunity to participate is important for children as a group (despite all the differences between children) as well as children as individuals. This relates to the minority group status of children discussed above, for while many socially marginal adults also lack such opportunities, it is not the case that adulthood in itself would be seen as an obstacle to participation.

Previous research about adult participation has pointed to the importance of recruitment efforts in mobilising participants (for example, Klandermans and Oegema, 1987, 1994; Jordan and Maloney, 1996). While some individuals seek out participation opportunities themselves, 'being asked' tends to be reported by participants as important in their mobilisation. This is particularly the case where the 'recruitment agent' is known to them through their existing social networks (Klandermans, 1984; Rosenstone and Hansen, 1993; Brady and colleagues, 1999). In practice, most opportunities for children to participate are created by adults or, at best, alliances of children and sympathetic adults. Guides to working with children on participation activities set out a variety of important points touching on recruitment and mobilisation. These include, for example, not imposing an adult agenda, listening to children's priorities and advice about methods of participation, and being inclusive. However, there appears to be little research that has traced the effects of different ways of recruiting children. Similarly, there is little research on children's self-organising activities, which tend to be invisible and unrecorded, and are at the moment accessed primarily by historical and ethnographic scholarship.

Finally, many writers have noted that matters to do with the dynamics of children's participation are important. Many of these issues, such as negotiating clear goals, roles and boundaries, are common to participation by adults but there are three topics, to do with the sustainability of participation, that seem particularly important in relation to children. The first concerns the inevitable growth of child participators, which creates '... continual "haemorrhaging" as children grow up' and requires building 'the capacity to involve new children and transfer of skills from older to younger children' (Lansdown, 2001, p 17). Although this kind of succession crisis is felt by many organisations, the timescale is likely to be different for children. Sustainability also requires that children's participation initiatives necessarily work with adults, especially those in positions of influence over decision making, who have to be recruited into the process and become convinced of the need to take children's inputs seriously. This involves overcoming prejudices against children and bringing about long-term organisational change so that this becomes part of the permanent structure and organisational culture (for discussion, see Chapter Six). Lastly, it is important that children's participation achieves at least some change. While this is probably true of all participative ventures, children face a particular problem identified by Baraldi (2003). Reporting research about a participative town planning initiative for children in Italy, he notes that while local politicians were supportive, even enthusiastic, about it, they regarded children's participation as primarily an educational activity for the children. They did not expect to have to take up the suggestions that it generated. The project became an exercise in reproducing social representations rather than one of participative democracy. Its dynamics were affected as the children and adults involved had to develop ways of surviving disappointment.

Implications for researching children's participation

The questions we have raised in this chapter could be addressed equally to both child and adult participation. Certainly, many of the issues raised by the research on the participation of adult public service users strongly echo those raised in research about children's participation. However, to our knowledge, research on children's participation has not brought these insights together into a comprehensive and general model of participation. Indeed, the theory that informs much research on children's participation seems relatively uninformed by the wider research on participation, even though the participation of both adults and children seems to raise many common issues and concerns. This is perhaps understandable when the main effort of those interested in children's participation has gone into the practical, and often local, tasks of building mechanisms for children's participation. Furthermore, the topic has received relatively little attention from the research community as a whole, which remains deficient in its adult-centricity.

We suggest, therefore, that MIT and the concept of the participation chain could form a useful research agenda for children's participation. They raise a number of key questions and relate them in a systematic way that is relevant to children's involvement in public services but extends to many other contexts. Employing such a common framework would encourage comparison to be made across different contexts, thus allowing differences and similarities between them to become more visible. The questions can be summarised as follows:

1. Motivation to participate

In a given context, who participates and who does not? What is the relative importance of children's individual and collective motives to participate? To what extent do children calculate the costs and benefits of participation? To what extent do they have shared goals, values and a sense of community? How do participants and non-participants compare on these dimensions? Do there seem to be different types or clusters of participants? What similarities and differences in these factors can be found between different contexts and between adults and children?

2. Resources

In a given context, what are the resources children need to participate? What is the role of money, time, skills and confidence? How do these different resources affect the degree to which different children participate? What similarities and differences are found between different contexts, different groups of children and between children and adults?

3. Mobilisation

In a given context, what opportunities for participation exist? How appropriate are these and what processes of recruitment into participation take place? What similarities and differences are found between different contexts, different groups of children and between children and adults?

4. Dynamics

In a given context, what are the dynamics of the participation process? How does the experience of taking part feed back into the process – negatively or positively? How are the frustrations and disappointments of participation handled and what are the consequences? What similarities and differences are found between different contexts, different groups of children and between children and adults?

Crucially, the participation chain suggests that these questions should be considered together. The 'chain' metaphor represents the fact that each individual link needs to be made as strong as possible if participation itself is to be strengthened. People, whether children or adults, might be motivated to participate and have sufficient resources, but remain unmobilised. They might have been asked to participate and be motivated to do so, but lack the necessary resources. Or they might have been asked to take part and have the resources to participate, but be insufficiently motivated. This raises the question of whether more can be done to ensure that people are properly resourced, mobilised and motivated – a weak link might cause the 'chain' to break. The potential for the dynamics of participation to feed back positively or negatively on each or any of these links also needs to be recognised. Beyond this, however, the chain metaphor also implies that the links must be connected up effectively if participation is not to fail. For instance, it is insufficient to say that we simply need to train people in the necessary skills, unless appropriate opportunities are going to be provided to use those skills. Similarly, it is insufficient to say that we should appeal to people's 'collectivistic incentives' in participation initiatives, but then fail to engage in active recruitment. The links in the chain need to be joined together, in a coordinated way, if participation is effectively to be strengthened.

We began this chapter by noting the relatively high degree of separation between the discussion of children's participation and that of adults, particularly adult public service user participation. It is as if there is an assumption that adult and child participation is different in principle. Such an *a priori* assumption seems to us to be unnecessary. At most it ought to be an empirical question rather than a foundational assumption. This is not to deny that there may be widespread differences between adults and children. There may be – but if there are, then they will be rendered visible by the use of a common framework of investigation. The approach we are advocating can be termed 'analytically symmetrical' between adults and children (see Prout, 2000, p xi; Christensen and Prout, 2002). Derived from actor network theory (see Callon, 1986) and implicit in the sociology of childhood (James et al, 2000; Prout, 2005), this radically deconstructive principle requires that a single analytical language be used to understand the activities of both children and adults. Differences must be allowed to *arise from* the analysis rather than being a condition of it. In the context of this chapter, it means that the issues and problems of participation are treated as comprehensible in the same terms for both children and adults, even if these issues and problems are not identical for both children and adults in a given context. Recognising this makes it possible to think of children's participation through insights drawn from studies of adult participation and vice versa.

Notes

[1] ESRC award number L215252002. Using multi-level, cluster sampling of user group participants ($n=392$) in three UK local authorities, quantitative data were collected using face-to-face interviews and an internally reliable (alpha = 0.7649) Scale of Collectivistic Motivations. A comparison group of non-participants ($n=106$), defined as service users who were aware of the opportunity to participate but had never been known to take it up, were also interviewed in the same manner. In addition, the main survey was supplemented with semi-structured interviews with key informants, such as local elected councillors, senior officers, front-line staff, voluntary organisations and service users. For a detailed exposition of the quantitative data produced by this study see Simmons and Birchall, 2005. It is important to note that this study concerned collective forms of participation, such as being in a tenants' organisation, self-help group, or service user consultative group. A separate follow-on study (Simmons et al, 2006; ESRC award number 143250040) gathering greater in-depth data, as well as further survey data, is being conducted at the time of writing. This study is concerned with identifying different 'cultures of participation' of service users and comparing them with those involved in the provision of services. It widens forms of participation, including bureau-political forms (such as contacting a political representative) and market-like mechanisms (such as going

through a complaints procedure), as well as participation in user groups and the like.

[2] There are, however, studies of children's motivations to participate in activities such as sport. See, for example, Longhurst and Spink, 1987.

References

Alford, J. (2002) 'Defining the client in the public sector: a social-exchange perspective', *Public Administration Review*, vol 62, no 3, pp 337-46.

Andrews, M. (1991) *Lifetimes of Commitment*, Cambridge: Cambridge University Press.

Argyle, M. (1991) *Cooperation: The Basis of Sociability*, London: Routledge.

Arnstein, S. (1969) 'Eight rungs on the ladder of citizen participation', *Journal of American Institute of Planners*, vol 35, pp 216-24.

Axelrod, R. (1984) *The Evolution of Cooperation*, New York, NY: Basic Books.

Baraldi, C. (2003) 'Planning childhood: children's social participation in the town of adults', in P. Christensen and M. O'Brien (eds) *Children in the City: Home, Neighbourhood and Community*, London: Routledge Falmer.

Baron, R., Kerr, N. and Miller, N. (1992) *Group Process, Group Decision, Group Action*, Buckingham: Open University Press.

Beck, U. (1992) *Risk Society: Towards a New Modernity*, London: Sage Publications.

Beresford, P. (2001) 'Participation and social policy: transformation, liberation or regulation?', *Social Policy Review 14*, Bristol: The Policy Press, pp 265-90.

Beresford, P. and Croft, S. (1993) *Citizen Involvement: A Practical Guide for Change*, London: Macmillan.

Birchall, J. and Simmons, R. (2004) *User Power*, London: National Consumer Council.

Blau, P. (1964) *Exchange and Power in Social Life*, New York, NY: Wiley.

Bochel, C. and Bochel, H. (2004) *The UK Social Policy Process*, Basingstoke: Palgrave Macmillan.

Brady, H., Schlozman, K. and Verba, S. (1999) 'Prospecting for participants: rational expectations and the recruitment of political activists', *American Political Science Review*, vol 93, pp 153-68.

Cabinet Office (1999) *Involving Users: Improving the Delivery of Local Public Services*, London: Service First Unit.

Callon, M. (1986) 'Some elements of a sociology of translation: domestication of the scallops and the fishermen of St Brieuc Bay', in J. Law (ed) *Power, Action and Belief: A New Sociology of Knowledge?*, London: Routledge.

Christensen, P.H. (2002) 'Why more "quality time" is not on the top of children's lists: the "qualities of time" for children', *Children & Society*, vol 16, no 2, pp 77-88.

Christensen, P. and Prout, A. (2002) 'Working with ethical symmetry in social research with children', *Childhood*, vol 9, no 4, pp 477-97.

Cress, D., McPherson, J. and Rotolo, T. (1997) 'Competition and commitment in voluntary memberships', *Sociological Perspectives*, vol 40, no 1, pp 61-79.

CYPU (Children and Young People's Unit) (2001) *Core Principles for the Involvement of Children and Young People*, London: Department for Education and Skills.

DETR (Department of the Environment, Transport and the Regions) (1998) *Guidance on Enhancing Public Participation in Local Government*, London: DETR.

DETR (1999) *Developing Good Practice in Tenant Participation*, London: DETR.

DH (Department of Health) (1998) *Moving in to the Mainstream*, London: DH.

DH (2001) *The Essence of Care*, London: DH.

DTI (Department of Trade and Industry) (2001) *Modern Markets: Confident Consumers*, London: DTI.

Ekeh, P. (1974) *Social Exchange Theory: The Two Traditions*, Cambridge, MA: Harvard University Press.

Finkel, S. and Muller, E. (1998) 'Rational choice and the dynamics of collective political action: evaluating alternative models with panel data', *American Political Science Review*, vol 92, no 1, pp 37-49.

Finkel, S., Muller, E. and Opp, K. (1989) 'Personal influence, collective rationality, and mass political action', *American Political Science Review*, vol 83, no 3, pp 885-903.

Giddens, A. (1990) *The Consequences of Modernity*, Cambridge: Polity Press.

Giddens, A. (1991) *Modernity and Self-identity*, Cambridge: Polity Press.

Hart, R.A. (1992) *Children's Participation, from Tokenism to Citizenship*, Florence: UNICEF

Hill, M., Davis, J., Tisdall, K. and Prout, A. (2004) 'Moving the participation agenda forward', *Children & Society*, vol 18, no 2, pp 77-96.

Homans, G. (1961) *Social Behaviour: Its Elementary Forms*, New York, NY: Harcourt, Brace and World.

Homans, G. (1974) *Social Behaviour: Its Elementary Forms* (2nd edn), New York, NY: Harcourt Brace Jovanovich.

James, A. Jenks, C. and Prout, A. (2000) *Theorizing Childhood*, Cambridge: Polity Press.

Jordan, G. and Maloney, W. (1996) 'How bumble bees fly: accounting for public interest participation', *Political Studies*, vol 44, pp 668-85.

Klandermans, B. (1984) 'Mobilization and participation: social-psychological expansions of resource mobilization theory', *American Sociological Review*, vol 49, pp 583-600.

Klandermans, B. (1997) *The Social Psychology of Protest*, Oxford: Blackwell.

Klandermans, B. and Oegema, D. (1987) 'Potentials, networks, motivations and barriers: steps towards participation in social movements', *American Sociological Review*, vol 52, pp 519-31.

Klandermans, B. and Oegema, D. (1994) 'Why social movement sympathizers don't participate: erosion and nonconversion of support', *American Sociological Review*, vol 59, pp 703-22.

Lansdown, G. (2001) *Promoting Children's Participation in Democratic Decision-making*, Florence: UNICEF Innocenti Research Centre.

Larter, L. (1998) *Youth Councils and their Influence on Local Government*, British Youth Council: Mimeo.

Liverpool CVS, The Children's Society and Save the Children (undated) *Citizens Now! A Report into Children's Participation in Liverpool: Does the City Need a Children's Bureau*, Liverpool: Liverpool CVS, The Children's Society and Save the Children.

Longhurst, K. and Spink, K.S. (1987) 'Participation motivation of Australian children involved in organised sport', *Canadian Journal of Sports Science*, vol 12, no 1, pp 24-30.

Lowndes, V. and Wilson, D. (1999) 'Social capital and local governance: exploring the institutional design variable', Paper presented to the Associational Engagement and Democracy in Cities Workshop, ECPR Joint Sessions, Copenhagen, 14-19 April.

Lowndes, V., Pratchett, L. and Stoker, G. (2001a) 'Trends in public participation: Part 1—Local government perspectives', *Public Administration*, vol 79, no 1, pp 205-22.

Lowndes, V., Pratchett, L. and Stoker, G. (2001b) 'Trends in public participation: Part 2—Citizens' perspectives', *Public Administration*, vol 79, no 2, pp 445-55.

Lowndes, V., Stoker, G., Pratchett, L., Wilson, D., Leach, S. and Wingfield, M. (1998) *Enhancing Public Participation in Local Government*, London: Department of the Environment, Transport and the Regions.

Maloney, W., Smith, G. and Stoker, G. (2000) 'Social capital and urban governance: adding a more contextualised "top-down" perspective', *Political Studies*, vol 48, no 4, pp 823-41.

McAdam, D. (1996) 'Conceptual origins, current problems, future directions', in D. McAdam, J. McCarthy and M. Zald (eds) *Comparative Perspectives on Social Movements*, Cambridge: Cambridge University Press.

McNeish, D. (1999) 'Promoting participation for children and young people: some key questions for health and social welfare organizations', *Journal of Social Work Practice*, vol 13, no 2, pp 191-203.

McNeish, D. and Newman, T. (2002) 'Involving children and young people in decision-making', in D. McNeish, H. Newman and H. Roberts (eds) *What Works for Children? Effective Services for Children and Families*, Buckingham: Open University Press.

Molm, L. (2000) 'Theories of social exchange and exchange networks', in G. Ritzer and B. Smart (eds) *The Handbook of Social Theory*, Thousand Oaks, CA: Sage.

Molm, L. (2003) 'Theoretical comparisons of forms of exchange', *Sociological Theory*, vol 21, no 1, pp 1-17.

Muller, E. and Opp, K. (1986) 'Rational choice and rebellious collective action', *American Political Science Review*, vol 80, no 2, pp 471-87.

Muller, E. and Opp, K. (1987) 'Rebellious collective action revisited', *American Political Science Review*, vol 81, no 2, pp 557-64.

NCC (National Consumer Council) (2001) *Involving Patients and the Public in Healthcare*, London: NCC.

NCC (2004) *Making Public Services Personal*, London: NCC.

Newman, J. (2001) *Modernising Governance*, London: Sage Publications.

Olson, M. (1965) *The Logic of Collective Action*, New York, NY: Schocken Books.

Parry, G., Moyser, G. and Day, N. (1992) *Political Participation and Democracy in Britain*, Cambridge: Cambridge University Press.

Peters, B. and Savoie, D. (1998) 'Introduction', in B. Peters and D. Savoie (eds) *Taking Stock*, London: McGill-Queens University Press.

Pierre, J. (1998) 'Public consultation and citizen participation', in B. Peters and D. Savoie (eds) *Taking Stock*, London: McGill-Queens University Press.

Prout, A. (2000) 'Foreword', in P. Christensen and A. James, *Research with Children*, London: Falmer Press.

Prout, A. (2005) *The Future of Childhood: Towards the Interdisciplinary Study of Children*, London: RoutledgeFalmer.

Ridge, T. (2002) *Childhood Poverty and Social Exclusion: From a Child's Perspective*, Bristol: The Policy Press.

Ridley, M. (1996) *The Origins of Virtue*, London: Penguin Books.

Rosenstone, S. and Hansen, J. (1993) *Mobilization, Participation, and Democracy in America*, New York, NY: Macmillan.

Scott, J. (2000) 'Rational choice theory', in G. Browning, A. Halcli and F. Webster (eds) *Understanding Contemporary Society: Theories of The Present*, London: Sage Publications.

Simmons, R. and Birchall, J. (2005) 'A joined-up approach to user participation in public services: strengthening the "participation chain"', *Social Policy and Administration*, vol 39, no 3, pp 260-83.

Simmons, R., Birchall, J. and Prout, A. (2006) 'Cultural tensions in public service delivery: implications for producer–consumer relationships', Working Paper 026, ESRC/AHRC Cultures of Consumption Programme (www.consume.bbk.ac.uk/publications.html).

Sinclair, R. (2004) 'Participation in practice: making it meaningful, effective and sustainable', *Children &Society*, vol 18, no 2, pp 106-18.

Smith, D.H. (1994) 'Determinants of voluntary association participation and volunteering', *Non-profit and Voluntary Sector Quarterly*, vol 23, no 3, pp 243-63.

Snow, D. and Oliver, P. (1993) 'Social movements and collective behaviour: social psychological dimensions and considerations', in K. Cook, G. Fine and J. House (eds) *Sociological Perspectives on Social Psychology*, New York, NY: Allyn and Bacon.

Snow, D., Rochford, E., Worden, S. and Benford, R. (1986) 'Frame alignment processes, micromobilization, and movement participation', *American Sociological Review*, vol 51, pp 464-81.

Sorokin, P. (1954) *The Ways and Power of Love*, Boston: Beacon Press.

Stewart, J. (1997) 'Innovation in democratic practice in local government', *Policy & Politics*, vol 24, no 1, pp 29-41.

Stoker, G. (1997) 'Local political participation', in R. Hambleton (ed) *New Perspectives on Local Governance*, York: Joseph Rowntree Foundation.

Thomas, N. (2002) *Children, Family and the State: Decision-making and Child Participation*, Bristol: The Policy Press.

Van Vugt, M., Snyder, M., Tyler, T.R. and Biel, A. (eds) (2000) *Cooperation in Modern Society*, London: Routledge.

Verba, S., Schlozman, K. and Brady, H. (2000) 'Rational action and political activity', *Journal of Theoretical Politics*, vol 12, no 3, pp 243-68.

Whiteley, P. and Seyd, P. (1992) *Labour's Grass Roots*, Oxford: Clarendon Press.

Whiteley, P. and Seyd, P. (1996) 'Rationality and party activism: encompassing tests of alternative models of political participation', *European Journal of Political Research*, vol 29, pp 215-34.

Whiteley, P. and Seyd, P. (1998) 'New Labour – new party?', Paper presented at the American Political Science Association Conference, Boston, 2-9 September.

Whiteley, P., Seyd, P., Richardson, J. and Bissell, P. (1993) 'Explaining party activism: the case of the British Conservative Party', *British Journal of Political Science*, vol 24, pp 79-94.

SIX

Included in governance? Children's participation in 'public' decision making

E. Kay M. Tisdall and Robert Bell

Peters (1996) comments: '... the very people who may have the most to gain from participation may be the same people who are least likely actually to participate in the policy process' (p 121). This comment is particularly true for children[1]. Children are subject to intense state and public intervention and are some of the highest users of public services but, until recently, they have been officially excluded from the policy process.

Now, children's participation *is* on the national policy agenda in the UK. Overviews of activities across the UK (Carnegie Young People Initiative, 2001; Cutler and Taylor, 2003) point to a general increase in participation activities and opportunities. The most recent evidence comes from a postal survey of statutory and voluntary organisations, undertaken in England (Oldfield and Fowler, 2004). Four out of five organisations reported involving children in decision making, with 89% of statutory and 74% of non-governmental organisations[2] (NGOs) reporting an increase in participation work over the past four years. Involvement, however, was not equally distributed across activities. Children were most likely to be involved in generating ideas about existing and new policies and services, and least likely to be involved in service delivery, monitoring and evaluation.

Respondents report that children had *some* influence on decisions made by their organisation (71% of statutory and 62% of NGOs). But only one in ten statutory and three in ten NGO respondents thought that children had a 'great deal' of influence on organisational decisions. Respondents differed considerably on the effectiveness of particular approaches, although a commonality was the view that all approaches could be effective – if undertaken properly.

As children's participation is taking hold in policy and practice, the question of how much impact such participation has on decision making is gaining volume (see also Kirby with Bryson, 2002). Concerns have been raised from children and adults alike, that children's involvement in decision-making can be tokenistic, a 'tick-box' exercise that fails to result in any substantive change (CIS, 2000; Sinclair, 2004). The arguments on children's participation now stretch beyond the mere recognition that children should participate, to demands that this participation result in 'political' change.

In the UK, discussions on children's participation have been largely separate from more generic debates that dominate the political and development studies literature – debates around changing forms of government and governance, policy networks and new institutionalism, social capital and civil society. These debates have been asking questions about how to understand policy making in the UK, who is involved (and who is not), and how to bolster 'public' participation. This chapter asks whether these literatures provide useful ways of understanding and challenging both policy and practice in children's participation in 'public' decision making. A previous article (Tisdall and Davis, 2004) applied a particular vein within political science, that of policy networks, to an example of children's participation in national decision making. This chapter builds on that article, this time considering the wider lenses of governance, 'participatory governance' and civil society.

Governance, participatory governance and civil society

Governance as a concept, as Magnette (2003) notes, is 'rarely defined with precision' (p 144). For this chapter, the concept is fruitful because of how it considers policy processes. Richards and Smith's explanation captures this:

> 'Governance' is a descriptive label that is used to highlight the changing nature of the policy process in recent decades. In particular, it sensitizes us to the ever-increasing variety of terrains and actors involved in the making of public policy. Thus, it demands that we consider all the actors and locations beyond the 'core executive' involved in the policy-making process. (2002, p 2)

Within the governance literature, strong claims are made that there has been a shift from government to governance in the UK. Governance is not only a new academic agenda – although it is – but an actual change in practice.

Across the literature, there is a common narrative that the current move to governance is a reaction to the difficulties caused by earlier moves to corporate management and marketisation. Control was lost to the centre, with problems of fragmentation, lack of accountability and the power to steer. One result is the current focus on 'joined-up government' and 'partnerships' to try to regain control and address fragmentation. These challenges, and resulting solutions, are neatly captured by the Westminster White Paper *Modernising Government*, which sets out three aims for government:

1. Ensuring that policy making is more joined up and strategic.
2. Making sure that public service users are the focus.
3. Delivering public services that are high quality and efficient. (Cabinet Office, 1999, p 6)

The second aim requires that service users' concerns are listened to and they should be involved in decisions about how services are provided (Cabinet Office, 1999, ch 3, para 6). Such an aim is captured theoretically by Lovan and colleagues' notion of 'participatory governance':

> Governance, in short, is a process of participation which depends on networks of engagement, which attempts to embrace diversity in contemporary society; which promotes greater responsiveness to service users and, in so doing, seeks to reshape accountability relationships. (2004, pp 7-8)

The development studies literature also utilises ideas of governance and participation, applied internationally. 'Good' governance has become a central issue in the past decade. Good governance is equated with democracy and a vibrant and active civil society is essential. NGOs are identified as particularly vital. International donors have deliberately substituted them for the state, as more efficient service providers and better able to reach 'the poorest of the poor'. NGOs are also supported as a 'counterbalance' to the state, as the creators and supporters of civil society (Clark, 1995; Edwards and Hulme, 1996; Deakin, 2001).

Civil or civic society may have become a concept widely used in the UK and internationally, both by academics and international funders, but like governance it is an imprecise concept with various definitions. Today, it is typically used as an 'oppositional pair' with the state – see above – although in fact the concept is highly reliant on the state. Much of civil society theory is about influencing the state and indeed civic society depends on the structural protection of the state (Hearn, 2001). Civil society is also dependent conceptually on there being a private–public divide, between the privacy of one's household and the 'public' sphere of engagement. Key definitional elements are the voluntary or 'uncoerced' associations made in this public sphere, captured by Walzer's much-quoted definition:

> The words 'civil society' name the space of uncoerced human association and also the set of relational networks – formed for the sake of family, faith, interest and ideology – that fill this space. (1995, p 7)

Certain authors resolve the differing definitions by focusing on civil society as a space or an arena, where various activities take place (Deakin, 2001; Hearn, 2001).

How can these ideas, literatures and debates be useful in understanding children's participation? Children are the quintessential 'non-governmental public actors' because they are largely prohibited from being *governmental* actors: due to age prohibitions, they are not allowed to hold public office, they cannot be employed to any substantial extent until the age of 16 in government positions, they cannot vote in democratic elections. But they *can* be part of civil society, and current legal and policy provisions construct them as independent actors in a range of settings, albeit with some ambiguities (Jones and Bell, 2000). The arguments for children's participation can be recast into claims for children to be recognised and supported as part of civil society; conceptually and practically brought out of the 'private' sphere of the family and institutions, into the 'public' sphere of policy making and debate. Then questions can be asked about their place within the purported moves towards participatory governance. The development literature leads to questions about understanding and evaluating NGOs as key organisers of children's public action and frequently crucial intermediaries between children and those in power. Civil society theory, however, has been criticised for its failure to analyse power relationships (Fisher, 1997) and its unsophisticated understanding of policy making (Deakin, 2001). Here, the debates on governance and policy networks may be useful in understanding how children's participation can (or cannot) influence policy making.

Two case studies pick up and explore these ideas, in light of children's participation in national policy making. The first describes an attempt to integrate children's participation into the workings of Whitehall (participatory governance) and do so across all its departments (joined-up government). This is the Children and Young People's Unit's *Learning to Listen* (DfEE, 2001a), explored from the perspective of one of the authors who worked in the unit. The second case study explores an NGO's attempt to support groups of disabled children in national policy making, where the NGO acted as an intermediary for children's participation in civil society, and its impact on 'the state'. Both examples thus relate to key elements of the literature above. As recent examples, they also allow for tracing through of (some) policy impacts – and an exploration of what facilitated or blocked these.

Learning to listen

In 2000, the Children and Young People's Unit (CYPU) was established, explicitly to address the lack of coordinated policy and structure across Whitehall departments, on children and young people's issues. Among its core tasks, the CYPU was given cross-departmental responsibilities to promote 'children's engagement in their services and communities' (DfEE, 2001b).

In response, the CYPU published *Learning to Listen* (DfEE, 2001a). This document sets out the core principles that central government departments should adopt in establishing a new relationship with children:

1. A visible commitment should be made to involving children and young people, underpinned by appropriate resources to build a capacity to implement policies of participation.
2. Children and young people's involvement should be valued.
3. Children and young people should have equal opportunities to get involved.
4. Policies and standards for the participation of children and young people should be provided, evaluated and continuously improved. (DfEE, 2001a, pp 10-11)

Learning to Listen, it was hoped, would support more effective engagement that would in turn lead to better policies and services, improvements in the prevention and tackling of children's social exclusion, and more children benefiting fully from the services and policies designed to help them. In the document, children are thus constructed primarily as policy and service *consumers*.

Learning to Listen therefore challenged the civil service to develop new ways of working. In the first wave, in 2002, 11 departments signed up to the principles. From the outset, there were issues about the capacity and skills base of the civil service. In each of the 11 departments, specific officials were given lead responsibility for producing annual action plans. Typically, this role was one among other responsibilities lead officials had to juggle. Often officials were relatively junior. There was thus frequently a trade-off between levels of energy and enthusiasm for a challenging new agenda, and the experience and influence necessary for individual civil servants to win the heart, minds and practical support of colleagues and ministers.

The cross-departmental vision set out in *Learning to Listen* challenges the isolated 'policy chimneys' of government departments (see Rhodes, 1997) but, in practice, those chimneys have been remarkably resistant to erosion. The CYPU took on a 'light-touch' coordination, aiming to nurture the goodwill of departments, rather than to hold them to account for their activity – or lack of activity. Staff in the CYPU supported individual officials from signatory departments to put together their action plans. In practice, the quality of action plans varied widely and there was no mechanism for quality assuring submissions.

In the first wave of actions plans (2002-03), departments and officials, burdened by competing policy priorities and demands, tended to adopt a defensive posture and concentrate on demonstrating that they were indeed already active. Only limited attention was given to how identified activities could be replicated and how they could permeate the breadth and depth of departmental activities. The scale of the task was acknowledged but, in general, no attempts were made to articulate clearly what *successful* implementation might look like. In the second year of action plans (2003-04), shifts could be seen. Longer-term considerations were beginning to be noted. There were more references to improved coordination across departments and to the desire to ensure that future action plans better reflected the ways children and young people wished to be involved, and aspirations for more deeply embedded work in departments' formal structures. In the Department for Work and Pensions, for example, a cross-departmental steering group was established, recognising that children and young people's needs demanded responses and engagement from other departments.

As an exemplar of 'joined-up working', the assumptions underpinning the action plan approach – the fundamental mechanism for implementing *Learning to Listen* – may be flawed within this new governance landscape. A departmental action plan and a small central delivery team require a department's civil service to be committed uniformly and to give priority to a participation action plan. This approach presumes that a small and influential team can drive change from a central point, often buried away within a bureaucracy. Far more effective might be an approach that concentrates on identifying senior actors within departments that together wish to, and can make, change happen. For example, Department for Environment, Food and Rural Affairs is piloting 'action learning' as a means of helping officials improve their thinking and practice, and better manage organisational change.

Most 'mainstreaming' policies trickle down from 'on high' in directorates and are rigorously monitored and improved. It could be argued that children's participation has been prematurely mainstreamed – set afloat while many of the basic elements are not in place, and hearts, minds and business managers not won over; left to sink or swim as policy makers' attention moves elsewhere. With doubts over the future coordinating role and central thrust behind *Learning to Listen*, participation could be said to be occupying the architecture of mainstreaming, but without the prerequisite substance. More optimistically, within this process, some departments have been innovative and understood the scale of the challenge they face. One approach used with some success has been the Office of the Deputy Prime Minister's use of external secondees to design its annual programmes.

Indeed, the use of external expertise was explicitly recommended by *Learning to Listen*, another example of the broadening of governance to include NGOs. Such organisations have come to occupy an unusual position in this new emerging governance landscape. Previously, civil servants had primarily related to children's NGOs in two ways: reacting to their campaigns for change or contracting them to undertake specific pieces of work. The participation agenda has altered these relations. The agenda was so new that the civil service did not have strategic or practical expertise to direct change. Therefore, government had a strong need for external assistance. Certain NGOs have greatly benefited from government largess, becoming deeply entwined in the governmental process through delivering consultations with children, running workshops, and producing guidelines. NGOs themselves, however, had not articulated a shared strategic vision for children's participation nor an organised approach to government requests, so that relationships between certain NGOs and government departments have frequently been based on serendipity or even personal contacts. Certain NGOs have therefore become deeply entwined in this 'participatory governance' and the civil service, while others have a considerably more marginal position.

Citizenship in practice

In 2000, Children in Scotland[3] (CIS) received monies from The Diana, Princess of Wales Memorial Fund to support the involvement of groups of disabled children in policy making[4]. Called Citizenship in Practice, the project sought to explore an alternative to the typical way children were involved in national policy making: that is, a one-off consultation process on government's already articulated policy ideas. Instead, the project sought to involve interested children with policy development over time, articulating their own policy agendas and seeking to influence policy makers on this agenda. Eight separate groups of children (46 children in total) were involved at this initial agenda-setting stage, resulting in *What Matters to Me* (see CIS, 2000). This proved an unexpectedly popular document and it and its accompanying rap were disseminated across Scotland.

Overall, children wanted to have more choice and control over aspects of their lives and school was an important arena for this. Children particularly wanted, for example, to have the opportunity to attend meetings about their own education. Thus, when Scottish Executive civil servants approached CIS to undertake consultations with children for the executive's policy review on special educational needs (SEN), CIS consulted with the original Citizenship in Practice groups and it was agreed to do this.

Part of the deal made with the Scottish Executive was that children should be involved as the policy developed. This took three stages (2001, 2001-02, and 2002-03), as policy became increasingly defined, and involved over 100 children aged 11 to 21 years, with a continuing core group of about 40 children. In each stage, a report was prepared by CIS and submitted to the executive. Immediate feedback to the groups was provided by CIS, in terms of meetings, copies of the reports and accessible summaries. In agreeing to facilitate the work, CIS had bargained with the Executive to provide some immediate feedback to those who had participated and that, in due course, interested children would have the opportunity to discuss their views with the Minister. These agreements were met, although it took some time to meet with the Minister. When the Education Committee of the Scottish Parliament came to consider the draft legislation, it picked up on the children's involvement. CIS was once again asked to assist and a 'civic engagement' day was held with committee members and groups of disabled children. This was included as part of the Education Committee's report on the Bill (Education Committee, Scottish Parliament, 2004a) .

One can trace through the influence – or not – of the children's views on policy development. As described in more detail in Tisdall and Davis (2004), the responses can be divided into three types: specific legislative proposals (for example, a minimum standard on information for children and young people); vague promises (for example, on children's right to express their views); and no action (for example, while children wanted play and recreation to be considered alongside schooling, this was not done).

Power within the policy process is illuminated by following through one particular demand. The majority of children said they would like to dispute an educational decision they felt was wrong, but few children felt able to do so. This demand was recognised and commented upon in the Executive's first responses (Scottish Executive, 2002, 2003). In 2002, the Executive proposed that education authorities should have in place arrangements to support children (for example, 'a named individual') (Scottish Executive 2002, p 22) with regard to meetings. Both parents and children should have the right to appeal against any part of the coordinated support plan (CSP)[5]. By the time of the draft Bill (Scottish Executive, 2003), however, the Executive was not proposing that children could appeal their plan – only parents would have that right. Instead, mechanisms to support children in expressing their views would be dealt with in guidance. With CIS continuing to raise the children's demands with Members of the Scottish Parliament (MSPs), the debates continued in the Scottish Parliament. Once the Executive agreed there would be a statutory Code of Practice (stronger, legally, than guidance), the mechanisms gained a potentially stronger footing as the Executive promised they would be agreed in the code. But the Executive refused to grant children appeal rights over its CSP. Instead, it promised a review of all relevant legislation on children's right to appeal and legal capacity.

How can this path be understood? At a technical level, the Executive's stance was incongruous: only four years before, it had recognised children's capacity to appeal their own school exclusions if they were 'legally competent' under Scots law. Similarly, 'competent' children already had the right to take forward their own education case under disability discrimination legislation. The Executive's stance, however, becomes very understandable when one considers the policy networks – and particularly the power of organised groups of parents. In special educational needs (now additional support needs) policy, parents' representatives are firmly part of the policy network. The Executive was careful to ensure that such representatives were part of its National Advisory Group on SEN[6] and the implementation group for the Bill[7]; they sought to ensure that parents' groups were consulted during all stages of the Bill's development. Nonetheless, when the Bill was published, other parent-led organisations became very active and brought considerable media and political criticism to the Bill – and accused the executive of failing to consult adequately. These organisations were thus very effective in using 'outsider' strategies to insert themselves (or at least some further representatives) into the policy network and certainly to influence the policy process itself. With parents' central role within SEN policy networks firmly (re)established, neither politicians nor civil servants were willing to promote children's independent right to appeal that might potentially clash with parents' views. This reason is given by Minister Euan Robson to the Education Committee:

> It seems that the amendments would create a situation in which … there could be tensions between the rights of the parents and those of the child. The amendments do not stipulate whose right would prevail in the event that a parent and a child disagreed on a matter. That could be a very significant point. Conflicting appeals, for example, would be particularly difficult. (Education Committee, Scottish Parliament, 2004b, cols 938-9)

Very effective mechanisms were used to defuse the politics of this issue. First, the Minister's explanations to the committee were legally inaccurate (Education Committee, Scottish Parliament, 2004b, cols 937-8) and these inaccuracies suggested that children's rights were more limited than they are in education and Scottish law more generally. Second, much would be left to the Code of Practice and a further review of legislation. Children's views thus become a more 'technical' issue, in the Code of Practice, a question of mechanisms rather than rights, in something that would receive less political and certainly less media scrutiny. The review provided a time breather, with the potential to build more political consensus through the policy networks as it was undertaken.

Both the state (the Executive/the Scottish Parliament) and civil society (in this case, a range of NGOs) can collude in presenting a consensual view of policy development. Policy networks are used by the state to limit the unexpected, to control the policy agenda, to have incremental rather than radical change (Maloney et al, 1994); civil society has more power to bargain with policy makers if it appears united, able to bring along its membership to support the policy and its implementation (Grant, 2000). But this appearance of consensus was blown by the very effective tactics by certain parental organisations mid-way through the process.

The development studies literature particularly notes the normative promotion of civil society, that associational networks are perceived as quintessentially positive. And within this literature are some queries about how such networks can exclude as well as include, and observations about how power acts externally on civil society as well as within it (for example, Howell and Pearce, 2001; Baker, 2002; Peterson, 2003). This chapter does not seek to present the particular parents' organisations as unduly negative. The political science literature instead encourages us to be more 'matter of fact'. Parents, in this case, exerted power more successfully than the coalition of certain NGOs with groups of children. Their power did not have a linear impact, as the parental concerns were not over children's rights to appeal. But the increasing sensitivity of the Executive, both civil servants and the Minister, can be evidenced and one result was to limit the extension of children's rights when they might particularly cause conflict with those of the parents.

The NGO coalition did bring children into the 'public' sphere of civil society, giving them some voice and indeed some influence within the policy debates. NGOs were key intermediaries between the hierarchies of those in power (the national policy makers of Ministers, other MSPs and civil servants) and the 'grass roots' of the groups of children. It was an example of the 'positive sum game' of power, where both the children and CIS gained power within the policy network to influence policy: the children were able to capitalise on CIS's access to funds and political contacts, while CIS gained additional credibility in its demands and status. But notably children were firmly not allowed into the 'insiders' of the policy process. They were not invited to sit on the advisory groups in the Scottish Executive, despite suggestions by CIS staff members that this be done. Children's participation waned as the process narrowed into the legislation, filled as it was with legal debates and technical discussions. But by then the battles were themselves narrowed, the agendas largely set.

Conclusion

The two case studies represent attempts to involve children in 'public' decision making at a national, governmental level. They exemplify the recent moves in UK governance, which challenge government machinery to be more 'joined up' and strategic and make public service users the focus. The government now needs to demonstrate the process of participation, for legitimacy of their policy recommendations and functions (Magnette, 2003). The case studies show that children's participation does have a new place in how the civil service works.

The case studies also show that children's views are but one set of views among those of other stakeholders, whether internally within government or externally within civil society. The case study on *Learning to Listen* describes how the agenda for children's participation had to compete with other, higher-level, policy agendas. There is generally warm support for involving children but that support quickly cools when resources and capacity are limited. Departments set out their target stakeholders as part of their strategic planning; children are rarely such target stakeholders. Then, children's inclusion is a 'favour' rather than an automatic activity. The case study on Citizenship in Practice demonstrates that children's views 'lost out' to the more powerful voices of certain parental organisations. A naïve promotion of 'civil society' hides differences in power between portions of it. The theorisation of policy networks, on the other hand, expects and explores different power relationships and their underlying resources. As Smith (1997) describes, a policy network or community tends to have a core and periphery, or a primary and secondary community. In Citizenship in Practice, the children involved became part of the secondary policy community, one that did 'not have enough resources to exert a continuous influence on policy' but has 'occasional access to the policy process' (Smith, 1997, p 81).

Both case studies show that civil servants – despite all the UK literature describing the 'hollowing out' of the state, the government's role as 'steering' rather than 'rowing', and the need for partnerships to ameliorate structural fragmentation – maintain a powerful role in policy networks and the national policy process. Magnette (2003) writes: 'Both the initiative of participation and the choice of the groups consulted remains firmly in the hands of the institutions' (p 150). This was certainly true in the *Learning to Listen* case study, as individual departments set out their strategic plans and invited certain groups to participate. In the case study of Citizenship in Practice, in fact, the first part of Magnette's statement was true (the involvement of children was initiated by the policy team) but not the second (this was negotiated between CIS and the policy team). What Magnette does not mention, in this particular quotation, is the power of the institutions to then sift out what messages from participation it will highlight, listen to and actually act on. Both Whitehall civil servants and the Scottish Executive made distinct decisions on whose and which views they would prioritise.

Civil servants may retain a powerful position in the new forms of governance but both case studies demonstrate the increased reliance on NGOs. *Learning to Listen* shows government's need for the expertise of NGOs, which brought particular organisations deeply into policy networks – or even incorporated in the governmental machinery itself. NGOs were also used in both case studies to 'deliver' civil society: that is, as an institutional form to reach out to children and to support their involvement. There is a serious challenge here – as the government uses NGOs increasingly for the delivery of its policies – for NGOs to avoid becoming 'incorporated' and their critical voice on participation quietened. At the same time as developing participatory networks, government must not see this as a substitute for investing in its own capacity to involve children; it should not 'contract out' cultural change but needs to recognise the imperative of up-skilling its own staff. A question also arises about the role of adult NGOs as intermediaries in children's participation; while Lansdown (see Chapter Eight) argues that adults should have a continuing role to support, the politics and development literature would at least encourage recognition that adult NGOs can very much benefit from this intermediary role, in finance, status and political power.

The activation of children as political actors has radical potential – to change the political and policy-making process and outcomes. But elements of the development literature point to civil society's controlling elements and the use of NGOs to deliver it. Does participation become a 'technical' problem, with 'technical' solutions, rather than political emancipation? For example, with no apparent irony, Maclure and Sotelo (2004) write of the role of non-governmental organisations to foster 'secondary' citizenship for those excluded from participating in state-centred politics (see also Reilly, 1995). Children's wish for avenues to dispute a decision, in Citizenship in Practice, was managed by policy makers, to take this demand out of political debate and deal with it quietly through hopefully non-controversial Codes of Practice and guidance. It is also a risk when children's participation is incorporated into departmental action plans, as in *Learning to Listen*, which conceptualise such involvement particularly around children as consumers. This leads to a limiting and limited model of participation, dominated by an emphasis on communicating to and consulting with children. With limited resources for participation, this results in far less ongoing engagement with children and fewer opportunities to shape policy at an early stage. The danger continues to be that children's engagement is perceived as an appealing, though disposable, addition to main governmental business.

This chapter thus charts the increased inclusion of children into previously closed policy networks in 'public' decision making – but also current caveats and future dangers. It suggests that literatures outwith childhood studies can help in understanding and conceptualising both, and thus have the potential to build on the positives and ameliorate the negatives. In particular, the chapter advocates that children's participation must not be reduced to a technical solution, so that policy makers can be responsive to children as consumers but not accountable to them. Instead, the potential for children's participation to be political, to challenge and insist on change, must be retained and promoted. Otherwise children remain on the margins of political and policy decision making, a form of social and political exclusion, of 'secondary citizenship'.

Notes

[1] In keeping with the meaning in United Nations Convention on the Rights of the Child, the term 'children' is used here to denote those up to the age of 18. It is recognised, however, that children themselves at the upper end of this age range prefer to use the term 'young people'.

[2] In the UK (and for this particular survey), the phrase 'voluntary organisations' is used, while, internationally, 'non-governmental organisations' (NGOs) is more common. For consistency, this chapter will use NGOs.

[3] The national membership agency for organisations and professionals working with children and their families (www.childreninscotland.org.uk). The views expressed in this chapter do not necessarily represent CIS's perspectives.

[4] For more information, see www.childreninscotland.org.uk/html/ microsites/whatmatters/bgnd.htm.

[5] The CSP '... will co-ordinate the support for those with additional support needs, arising from complex or multiple factors, who need a range of support from different services' (Scottish Executive, 2004, p 4).

[6] Members of the Scottish Parliament.

[7] For a list of members, see www.scotland.gov.uk/library2/doc15/ sen-07.asp?textonly=FALSE.

[8] For a list of members, see www.scotland.gov.uk/Topics/Education/ School-Education/19094/18688.

References

Baker, G. (2002) *Civil Society and Democratic Theory: Alternative Voices*, London: Routledge.

Cabinet Office (1999) 'Modernising government', Cm 4310 (www.archive.official-documents.co.uk/document/cm43/4310/ 4310.htm, accesssed 21 February 2005).

Carnegie Young People Initiative (2001) 'Taking the initiative: UK full report' (www.carnegieuktrust.org.uk/cypi/publications/ taking_the_initiative, accessed 25 September 2005).

CIS (Children in Scotland) (2000) 'Taking the initiative: Scottish report' (www.carnegieuktrust.org.uk/cypi/publications/ taking_the_initiative, accessed 25 September 2005).

Clark, J. (1995) 'The state, popular participation, and the voluntary sector', *World Development*, vol 23, no 4, pp 593-601.

Cutler, D. and Taylor, A. (2003) 'Expanding and sustaining involvement' (www.carnegieuktrust.org.uk/node/view/197, accessed 25 September 2005).

Deakin, N. (2001) *In Search of Civil Society*, Basingstoke: Palgrave.

DfEE (Department for Education and Employment) (2001a) 'Learning to listen' (www.dfes.gov.uk/listeningtolearn/ downloads/ LearningtoListen-CorePrinciples.pdf, accessed 25 September 2005).

DfEE (2001b) *Tomorrow's Future: Building a Strategy for Children and Young People*, London: DfEE.

Education Committee, Scottish Parliament (2004) 'Stage 1 report on Education (Additional Support for Learning) (Scotland) Bill', 14 January 2004 (www.scottish.parliament.uk/business/committees/ education/or-04/ed04-0202.htm#Col667, accessed 25 September 2005).

Education Committee, Scottish Parliament (2004b) 'Stage 2 of the Education (Additional Support for Learning) Bill', 25 February 2004 (www.scottish.parliament.uk/business/committees/education/or-04/ed04-0602.htm#Col919, accessed 20 August 2006)

Edwards, M. and Hulme, D. (1996) 'Too close for comfort? The impact of official aid on nongovermental organizations', *World Development*, vol 24, no 6, pp 961-73.

Fisher, W.F. (1997) 'Doing good? The politics and antipolitics of NGO practices', *Annual Review of Anthropology*, vol 26, no 1, pp 439-64.

Grant, W. (2000) *Pressure Groups and British Politics*, Basingstoke: Macmillan Press Ltd.

Hearn, J. (2001) 'Taking liberties: contesting visions of the civil society project', *Critique of Anthropology*, vol 21, no 4, pp 339-60.

Howell, J. and Pearce, J. (2001) *Civil Society and Development: A Critical Exploration*, London: Lynne Rienner Publishers Ltd.

Jones, G. and Bell, R. (2000) *Balancing Acts*, York: Joseph Rowntree Foundation.

Kirby, P. with Bryson, S. (2002) 'Measuring the magic? Evaluating and research young people's participation in public decision making' (www.carnegieuktrust.org.uk/cypi/publications/measuring_the_magic, accessed 12 March 2005).

Lovan, W.R., Murray, M., and Shaffer, R. (2004) 'Participatory governance in a changing world', in W.R. Lovan, M. Murray and R. Shaffer (eds) *Participatory Governance*, Aldershot: Ashgate, pp 1-20.

Maclure, R. and Sotelo, M. (2004) 'Children's rights and the tenuousness of local coalitions: a case study of Nicaragua', *Journal of Latin American Studies*, vol 36, no 1, pp 85-108.

Magnette, P. (2003) 'European governance and civic participation: beyond elitist citizenship', *Political Studies*, vol 51, no 1, pp 144-60.

Maloney, W.A., Jordan, G. and McLaughlin, A.M. (1994) 'Interest groups and public policy: the insider/outsider model revisited', *Journal of Public Policy*, vol 14, no 1, pp 17-38.

Oldfield, C. and Fowler, C. (2004) *Mapping children and young people's participation in England*, London: DfES.

Peters, B.G. (1996) *The Future of Governing: Four Emerging Models*, Kansas: University of Kansas Press.

Peterson, J. (2003) 'Policy networks', in A. Wiener and T. Diez (eds) *European Integration Theory*, Oxford: Oxford University Press, draft.

Reilly, C.A. (1995) 'Public policy and citizenship', in C.A. Reilly (ed) *New Paths to Democratic Devleopment in Latin America*, London: Lynne Rienner Publishers, pp.1-27.

Rhodes, R.A.W. (1997) *Understanding Governance*, Buckingham: Open University Press

Richards, D. and Smith, M.J. (2002) *Governance and Public Policy in the UK*, Oxford: Oxford University Press.

Scottish Executive (2002) 'Assessing our children's educational needs. The way forward? Scottish Executive response to the consultation' (www.scotland.gov.uk, accessed 4 March 2003).

Scottish Executive (2003) 'Consultation on draft Education (Additional Support for Learning) (Scotland) Bill' (www.scotland.gov.uk, accessed 4 March 2003).

Scottish Executive (2004) 'A guide for parents: the Education (Additional Support for Learning) (Scotland) Act 2004' (2nd edn) (www.scotland.gov.uk/library5/education/esa04gp.pdf, accessed 12 March 2005).

Sinclair, R. (2004) 'Participation in practice: making it meaningful, effective and sustainable', *Children & Society*, vol 18, no 2, pp 106-18.

Smith, M.J. (1997) 'Policy networks', in M. Hill (ed) *The Policy Process: A Reader*, Wheatsheaf Hertfordshire: Prentice Hall/Harvester, pp 76-86.

Tisdall, E.K.M. and Davis, J. (2004) 'Making a difference? Bringing children's and young people's views into policy-making', *Children & Society*, vol 18, no 2, pp 131-42.

Walzer, M. (1995) *Towards a Global Civil Society*, Oxford: Berghahn.

SEVEN

The Irish National Children's Strategy: lessons for promoting the social inclusion of children and young people

John Pinkerton

Children are at the heart of Irish life. They represent over one third of the population and are the centre of attention in over half a million Irish families. The way we care for our children is fundamental to what we stand for as parents, as communities and as a country....

For a Government to meet its part in this challenge we have to be clear sighted, set common goals and acknowledge the wide range of issues which have to be addressed. Political will to succeed is also vital. This is what the Strategy we are launching this morning is all about....

A lot of work went into developing the Strategy and I want to thank all of the organisations, researchers, officials and particularly the children who contributed to it.... (An Taoiseach, 2000)

Introduction

The focus of this chapter is the Irish National Children's Strategy published in 2000 (NCO, 2000). The strategy is a high mark in central government policy making with regard to Irish children. It was an internationally innovative attempt to address, within a national jurisdiction, the global agenda of the United Nations Convention on the Rights of the Child (UNCRC), ratified by Ireland in 1992. The 10-year strategy commits to three overarching and interlinked goals:

to give children a voice; to understand children's lives better; and to provide children with quality support and services. This chapter describes the origins, development and contents of the strategy, noting the links to the wider imperative of social inclusion within a society that, during the 1990s, saw rapid economic growth and cultural change. Attention will also be given to the place of participation within the development, content and early implementation of the strategy. Reflecting on the experience of the Irish National Children's Strategy from a critical perspective on societal structures and policy processes, it will be argued that within Irish society today there is an emerging policy space for a radical politics of childhood.

While presenting the National Children's Strategy as a benchmarking opportunity for pursuing the social inclusion of children and young people in Ireland, the chapter will also pose the question as to whether the strategy should be seen as 'the giant leap' (O'Morain, 2000) it was judged and welcomed to be when launched. In considering that question, it will be argued that this national case study highlights a central contradiction in advancing the global agenda of children's rights, which requires considered, strategic handling. The momentum for change behind government policy advances is as much about the management of change in the interests of securing the structures that create social exclusion, as it is an expression of the forces of change that challenge those structures.

The chapter concludes that for participation to advance the social inclusion of children and young people within Ireland, it must be much more than co-option of the few, adults and children into a 'policy community' close to government within the framework of social partnership. It must be about the direct involvement of the majority in an 'issues network' threading together a diverse and multi-levelled constituency for radical social, economic and political change. This is a politics of participation that, to borrow Moss and Petrie's provocative phrase, is about 'putting a stutter into powerful narratives' (2002, p 185) – not least that of linear progress towards an end-point vision of children's rights that underpins much governmental and non-governmental engagement with the UNCRC.

The Irish National Children's Strategy

Origins

The Ireland that entered the 21st century was a very different place from what it had been 10 years before. It had:

> ... been recognised as a success story in terms of macroeconomic characteristics by EU and OECD standards ... attained an impressive level of prosperity characterised by sustained population and employment growth, falling unemployment, increasing living standards for those in employment and sustained net immigration. (National Economic and Social Council, 1999, p 3)

By the end of that decade, Ireland had earned the reputation of being one of the most globalised economies in the world and, by reference to the dynamic economies of South East Asia, gained the tag of 'Celtic tiger'. The economic opening up of the country was matched by an increasingly confident social and cultural assertion of a new Irishness, proud of its roots but keen to develop new European and global characteristics. Ireland was a country renovating itself economically and socially and at the heart of the project was social partnership (National Economic and Social Council, 1999; Rush, 1999; Kirby et al, 2002).

The Irish state, both governments and civil service, has been committed to corporatism as an economic and social strategy since the late 1950s when it was seen as the only available response to the serious failures of post-independence protectionism and self-sufficiency evidenced by decades of slow economic growth, limited job creation and high levels of emigration. However, it was not until the late 1980s that the internal and external environment (with the European Union being of particular importance) allowed for modernisation to take off through social partnership within a corporate framework. During the late 1980s and 1990s, the country moved from 'green donkey to Celtic tiger' (O'Hearn, 2001) through extending its objectives beyond narrow national economic agreements between trade unions and employers. It placed social inclusion and social equality on the agenda and consolidated four 'pillars' of representation – farming organisations, trade unions, employers, and community and voluntary organisations. Support structures were put into place or revamped and technically sophisticated strategic documents preceded the negotiation of national economic and social programmes.

Children and young people had a significant place within the changes of the Celtic tiger years. Just by force of numbers they had to (Fitzgerald, 2004). With over a million children under 18 years of age in 2002, making up around 29% of the population, Ireland had the highest percentage of households with children in Europe. Yet that figure is 10% less than the 40% it was in 1981. Falling birth rates and smaller family size had changed a demographic profile more akin to those in the developing world than Europe. The combination of a lowering dependency ratio of child to adult plus the economic boom made it realistic to aspire to provide Irish children and young people with a lifestyle similar to that of their European peers. The changes of the 1990s created the opportunity for significant public investment in children. The need to take that opportunity reflected not only the benefits of the growing wealth of the country but also the reality of the undertow of that economic development. There has been a significant reduction in consistent poverty in Ireland but an increase in relative income poverty, making the divide between rich and poor one of the widest in Europe. Children formed a significant proportion of those marginalised and left (Combat Poverty Agency, 2000; Nolan, 2000).

The political will to realise the opportunity for children and young people offered by the Celtic tiger years gained momentum as a millennium gesture.

> Children are at the heart of every vibrant and successful society. Their happiness and security is a fundamental measure of the health and fairness of a society. In the past and even today, we have as a country often failed to act in the best interests of children. At the start of a new century, this is a goal which deserves our best national effort. (An Taoiseach, 2000)

Reflected in the Taoiseach's open admission of Ireland having 'often failed' its children is a second negative driver behind the development of a children's strategy. Child abuse within the state and religious residential institutions reaching back to the foundation of the state in 1921 surfaced as a major scandal in political and civic life during the 1990s (Raferty and O'Sullivan, 1999; Richardson, 1999). Those scandals were depressing reminders of the harsh days of a socially and culturally narrow national past dominated by an authoritarian and patriarchal

Catholic Church. The electorate needed to be reassured that those days had been left behind:

> At this point in our history, we are more aware than ever of the ways in which the State and other powerful institutions have failed children. In that light the National Children Strategy published by Government yesterday is particularly welcome. (*The Irish Times*, Editorial, 14 November 2000)

The children's strategy gave the opportunity for government to then map out a much brighter future, not just for children in state care, but for all children and young people.

There was also a vocal children's lobby to be managed politically (Richardson, 1999). Its voice was amplified by the logic of social partnership: 'Social investment is vital to continuing success and nowhere is that investment more important than in children' (Government of Ireland, 2000a, p 8). The concerns expressed by those advocating for children were reinforced by the comments from the UN Committee on the Rights of the Child to the first national report presented to it by Irish Government in 1996. In Ireland, as elsewhere, the UNCRC was demonstrating that globalisation brings with it not only inward economic investment but also progressive social policy standards to be met.

Development

In the summer of 1999, Frank Fahey, then the Minister for Children (a non-cabinet position with cross-departmental responsibility for children's issues created in the mid-1990s) established an Inter-Departmental Group (IDG) of senior civil servants representing eight key government departments and the Attorney General's Office. The primary role of the IDG was to oversee the development of a comprehensive 10-year strategy for children. The seniority of the members of the IDG and the involvement of departments beyond those that had children's issues as core business were important statements on the priority being given to the initiative. The IDG was supported by a small cross-departmental team (CDT) established solely for that purpose. A staff of eight was drawn from the four departments responsible for most children's services – health, education, justice and family affairs. The CDT also included an academic on full-time secondment (this chapter's author) and a freelance adviser on public consultation with a particular brief for engaging children and young people.

Two panels were established to provide expert advice: a research and information panel and a non-governmental organisation (NGO) panel. The former was made up of Irish academics along with a number of international advisers. The NGO panel included not only the large Irish childcare charities, like Barnardo's and the ISPCC (Irish Society for the Prevention of Cruelty to Children), but also smaller organisations with specialist interests such as children and the arts (The Ark) and the needs of traveller children (Pavee Point Travellers Centre). The Irish Children's Rights Alliance (www.childrensrights.ie) was also involved from early on in the process. The expertise of other key contributors, such as statutory health and social care providers and local government, was drawn on as required.

Through the work of the IDG and CDT, the government was in effect identifying, mobilising and consolidating a 'children's policy community' in a manner consistent with the practice of social partnership. Bochel and Bochel identify the following as characteristics of such policy communities (2004, p 59):

- a limited number of participants;
- participants are constant in their presence;
- participants are consistent in their values and policy preferences;
- significant consensus exists amongst participants about the policy process;
- participants share broad policy preferences;
- all participants have resources important to the area;
- interaction between participants is frequent and of high quality.

Involvement beyond this 'policy community' was sought through public consultation – a stable ingredient of Irish policy making (Iredale, 1999; O'Leary, 2002). As in the United Kingdom:

> ... this concern with involvement and participation has been echoed over the past decade in the much more wide spread use of the concepts of social exclusion and inclusion to aid our understanding of social policy and its outcomes, with the greater emphasis on exclusion through lack of a voice and the role of processes in reinforcing or challenging exclusion. (Bochel and Bochel, 2004, p S159)

Reflecting this, the CDT made considerable efforts to consult directly with children and young people (Boyle, 2000; Government of Ireland, 2000b). From the start, children and young people were regarded as the central, but not the only, legitimate stakeholders.

To engage children and young people, the newly appointed Minister for Children, Mary Hanafin, personally invited them to contact her directly by e-mail or letter giving answers to two questions: 'What is good about living in Ireland?' and 'What would make Ireland a better place?'. The invitation was publicised through schools, organisations working with children and the mass media. The minister was even quizzed by the star of a popular children's TV programme, a human-size turkey puppet. Five primary and five post-primary schools, selected to provide a range of experiences by age and social circumstance, were visited by the minister. Focus groups and forums were organised by children's organisations with the support of the Children's Rights Alliance and National Youth Council. The ISPCC used its four annual Regional Children's Forums to consult on the minister's two questions. Children as young as three years old took part in the consultation, though the majority, about two thirds, were 13 years or older. More girls than boys were involved by a ratio of three to two. Somewhere in the region of two and a half thousand children and young people directly responded to the minister's invitation by e-mail and letter (825), through their schools (600) and through organisations (1,063) – a figure almost 10 times that of the number of adult submissions produced by the traditional mechanism of advertisements in the national press.

Contents

The full National Children's Strategy (Government of Ireland, 2000a), in both its Irish and English versions, is a tightly packed, well laid out, hundred-page document, of seven chapters – the executive summary manages to reduce it to 34 pages and the children's version to less than 20. The first chapter opens with the basic assertion: 'Children matter' (p 6). It goes on to set out the rationale and guiding principles behind the strategy as well as outlining its contents and how it was developed (described more fully in a separate publication – Government of Ireland, 2000b). It is in this chapter too that that the heart of the strategy can be found in what aims to be a 'clear and unifying vision' (p 10):

> An Ireland where children are respected as young citizens
> with a valued contribution to make and a voice of their
> own; where all children are cherished and supported by
> family and the wider society; where they enjoy a fulfilling
> childhood and realise their potential.

This vision expresses a value base that is also explicitly stated: children
and young people's innate dignity as human beings; the central place
of family life; adult responsibility to provide protection and support. A
combination of respect for the autonomy of children and young people
with acceptance of adult responsibilities towards them underpins these
values and is expressed in the strategy's subsidiary heading: *Our Children
– Their Lives*. Conscious that a central government strategy needs to
concern itself as much with the 'how' as with the 'what' of policy
(Boyle, 2000), the first chapter also states the six operational principles
that commit the strategy to being: child-centred; family-oriented;
equitable; inclusive; action-oriented; and integrated (p 10).

The second chapter, 'Focusing on children', summarises the changing
context of children's lives in Ireland and presents a 'whole-child'
perspective that anchors the strategy and shape its goals. This 'whole-
child' perspective recognises that all children and young people live
their lives 'in the round' as 'active subjects', shaping their own lives as
they grow and develop just as much as they are shaped and supported
by the world around them. In addition to identifying nine interlinked
dimensions of development, attention is drawn to the complex mix of
support and services on which child development depends.

The next three chapters, which constitute over half the document,
deal with each of the national goals. These are expressed as outcomes
for children and none is given priority over the others as they are seen
as intrinsically intertwined.

- Children will have a voice in matters that affect them, and their
  views will be given due weight in accordance with their age and
  maturity (chapter 3).
- Children and their lives will be better understood and they will
  derive maximum benefit from evaluation, research and information
  on their needs and the effectiveness of services (chapter 4).
- Children will receive support and services to promote all aspects of
  their development through ensuring access and removing barriers
  (chapter 5).

For each of the goals, the relevant chapter provides a rationale, identifies central policy objectives and key measures that need to be acted on to advance achievement of the objectives.

The two final chapters, 'The engine for change' and 'Making a strong start', then address how to ensure that the objectives and measures are implemented. Both process and new administrative mechanisms are identified as crucial to effective follow-through. The suggested administrative mechanisms include a cabinet subcommittee chaired by the Taoiseach to oversee the strategy and a National Children's Office (NCO), accountable to the Minister for Children, with direct responsibility for implementation of the cross-departmental agenda set by the national goals and their associated objectives. Individual government departments are seen as retaining responsibility for implementing those measures within the strategy relevant to their role, with the NCO monitoring progress and supporting coordination where appropriate. External to government, the strategy suggests not only a Dáil na nÓg (National Children's Parliament) and Ombudsman for Children, but also a National Children's Advisory Council (NCAC) bringing together children's representatives, the social partners and the research community.

In concluding the strategy document, chapter 7 lists as the immediate actions to be taken to kick-start implementation: putting the suggested new infrastructure in place; embedding the national goals in current policy development and service delivery; allocating new funding for priority initiatives under each goal; and 'communicating the message'. All of these can be seen as placing priority on consolidating the identity and activities of a children's policy community. This final chapter in the strategy also stresses that effective, independent and routine monitoring must form part of implementation from the start.

Politics of participation

From the above account, it can be seen that, as a document, the Irish National Children's Strategy is a strong response to one of the United Nations Committee on the Rights of the Child's central concerns: 'If government as a whole and at all levels is to promote and respect the rights of the child, it needs to work on the basis of a unifying, comprehensive and rights-based national strategy, rooted in the Convention' (UN Committee on the Rights of the Child, 2003). What is more, the strategy explicitly declares itself to be a document that 'reflects the aspirations and concerns of children themselves' (UN Committee on the Rights of the Child, 2003, p 6). The recognition of children within the strategy document as social actors who 'actively shape their own lives and the lives of those around them' (UN Committee on the Rights of the Child, 2003, p 6) was apparent in the unprecedented level of direct participation by children and young people in formulating this piece of public policy. Participation also strongly features in the strategy's content – its vision, value base, operational principles, goals and engine for change. The decision to make 'giving children a voice' one of the three overarching, intertwined national goals was intended to give the strongest possible backing to Article 12 of the UNCRC.

However, with regard to policy documents no less than to legislation, it is important to heed the warning 'not to think that because the words had been enacted the conditions of children's lives have changed' (Freeman, 1992, p 52). The strategy recognises this and so includes the explicit statement on an 'engine for change' (chapter 6) and spells out what action needs to be taken to kick-start implementation (chapter 7). Monitoring is identified as having an important role to play in driving forward effective implementation. However, despite the commitment to an independent evaluation to be carried out by an international panel every three years (NCO, 2000, p 95), no such evaluation has taken place more than five years on from the strategy's launch. It could be argued that it is too early to make meaningful judgements on the impact of policy as ambitious in its scope as the strategy. Alternatively, it could be argued that if specific objectives are considered, it is already quite clear that insufficient action has been taken. A case in point is the commitment to providing the financial support necessary to eliminate child poverty. Following the 2004 Budget, the End Child Poverty lobby group starkly stated in a press release that the government had 'failed to introduce resources to end child poverty' (www.endchildpoverty.ie).

One of the objectives that has been achieved is the establishment of the National Children's Office (NCO). Although it was slow to become fully operational (the director was not appointed until 2002), it has proved to be, as planned, the centrepiece to the 'engine for change'. From its website (www.nco.ie), it can be seen that in 2004 with 141 action points to progress, a staff of 18 and a budget of just under three million euros, the NCO is making steady, though slow, progress. It has given considerable effort to advancing the child's voice national goal – the website includes a page titled 'Participation by children and young people'. The main participation projects that the NCO is working on include:

- Comhairle na nÓg (Local Children's Councils);
- Dáil na nÓg (National Young People's Parliament);
- Dáil na bPáistí (National Children's Parliament);
- a Student Council Working Group;
- guidelines on participation by children and young people;
- the establishment of an NCO Child and Youth Forum;
- the inclusion of children in the development of National Child Well Being Indicators;
- support for the Young Social Innovators Exhibition, a showcase for young people's involvement with social issues;
- support for the national television network's children's News2Day.

It is tempting to use such lists as the means of assessing what progress has or has not been made in implementing the strategy. Indeed, the NCO noted in its first annual report (NCO, 2003) that it had presented such an assessment to the Cabinet Committee on Children. It judged, on the basis of having considered 135 actions proposed in the strategy, that 'good progress' had been made on 19%, 'action was under way' on 79%, and in only 9% of actions was 'progress poor', making for 'a reasonable level of progress' overall.

There is something to be said for this apparently clear-cut approach to policy evaluation. Measuring progress against proposed action limits the room for evasive political manoeuvre that seems to dog implementation of government strategies. However, this approach assumes a linear sequence from recognising a policy problem (the need for an overarching strategy for children) to bringing together the necessary expertise and opinion to produce an accurate understanding of the problem (the IDG + CDT + consultation), to using that understanding to develop a policy solution (the National Children's Strategy), that is then applied and evaluated. Policy is seen as dealing solely with prescription, the desirable to be worked towards, with implementation being about what then happens, which is open to measurement against the desirable.

Such a traditional bureaucratic/rational framework of policy analysis assumes a 'top-down' relationship between policy and its implementation. Policy formulation and implementation is about linking policy input to implementation outcomes through technical problem solving from above with the goal of minimising 'implementation deficit' (Ham and Hill, 1993). Powerful policy makers use delivery staff at various lower levels as a conveyor belt to the powerless recipients of the policy outcomes. This may reflect the power imbalance that is deeply etched into the social and political structures of contemporary nation states but it also assumes unrealistically rigid, functional and manageable policy making and implementation systems. The desired degree of control is unobtainable and to pursue it runs counter to the democratic imperatives and the messy practicalities of open consultation and participation – particularly with children and young people (Pinkerton, 2001; Kirby and Bryson, 2002; McAuley and Brattman, 2002; Bochel and Bochel, 2004; NCO et al, 2005).

There is an alternative systemic/interactionist view of policy (and policy evaluation – Pinkerton, 2004) that is more in keeping with 'a belief that participation is a key element in ensuring a healthy democracy and society and a recognition that the full range of interests in society should be represented in the decision-making process' (Bochel and Bochel, 2004, p.163). Within this participatory democracy model, emphasis is placed on the policy process. Attention is given to the complexity and dynamics within and across the various levels and types of interaction between a diversity of stakeholders. Conflict is as valued as consensus and unintended consequences as much to be expected as achievement of objectives. This is not to lose sight of outcomes but to make the necessary intermingling link between them and process. Effective policy making and implementation is about enabling negotiated, dynamic, fluid and diverse communication and action at many levels. It recognises that as part of participatory democracy, 'there is a need to recognise the multiplicity of sites in which dialogue is conducted and interests and identities shaped' (Newman, cited in Bochel and Bochel, 2004, p 165). While there is an important place for consolidating and managing a policy community relevant to a particular area, more important is mobilising an 'issue network'.

Issues networks (Bochel and Bochel, 2004) can be distinguished from policy communities by the involvement of many more types and numbers of actors whose involvement fluctuates and among whom relationships are very varied. They encompass a far wider range of interests in the issue that connects them and, while there may be some general agreement around ideals, the network is held together as much by conflict as consensus. This much looser and inclusive perspective, on what constitutes engagement with an issue, values a variety of avenues for participation – from membership of political parties and pressure groups, voting in elections and referenda, giving user feedback on public services and 'direct action' protest, through to lifestyle choices. It also accepts 'that some people seek to be involved whilst others do not' (Bochel and Bochel, 2004, p 177).

The children's policy community convened around the children's strategy is only a part of a much more wide-reaching and tangled children's issues network. The children's policy community inside and outside of government is important, not least for its visibility, and yet relatively insignificant when compared with what lies beyond it in the multiple exchanges between adults and children where the conditions, the issues, of children and young people's lives are constituted and contested in the rich relationships, positive and negative, with one another and with adults. Indeed, the strategy document recognised as much.

> The National Children's Strategy is an opportunity to enhance the status and further improve the quality of life of Ireland's children. It is a statement of support to parents. It is an invitation to everyone who works with children, in whatever capacity, to work together more effectively. It is also an encouragement to become more formally involved in shaping their own lives. (Government of Ireland, 2000a, p 6)

The strategy, through supporting, inviting and encouraging, creates an opportunity, a policy space, in which an issues network can thrive and a politics of childhood can be more fully developed. This politics need not be shut down by the pursuit of a closed consensus so much a feature of Irish social partnership: 'the formalization throughout the 1990s of social partnership as a model of governance reflects the successful institutionalization of this consensus ideology in Ireland's political structures and within civil society' (Meade, 2005, p 355). Social partnership may be a strategy for the management of change in a fashion unthreatening to the prevailing inequitable economic, social and political structures in Ireland:

> The only redistribution which has taken place, as a result of Social Partnership, has been in favour of the rich and powerful and has been dictated by the interests of business and capital, with the working class and those excluded from Irish society being the ones to pay. (Irish Socialist Network, 2003, p 1)

However, as the children's strategy illustrates, within the forces of change and within the strategy of social partnership, '... there exist subversive potentials that hold the promise of a transformed future (Kirby et al, 2002, p 196). It may be that 'state intervention is designed to generate a particular kind of civil society – one that bolsters the neo-liberal consensus, compensates for public sector withdrawal and studiously avoids critical assaults on state power' (Meade, 2005, p 361). But there are alternative futures to be strived for: 'the public sphere needs to be grounded in strong communal solidarities and notions of freedom that generate respect for – and attachment to others, rather than just granting a licence to ourselves' (Dunne, cited in Kirby et al, 2002, p 198). The rights-based, developmental social ecology that underpins the whole child perspective within the strategy arguably requires just such a public, and indeed private, sphere. Pursuit of that future should prompt the children's movement to build alliances with the trade union and community sectors that also have an interest in building another Ireland. The politics of childhood is primarily a 'politics of recognition', aiming to enhance the status of children and young people as a social category, but it also needs to be a 'politics of distribution' that recognises the compounding of social exclusion by structurally determined economic inequality (Clarke, 2000, p 208).

Conclusion

As the final chapter of the Irish National Children's Strategy states: 'The publication of the Strategy provides a new framework for action by a wide range of agents. Each must now identify what they can do to contribute to the success of the Strategy' (Government of Ireland, 2000b, p 93). The strategy document can only be a contribution to what must be a flexible and evolving process. As policy and practice experience is gained within the policy space created by the strategy, it will be possible to further review the options and debates it opens up around both objectives and processes. At the same time, it must be recognised how much will be undocumented and outside the gaze of the state and the more formal children's policy community. The strategy document is self-consciously not an end in itself but a tool to be used in developing the diverse partnerships that can make up an issues network capable of delivering the rich mixture of communication and action needed to mobilise the forces for change. It is only that breadth of force that can express and develop the contingent, continuous, recursive, highly divergent and emergent processes of solidarity and self emancipation that are the lived realities of the struggles for children and young people's social inclusion.

References

An Taoiseach (2000) Speech by An Taoiseach, Bertie Ahern TD, at the launch of the *National Children's Strategy: Our Children – Their Lives*, Dublin, 13 November (www.nco.ie, accessed 27 March 2006).

Bochel, C. and Bochel, H.M. (2004) *The UK Social Policy Process*, Hampshire: Palgrave Macmillan.

Boyle, R. (2000) *The National Children's Strategy: Enhancing Policy Co-ordination: Key Structures and Process Issues*, Dublin: Institute of Public Administration.

Clarke, J. (2000) 'A world of difference ? Globalization and the study of social policy', in G. Lewis, G. Gewirtz and J. Clarke (eds) *Rethinking Social Policy*, London: Sage Publications.

Combat Poverty Agency (2000) *A Better Future for Children: Eliminating Poverty, Promoting Equality*, Dublin: Combat Poverty Agency.

Fitzgerald, E. (2004) *Counting our Children: An Analysis of Official Data Sources on Children and Childhood in Ireland*, Dublin: Children's Research Centre, Trinity College Dublin.

Freeman, M. (1992) 'Taking children's rights more seriously', *International Journal of Law and the Family*, vol 6, no 1, pp 52-71.

Government of Ireland (2000a) *The National Children's Strategy: Our Children – Their Lives*, Dublin: Stationery Office.

Government of Ireland (2000b) *Report of the Public Consultation – National Children's Strategy*, Dublin: Stationery Office.

Ham, C. and Hill, M. (1993) *The Policy Process in the Modern Capitalist State*, London: Harvestor Wheatsheaf.

Iredale, R. (1999) 'Public consultation and participation in policy making', in G. Kiely, A. O'Donnell, P. Kennedy and S. Quinn (eds) *Irish Social Policy in Context*, Dublin: University College Dublin.

Irish Socialist Network (2003) *Parting Company – Ending Social Partnership*, Dublin: Irish Socialist Network.

Kirby, P. and Bryson, S. (2002) *Measuring the Magic? Evaluating and Researching Young People's Participation in Public Decision Making*, London: Carnegie Young People Initiative.

Kirby, P., Gibbons, L. and Cronin, M. (eds) (2002) *Reinventing Ireland*, London: Pluto Press.

McAuley, K. and Brattman, M. (2002) *Hearing Young Voices – Consulting Children and Young People, Including Those Experiencing Poverty or Other Forms of Social Exclusion, in Relation to Public Policy Development in Ireland*, Dublin: Open Your Eyes to Poverty Initiative.

Meade, R. (2005) 'We hate it here, please let us stay! Irish social partnership and the community/voluntary sector's conflicted experiences of recognition', *Critical Social Policy*, vol 25, no 3, pp 349-73.

Moss, P. and Petrie, P. (2002) *From Children's Services to Children's Spaces – Public Policy, Children and Childhood*, London: Routledge Falmer.

National Economic and Social Council (1999) *Opportunities, Challenges and Capacities for Choice – Overview, Conclusions and Recommendations*, Dublin: National Economic and Social Council.

NCO (National Children's Office) (2000) *National Children's Strategy*, Dublin: NCO.

NCO (2003) *Annual Report 2002: Making Ireland a Better Place for Children*, Dublin: National Children's Office.

NCO, Children's Rights Alliance and National Youth Council of Ireland (2005) *YOUNG VOICES – Guidelines on HOW to Involve Children and Young People in your Work*, Dublin: Stationery Office.

Nolan, B. (2000) *Child Poverty in Ireland*, Dublin: Combat Poverty Agency.

O'Hearn, D. (2001) *The Atlantic Economy – Britain, the US and Ireland*, Manchester: Manchester University Press.

O'Leary, E. (2002) *Taking the Initiative: Promoting Young People's Involvement in Public Decision Making in Ireland*, London: Carnegie Young People Initiative.

O'Morain, P. (2000) 'A giant leap for children's services', *The Irish Times*, 14 November, p 16.

Pinkerton, J. (2001) 'Developing partnership practice', in P. Foley, J. Roche and S. Tucker (eds) *Children in Society – Contemporary Theory, Policy and Practice*, Hampshire: Palgrave, pp 249-57.

Pinkerton, J. (2004) 'Children's participation in the policy process: some thoughts on policy evaluation based on the Irish National Children's Strategy', *Children & Society*, vol 18, no 1, pp 119-39.

Raferty, M. and O'Sullivan, E. (1999) *Suffer the Little Children: The Inside Story of Ireland's Industrial Schools*, Dublin: New Island.

Richardson, V. (1999) 'Children and social policy', in S. Quinn, P. Kennedy, A. O'Donnell and G. Kiely (eds) *Contemporary Irish Social Policy*, Dublin: University College Dublin, pp 170-99.

Rush, M. (1999) 'Social partnership in Ireland: emergence and process', in G. Kiely, A. O'Donnell, P. Kennedy and S. Quinn (eds) *Irish Social Policy in Context*, Dublin: University College Dublin.

United Nations Committee on the Rights of the Child (2003) 'Monitoring Children's Rights', CRC/GC/2003/5, (www.unhchr.ch/html/menu2/6/crc).

EIGHT

International developments in children's participation: lessons and challenges

Gerison Lansdown

The years since the adoption of the United Nations Convention on the Rights of the Child (UNCRC) in 1989 have borne witness to an extraordinary proliferation of activity all over the world as professionals, academics, local activists, non-governmental organisations (NGOs), politicians, policy makers and children have sought to grapple with the implications of the principle embodied in its Article 12, which recognises children's right to express their views and be taken seriously in all matters affecting them. Understanding of what is meant by participation varies widely but, if it is to be meaningful, needs to be an ongoing process of children's expression and active involvement in decision making at different levels in matters that concern them. It requires information sharing and dialogue between children and adults, based on mutual respect and power sharing, and must give children the power to shape both the process and outcome. Furthermore, issues relating to their own evolving capacity, experience and interest should play a key role in determining the nature of their participation (O'Kane, 2003).

Within that definition, the expression of participation has taken many forms, with children engaged in advocacy, social and economic analysis, campaigning, research, peer education, community development, political dialogue, programme and project design and development, and democratic participation in schools. This wealth of experience provides an invaluable body of evidence from which to begin to draw together some of the critical lessons as to the determinants of effective participation, the barriers to its realisation and the challenges to be overcome.

Recognising and respecting children's evolving capacities

In order to understand Article 12, it is necessary to give closer scrutiny to the concept of evolving capacities of children, embodied within Article 5 of the UNCRC. This key, but, to date, much less familiar principle, asserts that the rights and responsibilities for children, with which parents are vested, must be directed to the exercise by the child of their rights 'in a manner consistent with their evolving capacities'. In other words, as the child acquires capacities, there must be a gradual transfer of the exercise of rights from care givers to children themselves. Not only are children entitled to express their views and have them taken seriously, but they also have the right to take those decisions for themselves that they are competent to take. This entitlement raises significant questions as to how that competence is assessed, respected and promoted.

Although childhood is defined and understood very differently across societies, all operate with certain assumptions about levels of children's capacities (Lansdown, 2005a). In the main, these assumptions derive not from evidence of what children are capable of doing, but from what they are enabled to do in any given environment. Thus, in the UK, children under 11 years old are widely deemed incompetent to go out without adult supervision (Hillman et al, 1991). By contrast, in many developing countries, there would be far higher expectations of responsibility from young children. For example, from the age of 10 years, in some communities in Zimbabwe, boys are expected to build their own house while girls are considered capable of running a household in the absence of a more senior woman (Reynolds, 1985). On the other hand, British children are afforded greater opportunities for personal decision making than their counterparts in, for example, South Asia, and accordingly, would tend to have more confidence in their capacities for doing so.

It is not that children in these contrasting environments have intrinsically different capacities: rather, it is that the expectations from and experiences of children inform their levels of competence. Denying children opportunities for taking responsibility serves to diminish the opportunity to develop the capacities for doing so, and the subsequent lack of capacity is then used to justify the original failure to allow children greater responsibility. In light of these differences, it becomes apparent that it is not possible to make universal assumptions about the capacities of children to participate in the decisions and actions that influence their lives (Lansdown, 2005). Children's competencies evolve, in large part, in response to the world in which they grow up.

Accordingly, the defence of excluding children from participation in decision-making processes on the grounds of inexperience and incompetence becomes open to challenge. It is increasingly apparent that, given the opportunities, children, even those of young ages, can provide unique expertise and experience on their situation, have capacities to contribute towards their own protection, and can advocate effectively for the changes they perceive as necessary to improve their lives. However, building an environment in which this happens will necessitate very real challenges to existing presumptions about children's capacities.

Addressing the relationships between adults and children

Meaningful participation is a goal that can only be attained if recognition is given to the importance of the quality and nature of relationships between adults and children. Traditional hierarchical models based on presumptions of adults always knowing best, with wisdom flowing only from adult to child, need to be challenged. Equally important is the need to acknowledge the continuing responsibilities of adults in the participation process.

Informal power relationships between adults and children

Although children, given appropriate access to information, space and opportunity, can be powerful and effective advocates, they can only do so where there are adults to facilitate the process. Sustained autonomous activity on the part of children is not, in most instances, a realistic goal and therefore necessitates ongoing commitment of supportive adults. In a recent study of child participation across South Asia, for example, children involved in projects and programmes, even those led by children themselves, highlighted a continuing need for support from adults in respect of access to information, administrative help, forging links with policy makers, maintaining a skills base and counselling and advice (UNICEF, 2004). However, children do want changes in the nature of the relationships they have with the adult community. Research with children repeatedly highlights the demand for relationships in which partnership and respect play a greater part.

This challenge to the more traditional paternalism is powerfully highlighted in the findings of a project in Uganda and Sudan in which young people interviewed 2,000 adolescents and adults about their experiences of living in situations of armed conflict (Women's Commission for Refugee Women and Children, 2001). The findings are stark: war, displacement, HIV/AIDS, lack of development and poverty have created a world of unimaginable misery. Without family support, children and young people are at greater risk of forcible recruitment into armed combat, becoming heads of households, and experiencing sexual violence. And these problems are heightened by the fact that, despite facing heavy responsibilities and rights violations, their opinions are ignored when decisions affecting them are made. They experience little control over their lives, with traditional authority structures having failed to adapt to the challenges young people face or the contributions they are making. The research revealed a strong desire and capacity from young people to be involved in advocating on their own behalf, and providing leadership for constructive societal change. At the same time, they also want more support from adults and an easing of their burdens. In other words, it is a greater degree of partnership based on respect that is sought by these young people. This demand is repeated by children and young people throughout the world.

It is not only children who benefit from more respectful and collaborative relationships with adults. Adults can and do learn through listening to children. This process is highlighted in an HIV/AIDS project in India where children felt that existing messages from health professionals actually increased the stigma associated with the illness[1]. The project involved children aged 12 to 15 years in an awareness campaign on HIV/AIDS at all levels of project management, planning, implementation, review and monitoring. It had considerable impact on community awareness about the stigma and discrimination associated with HIV/AIDS. Even more significant was the effect on the adults involved. Initial resistance from many parents became pride, as they saw what their children were capable of achieving. The staff also observed that the process had challenged their limited assumptions about children's capacities and strengthened staff's own skills, resulting in mutual benefit and learning.

Formal power relationships between adults and children

Ultimately, children need access to sources of political power. Without it, opportunities for their voices to make a difference will never be realised. Recognising the necessity for such access, considerable investment has been made by many organisations to enable children to participate at all levels in conferences and other public events – the children's forum at the UN General Assembly Special Session for Children being one of the most high profile and successful[2]. However, it is still relatively rare for children to achieve the institutionalised dialogue with policy makers or politicians, through which significant and sustainable change can be achieved.

Building such processes presents a challenge in most countries, and it is important to learn from those initiatives that have been effective in establishing political legitimacy for children. One successful example can be found in Concerned for Working Children, an Indian NGO, which has empowered children to influence decision making within local Panchayats[3]. A key objective is to ensure that these Panchayats are child-friendly and free from exploitative child labour[4]. The project involves three- to five-year interventions in which children are brought together to set up their own local governments. Central to the process is that they elect their own members, thereby ensuring that the process is managed and owned by the children themselves. Equally important is the need to work in collaboration with the adults with power in those communities. Accordingly, the elections for the children's local governments are held by the formal government administration. A secretary of the adult Panchayat acts as the secretary of the children's Panchayat and a task force that is chaired by the district minister links the adult and children's Panchayats. In addition, the young people select a 'friend', who acts as an ombudsman, protecting their rights and intervening on their behalf.

The projects have not only been highly effective in reducing child labour and promoting a more child-friendly environment, but also provide the children with the opportunity for organised participation in local governance, which in turn provides them with an identity, enhanced self-esteem and the capacity to hold the state accountable. Concerned for Working Children has now facilitated the participation of thousands of children and young people in the governance of their villages. Adults who were traditionally feudal, patriarchal and gender-insensitive have become advocates for children's rights. They recognise the value in the active and equal participation of children through witnessing its translation into overall benefit for the whole community (Ratna and Reddy, 2002).

In the same region, the children's clubs in Nepal began in 1991 as an organic response to the call of the UNCRC for children's own perspectives to be given consideration (Rajbandary et al, 2002). It is now estimated that as many as 10,000 such clubs exist, some based in schools, and others in local communities. Activities encompass recreation, community development, advocacy for realisation of rights and peer education to raise awareness of rights. Increasingly, clubs are seeking recognition with the Village Development Committees to establish a formal voice for children in local policy-making forums. Furthermore, they have been engaged in a successful struggle for legal recognition of their organisations. In 2001, the Supreme Court made a groundbreaking decision to grant children's clubs the right to register their organisation on the basis of Article 15 of the UNCRC, the right to freedom of association[5]. This establishes a precedent both nationally and globally.

Bridging local, national and international participation

The practice of facilitating children's access to high-level adult events has prompted considerable debate and controversy. It is, of course, important that children have access to policy makers. However, organising children's participation in these forums involves considerable investment, while the outcomes it produces are often limited. A predominant focus on external events at the expense of ongoing work on the ground carries with it a number of risks. The participating children may be servicing the goals of the agency rather than their own expressed goals. The number of children involved in such events is necessarily limited, and often relies on investment in a small number of children who are the most confident and articulate. Too often there is no linkage between what the children are engaged in at the forums and their day-to-day lives at home. Furthermore, high-level participation can detract from the more demanding, and less prestigious, but arguably more valuable and influential work at the grass-roots level, enabling children to explore and pursue their own priorities. In this way, it can be seductive and raise unrealistic expectations of capacity to create change.

One of the aims of participation is to empower children to challenge power elites and structures that oppress them, and in so doing to render them more accountable. The pattern of plucking children from their local environment, and offering them access to national, regional and global policy arenas, risks creating groups of children who are equally unaccountable to the constituencies from which they come. Where this happens, participation is serving to *replicate* rather than *challenge* those power structures. This process is not inevitable: there are some very positive examples of building structures from which children can contribute from a mandated base, such as the child clubs in Nepal described above. However, there are also examples of the creation of 'child professionals' who have no sustained links with networks of children. At the same time, it is also important not to demand from children a level of accountability and representation that is not equally demanded of adults. Children are more vulnerable to such criticisms because the legitimacy of their presence in those arenas is less well established. Avoiding these pitfalls necessitates careful consideration of:

- the way in which children are selected;
- the nature of their accountability to children within their local community;
- the support given to them to forge links between the issues raised in these arenas and their translation into action on the ground;
- the need to create opportunities for the widest possible numbers of children to participate at this level.

Children, alone, are unable to establish the necessary building blocks to ensure continuity of dialogue between themselves as individuals and their peers, and consequent legitimacy for their involvement. This imposes an obligation on supporting organisations to encourage the development of child-led initiatives at local level that can serve to generate cohorts of children able and mandated to speak on behalf of their peers.

Enabling children to determine their own agendas

Across the many participation initiatives, there exist very different levels of real engagement by children. At one end of the spectrum are projects initiated and largely designed by adults but that involve children at the implementation stage. At the other end, initiatives emerge from children's own expressed concerns and are designed, implemented and evaluated by children themselves. All these models have legitimacy and can, and do, produce beneficial outcomes for children. However, the evidence to date, although largely anecdotal, does indicate that where children have greater input into the identification of the issues of concern to them, the better the outcomes in terms of personal development, more appropriate programming and more effective advocacy.

Once children's views are given expression, it becomes clear that their priorities do not always coincide with those identified by adults, and, indeed, often reveal aspects of their lives over which adults have little understanding or recognition. The gulf between adults' assumptions about children's lives and children's own experiences was succinctly expressed by a 16-year-old in Bangladesh, who observed 'you can see and address our physical needs without talking to us, but you cannot know about our emotional and psychological needs' (UNICEF, 2003, p 3). It is imperative, therefore, that the engagement of children takes place not once a project or programme is already established, but at the very earliest planning stages.

Significantly, children often emphasise issues relating to emotional well-being and safety and protection over material needs such as housing, food and clothing. In Sri Lanka, for example, the involvement of children in the strategic planning process undertaken by Plan International highlighted the children's aspirations for protection from alcoholic fathers, improved health and educational facilities, positive attitudes from community members, and improved family relationships (UNICEF, 2004). The involvement of children in this process resulted in Plan shifting its emphasis away from the development of individual children towards a focus on community development in which children were helped to play a significant role at all levels. A research project in Bangladesh supported 11 children aged 10 to 15 years to undertake a survey of around 50 street children on priorities identified by them in their daily lives. Contrary to the professionals' expectations that the priorities would relate to the need for health, education and care programmes, the children were far more concerned with violations of their civil rights. The majority of issues they raised concerned torture, injustice, exploitation, cheating, name calling, never using the child's name, forcing the children to do unpleasant and 'bad' work and the lack of an adult guardian to assist them in realising their rights. The research provided clear evidence that children's views cannot simply be guessed by adults. It is imperative to involve children themselves in both the identification of problems and strategies for their solution (Khan, 1997, cited in Alderson (2000)).

Balancing participation and protection

One of the most fundamental challenges posed by the UNCRC is the need to balance children's rights to adequate and appropriate protection with their right to participate in and take responsibility for the exercise of those decisions and actions over which they have competence. While the current increased global awareness of the need for greater child protection is positive, it does need to be tempered both by respect for those capacities children have, and, also the failure of many adult-designed strategies to protect children that deny children opportunities to contribute towards their own welfare (Boyden and Mann, 2000).

There is, for example, growing evidence that children are capable of exercising agency and utilising their own resources and strengths in developing strategies for their protection. Furthermore, active recognition of and support for children's engagement enhances their developmental capacities while over-protection can serve to increase vulnerability by failing to equip children with the information and experience they need to make informed choices in their lives. Protective approaches that make children dependent on adult support leave children without resources when those adult protections are withdrawn (Myers and Boyden, 2001). And given the scale of many national crises that are undermining the traditional family and community networks that served to protect children's well-being, there is an acute need to harness children's own potential strengths in order to maximise their opportunities for survival and development.

Achieving an appropriate balance requires assessment of a range of factors, including the capacities of the child, the levels of risk involved, the degree of support available, the child's level of understanding of the nature of the risks involved, and, of course, the child's own views.

Involving children in their own protection

Not only do children have relevant evidence to provide, but they also have a key role to play in developing strategies for their own protection. For example, an initiative in Kampala involved 200 children in tackling child abuse in the community (Lansdown, 2003). The children were asked to identify their protection needs, on the basis of which they designed and implemented a range of activities. The children, aged from 10 to 14 years old, established a steering committee for planning activities to address protection needs, a management committee for handling the implementation of project activities, a child protection committee for investigating cases of abuse and neglect, and an advocacy committee responsible for community sensitisation of child rights and child abuse. Committee membership was achieved through election by other local children. Central to the success of the project was provision of information to children about their rights, together with support from adults to help them identify what needed to change and how to bring it about. With this input, they were empowered to take action to challenge negative cultural behaviour towards children.

Respect for children's participation in their own protection does not mean that adults can abdicate their responsibilities. They have a vital role to play in creating safe environments for children, and introducing mechanisms for challenging abuses when they arise. But they also need to recognise that children have relevant insights into their own well-being, valid solutions to their problems and an important role in their implementation. They must accept that children are not merely passive beneficiaries of adult intervention, or an investment for the future, but competent social agents in their own right (Boyden and Levison, 1999).

The risks associated with participation

On the other hand, the struggle for justice and respect for human rights, in which marginalised groups begin to challenge traditional power bases, can expose them to risk. For children, often the most vulnerable members of society, the risks can be high, particularly in environments where there is little or no acceptance of children expressing their views. It is important to recognise that whereas adults can make informed choices for themselves as to the nature of risk that they take, children, particularly younger children, may be less competent to do so. Supporting adults, therefore, have a duty to ensure that, in any initiative, they give careful consideration to children's best interests and take responsibility for assessing any risks to which they are exposed. Moreover, children will not necessarily use the right to be heard and to exercise choices in ways that adults expect or approve of. It is important, given children's relative vulnerability, to be explicit about the boundaries within which decisions can be made, and the reasons for those boundaries. On the other hand, any commitment to empowerment must involve a level of preparedness to respect the views expressed by children. The extent to which they are complied with must necessarily depend on an assessment of whether the child has the capacity to understand the implications of any choice being proposed.

Finally, there can be unintended and negative consequences of involving children in claiming their rights. They may lose as much as they gain. There can be no change without risk, no struggle without costs. One illustrative example of the potential negative consequences is the recent experience in Nepal, where the Maoist insurgents have sought to recruit child leaders from the child clubs, successfully persuading some children to join by convincing them that they were fighting for their rights.

Protecting through listening

By failing to listen to children, the adult world can be blind to the reality of children's vulnerability to harm. Adults cannot protect children without understanding their experiences. It is only in the past decade, as children themselves have begun to make their voices heard, that both the extent and impact of violence they regularly experience has begun to be understood, and responded to. In countless consultations around the globe, children have cited ending violence – at home, in school and in the street – as a priority concern[6]. In a survey undertaken by UNICEF (United Nations Children's Fund) polling 15,000 children across Europe and Central Asia, an average of six in 10 children reported experiencing violent or aggressive behaviour at home. And the seriousness with which they view this issue is reflected in the fact that 43% of those surveyed identified their primary aspiration for the future as a world without crime and violence (UNICEF, 2001). The findings emerging from the regional consultations of the United Nations Study on Violence serve to confirm these findings (Save the Children, forthcoming).

The lesson to be learned is that effective protection of children can only be achieved by listening to and taking them seriously. The conventional view of protection has been as a one-way process, with adults as agents and children as recipients. What is now needed is a more sophisticated approach, in which it is understood as a dynamic process in which adults take responsibility for keeping children safe by listening to and respecting their perspectives, while empowering them to contribute towards their own protection.

Recognising the equal rights of younger children

To date, most activity on participation has focused on older children, with relatively little emphasis given to children under the age of eight. Most of the players spearheading debate on children's rights have been NGOs that work predominantly with older children. The focus has tended towards the creation of new forums through which children can be heard, rather than on working within those institutions that have greatest impact on younger children's lives – family, school, healthcare, early years' provision. The lives of children under eight are managed by parents and carers, and a range of professionals – teachers, nursery teachers, playgroup leaders, health workers – who have, overall, been less proactive in the participation debates (although clearly many such professionals do promote participatory practices with children). The commitment to participation by NGOs has derived from a rights-based analysis of children's lives. This differs significantly from the emphasis on development that informs much of the work in early years. While the two are not intrinsically contradictory, they do result in profoundly different emphases, objectives and strategies for intervention. In addition, the lack of focus on young children's participation probably also reflects the challenges it poses. While promoting participation rights at any age necessitates fundamental change to traditional attitudes towards children, this challenge is far greater with younger children who, in their day-to-day lives have even less say in how those lives are managed (Lansdown, 2005b).

However, Article 12 extends the right to be listened to and taken seriously to *all* children capable of expressing views. And, of course, young children have an equally valuable contribution to make towards decisions and actions affecting them. For example, in one community in Uganda (Save the Children, 1995), it was the children at the primary school who became concerned that animals used the village pond, which was the main water supply. They spoke with the village leader who called a village meeting where the children presented poems and dramas about the value of clean water. As a result, children and adults worked together on cleaning the pond and building a fence to keep the animals out. In a consultation with young children in north-east Brazil, they highlighted their need for a safe place to play. In response, a local organisation worked with the children to locate a piece of land, design the equipment, mobilise community support to build a playground and provide ongoing supervision and support. It was recognised that the children had a vital role to play in creating a physical space that both met their needs and fulfilled their aspirations[7].

Balancing rights and responsibilities

The idea that children bear responsibilities alongside their rights is controversial within the children's rights community. Of course, the fulfilment, protection and promotion of rights can never be contingent on the exercise of responsibilities. However, there is an inherent tension embodied in a struggle to demand recognition of children's rights and capacities for active participation while simultaneously failing to acknowledge the corresponding responsibilities associated with such engagement.

The conceptualisation of rights without responsibilities counters the way in which children are viewed in many developing countries, and with many of the deeply rooted assumptions about what children are entitled to as human beings. In sociocentric cultures, children are not considered to be autonomous individuals who hold rights, but as beings who exist primarily in relation to others (Adams et al, 2003). Children's sense of belonging to a particular social group is seen as fundamental to their well-being and is often expressed and reinforced through the fulfilment of duties or responsibilities to the group. Accordingly, greater attention is paid to the individual's responsibilities, than to his or her rights. This applies to both children and adults, although children's responsibilities are normally different. Meeting these responsibilities can be vital to children's social integration, self-efficacy and self-esteem. It follows therefore that seeking to limit children's responsibilities to protect their rights, for example, taking them out of work so as to facilitate school attendance, can lead to unintended adverse consequences for children, undermining their integration within family and community. So, within a rights-based framework, it is important to consider not only the detrimental effects, but also the benefits that children can gain from fulfilling responsibilities.

This issue has equal relevance in developed societies where it is arguable that the effective removal of children from economic and social responsibilities has served to infantilise them, reduce their status, and remove opportunities for acquiring skills, independence and greater autonomy. The insistence within the rights discourse of constructing children as subjects of rights but lacking any associated responsibilities would appear to reinforce this construction of the status of children. The process of participation in decision making does necessarily carry with it certain obligations – human rights are universal and must necessarily, therefore, be reciprocal and mutual. Overall, this is an issue that requires further debate and analysis, not least with children themselves.

Measuring participation

To date, there are few agreed indicators against which to measure and evaluate participation. Without such tools, it is harder to assess or contrast the effectiveness of different approaches to participation. Furthermore, it is necessary to demonstrate its efficacy, if sustained commitments are to be made to invest in the necessary legal, social and economic supports to enable it to become a reality for children. A number of dimensions need to be addressed (Lansdown, 2004):

- **Scope** – what degree of participation has been achieved and at what stages of project or programme development?
- **Quality** – to what extent have participatory processes complied with recognised standards for effective practice? The International Save the Children Alliance has developed a set of draft practice standards that provide an valuable framework against which to assess the quality of participatory work with children (Theis, 2004).
- **Impact** – what has been the impact on young people themselves, families, and the supporting agency, and on the wider realisation of young people's rights within families, local communities and at local and national governmental level?

One of the difficulties is that, as a relatively new concept, there has been no long-term evaluation of the impact of participation to assess how to achieve sustainable outcomes. One important exception to this gap in knowledge has been the research into the New Schools (Escuela Nueva) in Colombia. These democratic schools, designed to address persistent problems facing poor rural children in sustaining their access to education, provide powerful testimony as to the benefits of such a participative approach. Research evidence (Colbert et al, 1999) indicates that in sociocivic behaviour, maths and language the children scored considerably higher than in comparable rural schools. And the fact that the self-esteem of girls equalled that of boys is particularly important, demonstrating the equalising effect of its participatory methodology. Furthermore, a recent study (Forero-Pineda and Escobar-Rodriguez, 2002), undertaken 30 years after the schools were first introduced, indicates that they produce a sustained impact on non-violent conflict resolution and the strength of civil society.

Conclusion

The challenges to be faced in realising the right to participation are broadly comparable across all societies, although the scale and particular nature of the barriers vary. Interestingly, many of the most radical initiatives in child participation have evolved in the developing world. In part, this may arise from the relative absence of the state as provider and protector in children's lives, leaving greater scope for innovation and engagement by children themselves. It is, however, paradoxical, that it is in those societies that are traditionally more hierarchical and authoritarian that children have so often achieved greatest headway. Nevertheless, there is considerable benefit in looking to these international developments to build a greater understanding of what is possible and why, and how to address the key challenges in achieving genuine and sustainable opportunities for children to be involved in the decisions and processes that affect them. Emerging common themes are that:

- all children can participate;
- children need to be able to define their own agendas;
- adults can learn and benefit from children's experience;
- participation enhances children's evolving capacities;
- experience is as significant as age in influencing capacity;
- respectful and continuing adult support is essential;
- participation is a protective process;
- children have strengths to offer other children;
- participation needs to be linked to children's own daily lives;
- access to people with power is a prerequisite to achieving sustained change.

These lessons now need to be understood and applied beyond participation in projects and programmes, to build a culture in which children are respected as contributors and partners in all aspects of their daily lives. Doing so will necessitate dismantling the cultural, political and legal barriers that currently impede children's access to decision making. It requires a preparedness to challenge assumptions about children's capacities, and to invest in those environments in which children can acquire those capacities. It also needs serious consideration of key issues of protection, respective responsibilities, sustainability and power. It represents a challenge, but as the examples described in this chapter indicate, it is a realisable goal.

Notes

[1] This project was described in an unpublished paper from Save the Children UK in 2003 (Lansdown, 2003).

[2] See www.unicef.org/specialsession for more details on the children's participation in the event.

[3] Panchayat is the lowest level of administration in the system of local government. The term Panchayat refers to both the geographical and administrative units, as well as the elected body, which acts as the local council. A Panchayat is composed of a cluster of villages.

[4] Free of child labour means:

- no children having to do work that is detrimental to their normal growth and development;
- no children migrating from the Panchayat for employment;
- all children in the Panchayat getting an education that is appropriate to them and compatible to the formal system.

[5] This was a decision of the Nepal Supreme Court, 2058/5/25.

[6] See www.endcorporalpunishment.org for sources of research with children.

[7] This project is one that has been visited by the author, but there is no written report on its work.

References

Adams, J., Boyden, J., Feeny, T., and Singh, N. (2003) *Country Review: Bangladesh, A Report for SCUK Sweden/Denmark*, Dhaka: International NGO Training and Research Centre.

Alderson, P. (2000) *Young Children's Rights: Exploring Beliefs, Principles and Practice*, London: Save the Children UK.

Boyden, J. and Levison, D. (1999) 'Children as Economic and Social Actors in the Development Process', Paper prepared for the Ministry of Foreign Affairs, Government of Sweden, Stockholm (unpublished).

Boyden, J. and Mann, G. (2000) 'Children's risk, resilience and coping in extreme situation', Background paper to the consultation on Children in Adversity, Oxford: Refugee Studies Centre.

Colbert.V., Chiappe, C. and Arboleda,J. (1999) *Early Childhood Counts: Programming Resources for ECCD*, Washington, DC: Consultative Group on ECCD, World Bank.

Forero-Pineda, C. and Escobar-Rodriguez, D. (2002) 'School rules, democratic behaviour and peaceful social interaction of Colombian children', Paper presented to the International Society for New Institutional Economics conference, Boston.

Hillman, M., Adams, J. and Whitelegg,J. (1991) *One False Move ... A Study of Children's Independent Mobility*, London: Policy Studies Institute.

Khan, S. (1997) *A Street Children's Research*, Dhaka: Save the Children.

Lansdown, G. (2003) 'Involvement of children in shaping and influencing the work of Save the Children UK', Unpublished paper for Save the Children UK.

Lansdown, G (2004) 'Criteria for the evaluation of children's participation in programming', *Early Years Matters*, no 103, pp 35-9.

Lansdown, G. (2005a) *The evolving capacities of the child*, Florence: UNICEF Innocenti Research Centre/Radda Barnen.

Lansdown, G. (2005b) *Can You Hear Me? The Right of Young Children to Participate in Decisions Affecting Them*, The Hague: Bernard van Leer Foundation.

Myers, W. and Boyden, J. (2001) *Strengthening Children in Situations of Adversity*, Oxford: Refugee Studies Centre.

O'Kane, C. (2003) *Young People and Young People as Citizens: Partners for Social Change*, Kathmandu: Save the Children, South and East Asia Region.

Ratna, K. and Reddy, N. (2002) *A Journey in Children's Participation*, Bangalore: Concerned for Working Children.

Rajbandary,J., Hart, R. and Khatiwada, C. (2002) *The Children's Clubs of Nepal: A Democratic Experiment*, Kathmandu: Save the Children Norway/ Save the Children US.

Reynolds, P. (1985) 'Children in Zimbabwe: rights and power in relation to work', *Anthropology Today*, vol 1, no 3, p 17.

Save the Children (no date) 'Involving children and young people in shaping the work of the South Zone Indian Office of Save the Children UK', Unpublished internal paper.

Save the Children (1995) *Towards a Children's Agenda: New Challenges for Social Development*, London: Save the Children UK.

Save the Children (forthcoming) *Betrayal of Trust*, Stockholm: Save the Children.

Theis, J. (2004) *Promoting Rights-based Approaches: Experiences and Ideas from Asia and the Pacific*, Bangkok: Save the Children Sweden.

UNICEF (United Nations Children's Fund) (2001) *Young Votes: Opinion Survey of Children and Young People in Europe and Central Asia*, Geneva: UNICEF Regional Office for Europe.

UNICEF (2003) *Give Us Voice: We Know What We Want: Children and Young People's Perceptions of Implementation of their Rights in Bangladesh*, Dhaka: UNICEF.

UNICEF (2004) *Wheel of Change: Children and Young People's Participation in South Asia*, Kathmandu: UNICEF Regional Office for South Asia.

Women's Commission for Refugee Women and Children (2001) *Against all the Odds, Surviving the War on Adolescents: Promoting the Protection and Capacity of Ugandan and Sudanese Adolescents in Northern Uganda*, New York, NY: Women's Commission for Refugee Women and Children.

Part Three
Opening up theoretical spaces for inclusion and participation

NINE

Spaces of participation and inclusion?

Michael Gallagher

Introduction

This chapter presents a series of reflections on children's participation and inclusion from a geographical perspective. It begins by giving a brief overview of recent work on children's spaces in human geography, going on to explore some of the key concepts the geographical imagination has to offer the theorisation of children's participation and inclusion. With this conceptual framework in place, it then looks at research on children and their relationships to school spaces. It concludes by drawing out some problems that this literature raises for the creation of participatory and inclusive spaces. Throughout, the intention is not to provide a fully worked-out argument or a set of answers, but rather to open up and explore some questions about participation and inclusion, with the help of conceptual resources derived from human geography.

Children's geographies

As early as the 1970s, suggestions were made for a possible geography of children (see Bunge, 1973), and during the seventies and eighties a small literature developed around this topic within the discipline of geography (see, for example, Blaut and Stea, 1971; Hart, 1979; Matthews, 1984, 1987; Gold and Goodey, 1989). However, at the start of the nineties, James (1990) identified the need for geographers to pay much more attention to the social-spatial dimensions of childhood, calling for research 'which critically examines the ways in which children's lives, experiences, attitudes and opportunities are socially and spatially structured' (p 278). By the turn of the century, this call seemed to have been answered, and a recognisable sub-discipline of children's geographies formed (Holloway and Valentine, 2000; Matthews, 2003).

Some geographers have paid attention to the history of children spaces (Ploszajska, 1994, 1998; Gagen, 2000a, 2000b). However, human geographers' most distinctive contribution to childhood studies has been the exploration of how spaces and places are involved in the construction of childhood and children's lives. Thus, for example, there has been much recent work on urban childhoods (for example, Katz, 1994; Lynch, 1997; Chawla, 1998; Kong, 2000; O'Brien et al, 2000) and, following Philo's (1992a) call, a corresponding interest in children in rural places (e.g. Katz, 1991; Valentine, 1997; Jones, 1999, 2000; Matthews et al, 2000a; Tucker and Matthews, 2001). This focus on the urban–rural divide has also given rise to some comparative work (for example, Katz, 1994; Nairn et al, 2003). Much attention has also been paid to children's negotiation of public–private boundaries in space, and how this process constructs children's identities (Valentine, 1996; Aitken, 2000; Harden, 2000). There is also a wider and more disparate literature beyond geography that has contributed to academic understandings of children's spaces. For example, while work on children's experiences of educational institutions has been slow to develop within geography, there has been a growing interest in the spaces of education within educational sociology.

The children's geographies literature has drawn much of its inspiration from the 'new social studies of childhood' paradigm (James and Prout, 1997; James et al, 1998). Central to this paradigm is the attempt to see children as competent social actors, able to take an active part in the construction of their own lives and the cultures in which they live. This is intended to counteract the common tendency of adults to presume that children are incompetent, passive, powerless and dependent on their elders.

In turn, geographers have helped to inject an awareness of spatiality into these new social studies of childhood. A central idea in human geography is that spaces, bodies and identities are mutually constitutive, and children's geographers have attempted to demonstrate not only the difference that space and place make to childhood, but also the difference that children make to the spaces and places in which they live. Rather than viewing space as an empty container in which social relations take place, human geographers have drawn on theorisations of space and its relationship to society that are much more dynamic. The conceptualisation of space that geographers have brought to childhood studies has been strongly influenced by their discipline's engagement with, and selective reinterpretation of, the work of Lefebvre and Foucault. An examination of what geographers have borrowed from these two theorists will serve to clarify how children's geographers understand space, and what this understanding has to offer childhood studies, particularly in terms of its implications for participation and inclusion.

Lefebvre and Foucault: theorising society and space

Space, for human geographers, is generally understood as a social rather than a physical phenomenon. At its simplest, the term 'social space' can be seen as a way of recognising that space is produced by people (rather than pre-existing), and that spaces in turn shape people (rather than being inert or neutral). Very schematically, this chapter suggests that for geographers, Lefebvre has been a key source of inspiration for conceptualising how people produce space, while Foucault has been used to theorise how people are produced by space. This division is problematic for several reasons, but it will serve in this context as a heuristic, through which to give a brief overview of what geographical thought can contribute to the study of children, participation and inclusion.

According to Merrifield (2000), Lefebvre was a Marxist who applied Marx's logic to the analysis of space. Instead of treating space as a pre-given object, he wanted to analyse space as the product of social relations (Lefebvre, 1991). For Marx, class differences were the key factor in shaping the social relationships through which goods are produced. In the study of childhood, however, the adult–child divide takes the place of the Marxian bourgeoisie–proletariat divide to become the primary focus of interest. Accordingly, there is now a wealth of work in children's geographies looking at how the relationships between children and adults shape the production of space: for example in the negotiation of boundaries in the home (Sibley, 1995; Aitken, 2000; Christensen et al, 2000); the colonisation and policing of public spaces such as streets and shopping malls (Matthews et al, 1999, 2000b, 2000c; Young, 2003); and the creation of play spaces (Talen and Anselin, 1998; Hall et al, 1999; Smith and Barker, 2000; McKendrick et al, 2000). However, much of this work also pays attention to the ways in which differences among children – of class, ability, race, gender, and so on – affect the processes through which the spaces of children's lives are produced as inclusive or exclusive of certain groups. In theorising such relations between identity and space, Aitken and Herman (1997) explicitly draw upon Lefebvre, connecting his ideas with those of Winnicott, a psychoanalytic object relations theorist. In particular, they emphasise the importance of Lefebvre's notion of the 'trial by space' for children's geographies. The argument here is that only by producing a space for themselves can people constitute themselves as 'subjects'. Children's production of social space can thus be seen as central to the formation of their identities.

The implications for children's participation and inclusion of this understanding of space as socially produced are twofold. On the one hand, the literature repeatedly illustrates the myriad ways in which young people regularly play an active part in the production of the spaces in which they live. On the other hand, this literature is also shot through with anxieties about the ways in which children are often excluded from and marginalised within the production of social spaces, both on account of their age, and on account of other factors such as gender, race and disability. Vanderbeck and Dunkley (2004) state that: 'One of the central projects of recent work in children's geographies … has been the analysis of young people's exclusion from full participation in society's everyday activities and spaces by both formal legal frameworks and everyday practices that serve to naturalise adult authority' (p 177). Thus recognition of children's agency is tempered by an awareness of its limits: social space is produced through relationships that, in the main, subordinate children to adults. This produces a deep-seated tension in geographical accounts of childhood. While most studies draw attention to instances of children participating in the production of space, there is an underlying implication that such instances must be seen as exceptions within the wider context of children's general exclusion from such processes.

While Lefebvre's interest was in how subjects produce space, Foucault's was in the production of subjects by space. Here, 'subject' connotes an individual in possession of a particular personal identity, who is able to direct his or her own actions independently, and thus be autonomous. While some people may assume that humans simply 'are' autonomous, individual subjects in a pre-given, natural way, Foucault thinks that we have in fact been produced as such by the social, cultural and historical contexts within which we live.

The elements of these contexts to which Foucault attaches the greatest importance in producing human subjects are knowledge and power. However, as a number of geographers have pointed out (Philo, 1992b; Driver, 1994; Elden, 2001, 2003), there is also a profound spatial sensibility in his work. Several of his historical studies (Foucault, 1967,

1973, 1977) chart the development of spatial techniques of power, showing how ways of distributing and organising human bodies within institutional spaces have come to play a central role in forging humans as subjects. For example, Foucault (1977) sees cellular forms of spatial organisation, such as prison cells, school classrooms, hospital beds and factories, as crucial in the production of human subjects as *individuals*.

The implications of this conception of space for children's participation initially appear to be rather grim. One could argue that there is something sinister about the idea that spaces 'make' people; the implication seems to be that those people will be unable to exert any influence on this process, being subject to a controlling and dominating power. This theme of space as a form of control is recurrent within the childhood studies literature. It figures prominently in James et al's (1998) treatment of space, and can be discerned in a number of empirical studies. For example, those such as Matthews et al (1999) and Collins and Kearns (2001) examine age-based child curfews, one of the most overtly spatial techniques for the control of children. However, this chapter questions this reading of Foucault and its pessimistic consequences for children's participation.

Power as production, power as government

As those such as Moss and Petrie (2002) and Allan (1999) have sought to emphasise, Foucault conceived power as a predominantly productive rather than a repressive force. In its modern disciplinary forms, social power attempts to produce human subjects who will be so effective at regulating their own conduct that they will ultimately have no need of any external supervising power. Persuading people to participate in their own subjection in this way can be seen as the most cunningly efficient mechanism of power, enabling those who govern to do so with the bare minimum of intervention. Yet equally it can be argued that the ability to subject oneself to a set of behavioural principles – in Foucault's terms, an ethics of the self – is in fact the very basis of autonomy. In other words, by developing human beings' ability to govern themselves, disciplinary power actually ends up equipping those humans to become independent agents, no longer beholden to externally imposed system of rules. As Ransom (1997) puts it: 'The fact that we are *vehicles* of disciplinary power reveals ... not the omnipotence of power but its fragility. Such vehicles might go off the designated path in directions that frustrate the purpose for which they were originally developed' (p 36).

This ambiguity at the heart of Foucault's conception of modern power has important implications for the common distinction made in social science between structure and agency. Agency, understood as the ability to rule oneself autonomously by acts of will power, can no longer be seen merely as part of human nature. Rather, it is the outcome of the processes of subject formation carried out by institutional structures – particularly through their spatial practices. Thus we arrive at the troubling proposition that we owe what agency we have to structures of domination and control. Yet at the same time, those structures face the difficulty of governing human agents. Only if the agents that make up a structure are willing to comply with its aims can a structure achieve them. The autonomy of those agents means that there is always the possibility of insubordination. The power of structures thus depends on the agencies of all individuals involved. Understood in this way, the power of agents and the power of structures appear not as mutually exclusive opposites, but rather as entirely co-dependent.

In political terms, this conception of the process of governing people is liberal-democratic. Recognising that effective government depends on securing the complicity of the subjects being governed, liberal-democratic institutions attempt to harness the agency of those subjects by allowing them some control over the process of government. In general, the governed agitate for more control, while the governors attempt to place limits on this. The result is a compromise that is continually renegotiated through strategies and counter-strategies. The art of government thus involves judging how much control to cede to the governed, and determining what kinds of control to give them to make them more willing to be governed. This applies not only to political government, but also to social institutions. The rise of participatory initiatives such as school councils is one example of this. As Rose (1999) notes:

> This kind of 'government through freedom' multiplies the points at which a citizen has to play his or her part in the processes that govern him [sic]. And, in doing so, it also multiples the points at which citizens are able to refuse, contest, challenge those demands placed upon them. (p xxiii)

So what are the implications of all this for theorising children's relationship to space, particularly in relation to participation? It seems that the notion of power as governmental offers a way to reconcile the apparent contradiction between understanding children as the victims of controlling spatial regimes, and understanding them as agents in the production of space. Both Lefebvre and Foucault provide conceptual tools that refuse this dichotomy, by insisting that matters are always more complicated. On the one hand, children's participation in the production of social space always takes place through unequal relations of power, and therefore through power struggles. On the other hand, the ways in which spaces mould and produce children are both responsible for and beholden to their agency as human subjects.

In this context, it becomes clear that children's participation is a wholly ambiguous process. It does not, as some might like to believe, guarantee the unconditional exercise of children's free agency, but neither is it a tokenistic ruse designed to disguise and legitimate the dominating tendencies of institutions. To use a spatial metaphor, we could say that participation is the political domain in which the distinction between structure and agency breaks down. It is the frontier on which the wills of individuals and the wills of institutions directly confront one another, and are forced to acknowledge their mutual dependence. For an institution, the recognition that involving their subjects in decision making will improve the efficiency of its governance is a tacit admission of its dependence on the agency of its subjects. For the subjects, the very act of taking part in institutional decision making likewise constitutes a tacit recognition of the limits of their individual agency, and their dependence on institutional power to achieve their aims. Participation is thus the locus of an ongoing struggle, where the will of an organisation and the will of its subjects engage with and attempt to influence and realign one another.

Children in school spaces

This chapter now examines in more detail at some of the ways in which social researchers have looked at the relationships between young people and social space, with a view to raising some important questions about participation and inclusion. It focuses on studies that examine schools for two reasons. First, spatiality is so overt in schools. The school itself is an enclosed space partitioned off from the rest of society, while within schools the creation of different kinds of spaces for different activities makes the social production of space easy to observe. For example, thinking about a typical school hall, we can see that this physical space can support a number of different kinds of social space, depending on whether it is being used for an assembly, a drama class, a gym class, a school play, examinations or even as a polling station on election day. Second, schools have become a key site for formal initiatives promoting children's participation and inclusion, such as school councils, citizenship education, mainstream provision for children with special educational needs, and so on.

While a few human geographers have engaged with the social production of school spaces (for example, Krenichyn, 1999; Fielding, 2000; Holt, 2004; Gallacher, 2005), much of the interesting work on this topic has been produced within sociology and education research. A number of studies focus on space and gender, looking at how gender norms are reproduced, reinforced, negotiated and contested through the production of school spaces. For instance, Shilling (1991) showed how male pupils enact patriarchal rules by monopolising resources such as classroom space, learning materials, computers and leisure spaces. Likewise, Paechter (1998) noted how classroom-based studies have shown, for example, that boys tend to occupy the immediate zone around the teacher during demonstrations, to the exclusion of girls. She also describes how boys use sports activities as an aggressive means of colonising playground space as a masculine domain. Krenichyn (1999) came to similar conclusions in her study of how adolescents' gender identities in a New York high school. Krenichyn observed how the students' assertion of their gender identities often took the form of struggles over physical space. For example, at lunch times, the school's small gymnasium was dominated by boys playing basketball, to the exclusion of girls and other boys who did not conform to the masculine sportsman stereotype. Echoing Aitken and Herman's (1997) account of Lefebvre's 'trial by space', the excluded groups tried to establish other spaces for the expression of their identities, breaking the school rules by hanging out in public areas such as stairways, and thereby coming into conflict with the head teacher. The girls also attempted to organise a cheerleading group and lobbied the head teacher to make the necessary spatial resources available to them. However, the head resisted, arguing that this would only reproduce the rules of traditional gender roles, casting the boys as active sports players and the girls as mere onlookers.

The ways in which school spaces are regulated, both by staff and by pupils, is a key theme throughout the literature. Shilling and Cousins (1990) examined the social use of two school libraries, noting how school staff regulated the libraries by disciplining pupils whose behaviour was not conducive to the production of a quiet space for work. This involved techniques such as strict adherence to a timetable specifying the days and times when particular year groups were allowed to use the library, the arrangement of library furniture so as to maximise visibility for surveillance, and verbal reprimands and physical expulsion used in response to behaviour considered inappropriate, such as eating, talking and playing games. However, Shilling and Cousins showed how these institutional forms of power co-existed with many forms of agency exercised by pupils. For example, in one of the schools, a number of the older male pupils had colonised the library as a masculine social space for chatting and playing games. As well as imposing such activities on the space, these students also policed other kinds of activities, openly ridiculing pupils who tried to read or work in the library, particularly younger children and girls. Shilling and Cousins suggested that the concept of colonisation is useful as a more spatial and less glamorous way of understanding pupils' strategies of power that are more usually described as resistance, as in the classic ethnographies of school counter-cultures (for example, Willis, 1977; Corrigan, 1979).

Shilling and Cousins also drew attention to more covert forms of agency exercised by pupils. For example, some children enjoyed the peaceful atmosphere of the library but did not want to work. Accordingly, they found ways of evading surveillance by appearing to work while indulging in illicit activities. For example, pairs of students would look at books on shelves while quietly chatting to each other. Others used the shelves as cover behind which to eat without being seen, or sat in corners to converse quietly without being overheard by the librarians. These kinds of spatial tactics are interesting because they do not fit into a simplistic oppositional schema of power. They cannot easily be categorised as resistance tactics (they do not involve any conflict), colonisation (they are not an imposition on other students) or conformism.

Along similar lines, Gordon et al (2000) analysed the time–space paths taken by teachers and pupils in schools. They described how schools' organisational frameworks, rules and timetables strictly regulate pupils' time–space paths; one is expected to be in a certain place at a certain time, and there will be serious consequences if one is not. Yet, they also showed how such routines were regularly challenged by pupils, through a multiplicity of persistent small-scale tactics, such as students persuading their teacher to let them out of a class a few minutes early. Some children moved around when they should have been sitting still, or hid under tables. One student was observed to delicately sidestep the prescribed space–time path in a maths lesson. Through a careful combination of moving around the room collecting and depositing materials, and sitting quietly at his desk, he managed to do no work at all and escape detection by the teacher.

A few studies have looked at the spatial dimensions of the inclusion and exclusion of children classified as having special educational needs. Holt's (2004) study neatly illustrates the dependence of school structures on the agency of their subjects. She concluded that while school organisational frameworks may play a significant part in encouraging inclusion, such intentions are often frustrated by the actions of teachers and pupils. The research was based in a school that had a strong organisational commitment to inclusion, yet this did not prevent disableist practices from being reproduced by teachers and pupils. This is consonant with the work of education researchers such as Allan (1999), who demonstrated how children with additional needs are constructed as incompetent and dependent by their (often well-meaning) peers.

There is also a growing body of work looking at children's formal participation in school spaces. For example, Valentine (2000) examines school meal practices, arguing that since the 1980 Education Act, which emphasised consumer choice over schools' responsibility for pupil welfare, healthy eating policies have been replaced by a student-centred approach, based around providing what children want to eat. The school thereby 'constructs itself as an informal, "home-like" space, rather than an authoritarian space, where no-one is policing the pupils' corporeal consumption or performances and they are free to articulate their individuality' (p 260). In such an environment, teacher–pupil relations 'are based on principles that owe more to equality and dissolving divisions between adults and children, than hierarchy and deference' (p 260).

This picture, while attractive, must be questioned. Instructive here is Devine's (2002) examination of the regulation of children's time and space in three Irish primary schools. She solicited pupils' views on the way in which the schools controlled their space and time, and found (unsurprisingly) that many children resented their powerlessness and the lack of consultation in the process of planning classroom layouts, timetabling and rule making. Though in general they liked their teachers and wanted to have good relationships with them, the children were dissatisfied with their status as subordinate and inferior to the teachers. It is perhaps important to note that participation may take many different forms. Thus returning to Valentine's example of school meals, it is possible that children may be encouraged to make *individual* choices about what to eat from the range of food offered, but would not be *collectively* consulted about what that range of choices ought to be.

Pupil councils are the most obvious recent example of children's formal collective participation in schools, on which there is a growing literature, much of it highly critical. Drawing on questionnaire research, Alderson (2000) presented a range of comments in which pupils indicated that their school councils were highly undemocratic. Likewise, a recent small-scale study (Borland et al, 2001) found that while some young people felt that their pupil councils made real changes, many identified problems: older pupils dominating, subservience to teachers, limited power given to pupils and the involvement of a select minority of children from any year group. The young people in Morrow's (2001) study complained that formal structures, such as school councils and youth forums, were dominated by an elite comprised solely of high-achieving pupils, while Wyse (2001) found that: 'There was a perception that most issues raised by the school council members resulted in a lack of action combined with a lack of communication over the reasons for this lack of action' (p 211).

Cotmore (2004) paints a more ambivalent picture of a school council in a small rural junior school. This council was perceived by teachers and pupils to be highly effective on a range of issues. A teacher oversaw the council meetings, but pupil councillors found ways to 'manage' this teacher. Comments from both the teacher and the councillors suggested that they had created a distinctive social space for the school council, in which the usual hierarchical teacher–pupil relationships were questioned (though by no means dissolved). Yet the councillors also had to make numerous concessions to the established school system. They had to carry out all council business outside of lesson times, and there were also clear boundaries around what the council could and could not do. Its activities mainly concerned environmental issues, facilities and fundraising, and it had almost no formal control over timetabling, curriculum and classroom practices. Cotmore concluded that the children were placed in an intermediary position between the demands of the pupils and the demands of the school as an institutional system: 'While having to adapt to adult decision-making structures, councillors were also learning ways of managing adults in order to secure their desired aim' (p 63).

It seems that the work reviewed here exemplifies the pervasive tension described earlier, between the notion of children as competent social actors, and the notion of children as subject to the institutional power of schools. All of this work shows how children actively participate in producing the social spaces of schools. Mostly, this is through informal, spontaneous exercises of power, often carried out by individuals. But at the same time, this literature recognises that more formal, collective forms of children's participation in structuring school spaces are limited and compromised. The formal culture of schools is often represented as one of an oppressive disciplinary power that is generally indifferent to children's views. For example, Aitken (1994) noted that schools aim 'to socialize children with regard to their roles in life and their places in society ... inculcating compliant citizens and productive workers who will be prepared to assume roles considered appropriate to the pretension of their race, class and gender identities' (p 90). Similarly, for all their emphasis on children's agency, James et al (1998) portrayed the school as a space 'dedicated to the control and regulation of the child's body and mind through regimes of discipline, learning, development, maturation and skill' (p 38). Meanwhile, Holt (2004) suggested that 'classrooms represent panoptic principles, with emphasis placed on the regulation of children's bodies through disciplining gazes' (p 227).

In conceptualising this ambivalence around power, the model of power as governmental, outlined earlier in this chapter, might be a helpful tool. As Thomas (2000) remarked, schools are peculiarly paradoxical spaces: they 'are structured to encourage kids to become independent and self-reliant, yet most institutions curb expressions of nonconformity' (p 579). For Foucault, this is governmental power, a set of subtle games played between the institution as a whole and the agency of the individuals that comprise it. The nature of these games is such that in the very act of playing them, each party tacitly acknowledges its dependence on the other.

School spaces: some problems for participation and inclusion

Understanding structure and agency as co-dependent raises problems for both participation and inclusion. On the one hand, there is the problem that structural attempts to promote formal, collective participation and inclusion depend on co-opting children into exercising their agency in certain ways, as in Cotmore's (2004) study. This process of co-option seems antithetical to an ethics of participation. On the other hand, there is the problem that children often use their agency to resist, evade or circumvent such tactics of co-option, thus foiling them. Furthermore, the literature shows how the agency exercised by children may work to perpetuate social exclusion. This chapter concludes by exploring these problems a little further.

Children's agency has been repeatedly asserted and often celebrated in childhood studies, following James and Prout's (1997) new paradigm for the social study of children. The literature reviewed earlier typifies this in its lively illustrations of the many ways in which children do participate, usually informally and sometimes covertly, in the production of the spaces in which they live. However, in this literature, it is also sometimes possible to detect the assumption that these various kinds of agency will produce spaces that are inclusive.

This does seem logical from a certain point of view. Let us define an inclusive space as a space that has been, and continues to be, produced and reproduced so as to reflect the various interests of all those who might wish to use that space. If all children were able to participate in the production and reproduction of a particular space, it should reflect the interests of all those involved, and it would thus be inclusive according to the definition just given.

However, Lefebvre is instructive here. For him, social spaces always reflect the social relations through which they are produced. And if those relations are inegalitarian, then the spaces produced by them will also have this character. It is clear from the literature that the social relations of schools are extremely inegalitarian: in school cultures, certain pupils are always marginalised, stigmatised and excluded more than others. Perhaps schools are the best example of such inequalities, because they cannot easily be written off as unpleasant but accidental characteristics of their organisational structures. Schools govern by producing knowledge of pupils, assessing and examining them, classifying and ranking them, quantifying their personalities and abilities. Discrimination of this sort is therefore central to the purpose of schooling, and it is difficult to see how schools could perform this function so effectively and yet not reproduce, at least to some extent, discriminatory attitudes among their populations.

It is perhaps for such reasons that the childhood studies literature tends to identify exclusion as an effect of the dominating power of structures, while children's agency is sometimes represented in opposition to this, as a force that will produce more inclusive spaces. For instance, Vanderbeck and Dunkley (2004) argue that young people 'often reproduce broader societal discourses and practices which serve to "other" particular groups of young people, but they are also active cultural producers in their own right, capable of challenging exclusionary discourses and practices and creating their own complex systems of inclusion and belonging' (p 177). The implication here is that the reproduction of exclusionary discourses and practices is a *passive* process, which happens when children are 'duped' by institutional structures. Where children are *active*, these authors seem to be suggesting, their activity will involve challenging exclusion and fostering inclusion.

This is an attractive proposition, but it is clearly mistaken. One must beware of romanticising children as benign agents. As this chapter has already argued, structures depend on the agency of their subjects. Thus exclusionary cultures can only be perpetuated if people actively reproduce them. How, for example, could one be passively racist or sexist? Such cultures of exclusion may, of course, be re-enacted completely unconsciously, but this does not mean that their re-enactment is passive. Passive reproduction is an oxymoron: to reproduce something passively would be to not reproduce it at all. This means that there is no reason to suggest that children will use their agency to challenge exclusion. Indeed, some of the studies reviewed here suggest that children may use their agency precisely to perpetuate forms of exclusion, whether intentionally or not.

Thus as Davis and Watson (2001) have argued, inclusion demands attitudinal change at both cultural and individual levels. The problem for practitioners and policy makers is how to effect such change. One of the limitations of formal participation initiatives such as school councils is that they may make little or no difference to informal cultures of exclusion. To change such a culture, a school council would have to find a way to persuade children to change their attitudes. And within schools, it is probable that attempts to achieve this would involve the very kinds of disciplinary techniques for regulating children – systems of punishment and reward, exclusionary sanctions, and so – that most advocates of inclusion find so objectionable. In this author's own experience, these kinds of disciplinary techniques are so predominant in schools that they tend to be used automatically as the solution to most problems. One example is that of a well-meaning teacher reprimanding a child for singing the sash (an Irish loyalist song associated with sectarianism, which is a common within the culture of Scottish premier league football), and insisting that sectarian displays would not be tolerated in her school. Such tactics are clearly intended to make school spaces more inclusive, but they do so precisely by excluding exclusionary discourses and, ultimately, by excluding individuals who do not conform to inclusive norms. There is something profoundly contradictory about using exclusionary tactics as a means of promoting inclusion. And yet to tolerate exclusionary attitudes such as sectarianism in the name of including a diverse range of attitudes is also contradictory: one accepts exclusion as a means of promoting inclusion. Both strategies seem equally problematic.

To summarise, working from a Lefebvrean and Foucaultian conception of space as socially produced, this chapter argues that participation and inclusion present us with a peculiar double bind. On the one hand, the promotion of children's participation and inclusion in the production of social spaces depends on an understanding of children as agents, able to play an active part in producing and reproducing space. But this carries with it the burden of accepting, first, that children, as agents, may use their agency in ways which exclude themselves or others from the production of space, and second, that attempts to coerce or co-opt children into using their agency to create inclusionary spaces are likely to contravene the very ethics of inclusion. It is within this uneasy double bind that advocates of children's participation and inclusion must work.

References

Aitken, S.C. (1994) *Putting Children in their Place*, Washington, DC: Association of American Geographers.

Aitken, S.C. (2000) 'Play, rights and borders: gender-bound parents and the social construction of children', in S.L. Holloway and G. Valentine (eds) *Children's Geographies: Playing, Living, Learning*, London: Routledge, pp 119-38.

Aitken, S.C. and Herman, T. (1997) 'Gender, power and crib geography: transitional spaces and potential places', *Gender, Place and Culture*, vol 4, no 1, pp 63-88.

Alderson, P. (2000) 'School students' views on school councils and daily life at school', *Children & Society*, vol 14, no 2, pp 121-34.

Allan, J. (1999) *Actively Seeking Inclusion: Pupils with Special Needs in Mainstream Schools*, London: Falmer.

Blaut, J. and Stea, D. (1971) 'Studies of geographic learning', *Annals of the Association of American Geographers*, vol 61, no 2, pp 387-93.

Borland, M., Hill, M., Laybourn, A. and Stafford, A. (2001) *Improving Consultation with Children and Young People in Relevant Aspects of Policy-making and Legislation in Scotland*, Edinburgh: Scottish Parliament.

Bunge, W. (1973) 'The Geography', *The Professional Geographer*, vol 25, no 4, pp 331-7.

Chawla, L. (1998) 'Growing up in the cities: a project to involve young people in evaluating and improving their urban environments', *Environment and Urbanisation*, vol 9, no 2, pp 247-51.

Christensen, P., James, A. and Jenks, C. (2000) 'Home and movement: children constructing "family time"', in S.L. Holloway and G. Valentine (eds) *Children's Geographies: Playing, Living, Learning*, London: Routledge, pp 139-55.

Collins, D. and Kearns, R. (2001) 'Under curfew and under siege? Legal geographies of young people', *Geoforum*, vol 32, no 3, pp 389-403.

Corrigan, P. (1979) *Schooling the Smash Street Kids*, London and Basingstoke: MacMillan.

Cotmore, R. (2004) 'Organisational competence: the study of a school council in action', *Children & Society*, vol 18, no 1, pp 53-65.

Davis, J.M. and Watson, N. (2001) 'Where are the children's experiences? Analysing social and cultural exclusion in "special" and "mainstream" schools', *Disability and Society*, vol 16, no 5, pp 671-87.

Devine, D. (2002) 'Children's citizenship and the structuring of adult–child relations in the primary school', *Childhood*, vol 9, no 3, pp 303-20.

Driver, F. (1994) 'Bodies in space: Foucault's account of disciplinary power', in C. Jones and R. Porter (eds) *Reassessing Foucault. Power, Medicine and the Body*, London and New York, NY: Routledge, pp 113-31.

Elden, S. (2001) *Mapping the Present: Heidegger, Foucault and the Project of a Spatial History*, London and New York, NY: Continuum.

Elden, S. (2003) 'Plague, panopticon, police', *Surveillance and Society*, vol 1, no 3, pp 240-53.

Fielding, S. (2000) 'Walk on the left! Children's geographies and the primary school', in S. Holloway and G. Valentine (eds) *Children's Geographies*, London and New York, NY: Routledge, pp 230-44.

Foucault, M. (1967) *Madness and Civilization. A History of Insanity in the Age of Reason*, London: Tavistock.

Foucault, M. (1973) *The Birth of the Clinic. An Archaeology of Medical Perception*, London: Tavistock.

Foucault, M. (1977) *Discipline and Punish. The Birth of the Prison*, London: Allen Lane.

Gagen, E.A. (2000a) 'An example to us all: child development and identity construction in early 20th century playgrounds', *Environment and Planning A*, vol 32, no 4, pp 599-616.

Gagen, E.A. (2000b) 'Playing the part: performing gender in America's playgrounds', in S.L. Holloway and G. Valentine (eds) *Children's Geographies: Playing, Living, Learning*, London: Routledge, pp 213-29.

Gallacher, L. (2005) '"The terrible twos": gaining control in the nursery?', *Children's Geographies*, vol 3, no 2, pp 243-64.

Gold, J.R. and Goodey, B. (1989) 'Environmental perception: the relationship with age', *Progress in Human Geography*, vol 13, pp 99–106.

Gordon, T., Holland, J. and Lahelma, E. (2000) *Making Spaces: Citizenship and Difference in Schools*, Houndmills and London: MacMillan Press.

Hall, T., Coffey, A. and Williamson, H. (1999) 'Self, space and place: youth identities and citizenship', *British Journal of Sociology of Education*, vol 20, no 4, pp 501-13.

Harden, J. (2000) 'There's no place like home: the public/private distinction in children's theorizing of risk and safety', *Childhood*, vol 7, no 1, pp 43-59.

Hart, R. (1979) *Children's Experience of Place*, New York, NY: Irvington.

Holloway, S.L. and Valentine, G. (2000 'Children's geographies and the new social studies of childhood', in S.L. Holloway and G. Valentine (eds) *Children's Geographies: Playing, Living, Learning*, London: Routledge.

Holt, L. (2004) 'Children with mind–body differences: performing disability in primary school classrooms', *Children's Geographies*, vol 2, no 2, pp 219-36.

James, S. (1990) 'Is there a "place" for children in geography?', *Area*, vol 22, no 3, pp 278-83.

James, A. and Prout, A. (1997) 'A new paradigm for the sociology of childhood? Provenance, promise and problems', in A. James and A. Prout (eds) *Constructing and Reconstructing Childhood: Contemporary Issues in the Sociological Study of Childhood* (2nd edn), London and Washington, DC: The Falmer Press, pp 7-33.

James, A., Jenks, C. and Prout, A. (1998) *Theorizing Childhood*, Cambridge: Polity Press.

Jones, O. (1999) 'Tomboy tales: the rural, nature and the gender of childhood', *Gender, Place and Culture*, vol 6, no 2, pp 117-36.

Jones, O. (2000) 'Melting geography: purity, disorder, childhood and space', in S.L. Holloway and G. Valentine (eds) *Children's Geographies: Playing, Living, Learning*, London: Routledge, pp 29-47.

Katz, C. (1991) 'Sow what you know: the struggle for social reproduction in rural Sudan', *Annals of the Association of American Geographers*, vol 81, no 3, pp 488-514.

Katz, C. (1994) 'Textures of global change: eroding ecologies of childhood in New York and Sudan', *Childhood*, vol 2, pp 103-10.

Kong, L. (2000) 'Nature's dangers, nature's pleasures: urban children and the natural world', in S.L. Holloway and G. Valentine (eds) *Children's Geographies: Playing, Living, Learning*, London: Routledge, pp 257-71.

Krenichyn, K. (1999) 'Messages about adolescent identity: coded and contested spaces in a New York high school', in E.K. Teather (ed) *Embodied Geographies: Spaces, Bodies and Rites of Passage*, London: Routledge, pp 43-58.

Lefebvre, H. (1991) *The Production of Space*, Oxford: Basil Blackwell.

Lynch, K. (1997) *Growing up in Cities*, Cambridge, MA: MIT Press.

Matthews, M.H. (1984) 'Environmental cognition of young children: images of journey to school and home area', *Transactions of the Institute of British Geographers*, vol 9, no 1, pp 89-105.

Matthews, M.H. (1987) 'Gender, home range and environmental cognition', *Transactions of the Institute of British Geographers*, vol 12, no 1, pp 43-56.

Matthews, M.H. (2003) 'Inaugural editorial: coming of age for children's geographies', *Children's Geographies*, vol 1, no 1, pp 3-5.

Matthews, M.H., Limb, M. and Taylor, M. (1999) 'Reclaiming the street: the discourse of curfew', *Environment and Planning A*, vol 31, no 1, pp 1713-30.

Matthews, M.H., Taylor, M., Sherwood, K., Tucker, F. and Limb, M. (2000a) 'Growing-up in the countryside: children and the rural idyll', *Journal of Rural Studies*, vol 16, no 2, pp 141-53.

Matthews, M.H., Limb, M. and Taylor, M. (2000b) 'The street as thirdspace: class, gender and public space', in S.L. Holloway and G. Valentine (eds) *Children's Geographies: Living, Playing, Learning*, London: Routledge, pp 63-79.

Matthews, M.H., Taylor, M., Percy-Smith, B. and Limb, M. (2000c) 'The unacceptable *flaneur*: The shopping mall as a teenage hangout', *Childhood*, vol 7, no 3, pp 279-94.

McKendrick, J.H., Bradford, M.G., and Fielder, A.V. (2000) 'Kid customer? Commercialization of playspace and the commodification of childhood', *Childhood*, vol 7, no 3, pp 295-314.

Merrifield, A. (2000) 'Henri Lefebvre: a socialist in space', in M. Crang and N. Thrift (eds) *Thinking Space*, London and New York, NY: Routledge, pp 167-82.

Morrow, V. (2001) 'Young people's explanations and experiences of social exclusions: retrieving Bourdieu's concept of social capital', *International Journal of Sociology and Social Policy*, vol 21, no 4, pp 37-63.

Moss, P. and Petrie, P. (2002) *From Children's Services to Children's Spaces: Public Policy, Children and Childhood*, London: Routledge Falmer.

Nairn, K., Panelli, R., and McCormack, J. (2003) 'Destabilizing dualisms: young people's experiences of rural and urban environments', *Childhood*, vol 10, no 1, pp 9-42.

O'Brien, M., Jones, D., Sloan, D. and Rustin, M. (2000) 'Children's independent mobility in the urban public realm', *Childhood*, vol 7, no 3, pp 257-77.

Paechter, C.F. (1998) *Educating the Other: Gender, Power and Schooling*, London and Washington, DC: Falmer Press.

Philo, C. (1992a) 'Neglected rural geographies: a review essay inspired by Colin Ward's "The Child in the Country"', *Journal of Rural Studies*, vol 8, no 2, pp 193-207.

Philo, C. (1992b) 'Foucault's geography', *Environment and Planning D: Society and Space*, vol 10, no 2, pp 137-61.

Ploszajska, T. (1994) 'Moral landscapes and manipulated spaces: gender, class and space in Victorian reformatory schools', *Journal of Historical Geography*, vol 20, no 4, pp 413-29.

Ploszajska, T. (1998) 'Down to earth? Geography fieldwork in English schools, 1870-1944', *Environment and Planning D: Society and Space*, vol 16, no 6, pp 757-74.

Ransom, J.S. (1997) *Foucault's Discipline. The Politics of Subjectivity*, Durham and London: Duke University Press.

Rose, N. (1999) *Governing the Soul* (2nd edn), London and New York, NY: Free Association.

Shilling, C. (1991) 'Social space, gender inequalities and educational differentiation', *British Journal of Sociology of Education*, vol 12, no 1, pp 23-44.

Shilling, C. and Cousins, F. (1990) 'Social use of the school library: the colonisation and regulation of educational space', *British Journal of Sociology of Education*, vol 11, no 4, pp 411-30.

Sibley, D. (1995) 'Families and domestic routines: constructing the boundaries of childhood', in S. Pile and N.J. Thrift (eds) *Mapping the Subject: Geographies of Cultural Transformation*, London: Routledge, pp 123-37.

Smith, F. and Barker, J. (2000) 'Contested spaces: children's experiences of out of school care in England and Wales', *Childhood*, vol 7, no 3, pp 315-33.

Talen, E. and Anselin, L. (1998) 'Assessing spatial equity: an evaluation of measures of accessibility to public playgrounds', *Environment and Planning A*, vol 30, no 4, pp 595-613.

Thomas, M. (2000) 'Guest editorial: from crib to campus: kids' sexual/ gender identities and institutional space', *Environment and Planning A*, vol 32, no 4, pp 577-80.

Tucker, F. and Matthews, H. (2001) '"They don't like girls hanging around there": conflicts over recreational space in rural Northamptonshire', *Area*, vol 33, no 2, pp 161-8.

Valentine, G (1996) 'Children should be seen and not heard: the production and transgression of adults' public space', *Urban Geography*, vol 17, no 3, pp 205-20.

Valentine, G. (1997) 'A safe place to grow up? Parenting, perceptions of children's safety and the rural idyll', *Journal of Rural Studies*, vol 13, no 2, pp 137-48.

Valentine, G. (2000) 'Exploring children and young people's narratives of identity', *Geoforum*, vol 31, no 2, pp 257-67.

Vanderbeck, R.M. and Dunkley, C.M. (2004) 'Introduction: geographies of exclusion, inclusion and belonging in young lives', *Children's Geographies*, vol 2, no 2, pp 177-83.

Willis, P.E. (1977) *Learning to Labour: How Working Class Kids Get Working Class Jobs*, Westmead: Saxon House.

Wyse, D. (2001) 'Felt tip pens and school councils: children's participation rights in four English schools', *Children & Society*, vol 15, no 4, pp 209-18.

Young, L. (2003) 'The "place" of street children in Kampala, Uganda: marginalisation, resistance, and acceptance in the urban environment', *Environment and Planning D: Society and Space*, vol 21, no 5, pp 607-27.

TEN

From children's services to children's spaces

Peter Moss

This chapter[1] is about 'public provisions for children'. This term is used here to encompass a wide range of out-of-home settings where groups of children come together, from schooling, through a range of early childhood, play and out-of-school services as well as group residential settings, to lightly structured spaces for children's outdoor, unsupervised play. It excludes, for the purposes of this chapter, a wide range of provisions working with children and young people on an individual basis, such as, for example, foster care, social work and counselling.

The need to use this clumsy term arises because of the desire to question a more commonly used term: 'children's services'. There is a dilemma about how to refer to the field to be contested – environments provided through the agency of public policy for groups of children – without using a term ('children's services') that, it is argued, already carries certain meanings and values. The chapter therefore uses the term 'public provisions for children', while recognising that in practice there can be no neutral terminology.

The chapter explores a particular social construction of public provisions for children: public provisions understood as 'children's services'. This is treated as a dominant understanding in the UK today, producing public provisions as primarily technical and disciplinary undertakings, concerned with regulation, surveillance and normalisation, and instrumental in rationality and purpose. But the chapter also considers *an* other social construction with a different rationality and purpose: public provisions understood as 'children's spaces'. It argues that the meanings we attach to public provisions for children are inextricably linked with social constructions of childhood and our image of the child, which are taken to be contestable subjects produced in the social arena rather than essential truths revealed through science. A different child comes into view with different constructions of public provisions, and so too does a different worker.

This line of exploration throws up various questions: Why does policy pay so much attention to children at certain times? Is it a case of either 'children's services' or 'children's spaces' – or is it not so clear-cut in practice? What can be expected from children's services as technologies for addressing exclusion, poverty or inequality? In providing for children, what is the place of the local and the particular, and what is the place of the national and the uniform?

This chapter does not address directly the concept of social inclusion and its relationship to concepts such as poverty and inequality, which is covered elsewhere in the book. The working hypothesis here is that a central role of public provisions for children has been to tackle an array of socially constructed problems that take various names and forms at various times. These have in common a capacity to disturb the powers that be – because they threaten the ability of the nation state to compete globally (whether economically or militarily) and/or because they threaten the security of the nation state internally (for example, by spreading poor health, crime or other dangerous habits). Many are related to exclusion or inequality, but the central interest is in this role of problem solving, rather than with how the problems are understood, explained or named.

From children's services ...

Public provisions for children have both universal and targeted purposes. The school best personifies the universal purpose in its concern with the child constructed primarily as a becoming adult. As Readings (1997) observes: 'The long narrative of education that the Enlightenment inculcated [was] that knowledge would make mankind free, that education is a process of transforming children into adults. Education, that is, transforms children, who are by definition dependent upon adults, into independent beings, the free citizens that the modern state requires' (p 158).

This role continues to the present day, albeit with new technologies and disciplines:

> 'Developmentally appropriate curricula' [is] a widely applied curriculum theory that correlates lesson plans with a sequence of capabilities.... It appeals to developmental psychology for its scientific base, it inscribes assumptions of progressive efficiency, and it assumes a behaviourist

> approach to establish educational objectives.... [This]
> interweaving of developmental psychology, efficiency, and
> behaviourism in educational curricula becomes a
> technology of normalization. I call this technology
> *developmentality* as a way of alluding to Foucault's
> governmentality, and focusing on the self-governing effects
> of developmental discourse in curriculum debates.
> Developmentality, like governmentality, describes a current
> pattern of power in which the self disciplines the self.
> (Fendler, 2001, p 120)

Fendler further argues that much current educational practice is
intended to meet new demands from the state and the economic
system, in particular for 'flexible ways of being', with flexibility viewed
as the 'cutting edge solution to the challenges of productivity' (2001,
p 119). Like others (for example, Foucault, Popkewitz, Rose), she also
refers to the capability of modern technologies, deployed through
public provisions such as schools, to 'govern the soul'. The term 'soul'
here refers to what has been held as the innermost qualities of being
human. It is used (for example, by Rose, 1989) to emphasise the depth
to which modern technologies of discipline have extended.

> The thrust of whole child education is that the child's entire
> being – desire, attitudes, wishes – is caught up in the
> educative process. Educating the whole child means not
> only the cognitive, affective and behavioural aspects, but
> the child's innermost desires.... No aspect of the child must
> be left uneducated: education touches the spirit, the soul,
> motivation, wishes, desires, dispositions and attitudes of the
> child to be educated. (Fendler, 2001, p 121)

The general role of public provisions is not, therefore, just about
transmitting knowledge, inculcating values or preparing the child for
citizenship. The argument is that they are means by which subjectivity
is formed and by which we learn to govern ourselves: for 'a condition
of governance in a liberal democracy [is that] the educated subject is
self-disciplined ... [so that] the subject understands and reflexively
disciplines desires, feelings, loves, wishes and fears' (Fendler, 2001, p
124).

The targeted role of public provision, and the hopes invested in it,
are well captured by Hatch and Rose:

Rising expectations of science and technology in the 19th century coupled with a romantic view of the purity and perfectibility of the child, led to the perception that children are appropriate vehicles for solving problems in society. The notion was that if we can somehow intervene in the lives of children, then poverty, racism, crime, drug abuse and any number of social ills can be erased. Children become instruments of society's need to improve itself, and childhood became a time during which social problems were either solved or determined to be unsolvable. (Hatch, 1995, pp 118-19)

[The family of the labouring classes was] to be shaped, educated and solicited into a relation with the state if it was to fulfil the role of producing healthy, responsible, adjusted social citizens. The political task was to devise mechanisms that would support the family [of the labouring classes] in its 'normal' functioning and enable it to fulfil its social obligations most effectively without destroying its identity and responsibility. The technical details of the internal regime of the working-class family would become the object of new forms of pedagogy, for example through medical inspection of schoolchildren and the invention of 'health visitors', to instil norms of personal hygiene and standards of child care. While the mothers of the wealthier classes had been solicited into alliances with medics in the nineteenth century ... one sees a new specification of the role of the working-class mother as one who was to be educated by educationalists, health visitors and doctors into the skills of responsible government of domestic relations (Rose, 1999, pp 128-9).

These descriptions of expectations and developments at the turn of the 19th century resonate today. For they readily apply to expectations and developments at the turn of the 20th century: little has changed. Taking a historical perspective, programmes like Sure Start are the latest in a long line of interventions aimed at instilling norms and skills into a marginalised underclass, and so to include them in advanced liberal society.

Both these general and targeted purposes for public provisions for children are produced from a very specific social construction of these provisions: what Pat Petrie and I refer to as 'children's services' (Moss and Petrie, 2002). The word 'services' has many meanings. It can have the sense of offering yourself to the other, the performance of a duty or obligation, being of service. A 'service ethic' has been an important motivation for many people working with children. Our use of 'services' links to other meanings, in particular dictionary definitions of 'service' such as 'performance of a function' and 'the checking and (if necessary) repairing and/ or replacing of parts to ensure efficient operation' (Chambers Dictionary, 1998). It is our contention that the use of the term 'services' is often (though not invariably) associated with this sense. In any case, by questioning the term 'children's services', by suggesting it is problematic, we intend to show that it cannot be taken as neutral nor can its meaning be assumed to be self-evident.

The task of public provisions understood as children's services is regulation through governing the child. Their rationality is instrumental and calculative. They operate as sites for what Rose (1999) terms technologies of government or 'human technologies', 'imbued with aspirations for the shaping of conduct in the hope of producing certain desired effects' (p 52), which act on children, or rather on parts of the atomised child, to produce specific, predetermined and adult-defined outcomes. They embody beliefs and assumptions of modernity, in particular the possibility and desirability of an ordered and mastered world that is certain, controllable and predictable.

Public provisions as children's services assume particular social constructions of the child. The child of children's services is incomplete and immature, a becoming adult who will attain complete personhood through processes of development and through the transmission of knowledge, culture and values. The child of 'children's services' is a 'poor' child: she is 'the child in need', 'the child at risk', 'the vulnerable child', 'the child needing to be readied to learn' (Moss et al, 2000). The child of children's services is also a redemptive agent, who will grow up to rescue society – but first needs to be saved. Popkewitz (1998), writing about a 19th-century secular culture of redemption in American education, comments on how 'it was believed that personal as well as social development could be purchased....The school brought progress through rescuing the soul using theories and technologies constructed with psychology.... Discourses of salvation 'make' the child an individual who is not reasonable, capable and competent *but who – with the proper care and nurturance – can be saved*' (p 25, emphasis added).

An understanding of public provision as 'children's services' requires a particular understanding of those who work in these services.

Irrespective of their level of qualification and whether or not they are deemed professionals, they are technicians, whose task is to apply as precisely as possible technologies that are believed to work effectively in delivering predetermined outcomes. Control systems such as instructions, targets and regular inspections are a necessary part of ensuring that the performance of these technicians conforms to standard.

It has been part of the argument in this chapter that such understandings have been around a long time, indeed are inscribed with the thinking of modernity, a mindset or intellectual paradigm that has been dominant for several centuries (Dahlberg et al, 1999; Dahlberg and Moss, 2005). These understandings, however, become particularly prominent at certain historical moments – and we are living through one of these historical moments. Speaking of contemporary Britain, Prout (2000) observed that 'despite the recognition of children as persons in their own right, public policy and practice is marked by an intensification of control, regulation and surveillance around children' (p 304).

The New Labour Government has paid great attention to interventions involving children (and their parents). Some of these, in particular 'childcare services', are partly motivated by more immediate policy concerns, in particular the importance attached to paid work and the labour force. But much child-related policy is future-oriented; it is about using children as the means to tackle widespread problems in society, the notion being (to repeat an earlier quotation by Hatch) that 'if we can somehow intervene in the lives of children, then poverty, racism, crime, drug abuse and any number of social ills can be erased' (Hatch, 1995, p 119).

Why this current attention to 'children's services'? There are two intersecting influences, linked by the growing dominance of a particular form of capitalism over the past 30 years or so: market capitalism or neo-liberal capitalism. First, 'children's services' are a means to produce the kind of competitive, flexible workforce deemed necessary to compete successfully in an increasingly competitive and ruthless global economy – Fendler's 'flexible souls'. Second, 'children's services' are a means to tackle the serious consequences that market capitalism has had for the social fabric (Hutton, 1995; Sennett, 1998; Bauman, 1999; Gray, 1999). As Gray has observed:

> It is odd that there are still those who find the association
> of free markets with social disorder anomalous. Even if it
> could itself be rendered stable the free market is bound to

be destructive of other institutions through which social
cohesion is achieved. By privileging individual choice over
any common good it tends to make relationships revocable
and provisional. (Gray, 1999, pp 36-7)

So 'children's services' are a means to construct the future worker and
to bring order out of acute disorder. For both purposes, technologies
act on the child as a redemptive vehicle for the future. As Prout (2000)
puts it: 'I suggest that in a world seen as increasingly shifting, complex
and uncertain, children, precisely because they are seen as especially
unfinished, appear as a good target for controlling the future' (p 306).

Motivation to intervene is combined with a new confidence in the
possibilities of intervention: 'neo-liberalism does not abandon the "will
to govern"': it maintains the view that the failure of government to
achieve its objectives is to be overcome by inventing new strategies of
government that will succeed' (Rose, 1996, p 53). Central to the
strategies of the Labour government in Britain has been the application
of the procedures and techniques of new managerialism. Linked to
the application of selected knowledge and research, mostly situated
within a positivistic, empirical-analytic paradigm, managerialism
promises human technologies able to produce more certain outcomes.
It offers 'calculative technologies ... [that] provide a foundation for
enacting the new logics of rationing, targeting and priority setting'
(Clarke, 1998, p 177).

Managerialism is not the only technology underpinning advanced
liberalism's new-found belief in the processing qualities of 'children's
services'. For example, there are what Rose refers to as the 'psy
sciences', which he claims 'play a key role in rationalities and techniques
of government, with legitimacy claimed by "engineers of the soul"
on the basis they can deal truthfully with the real problems of human
existence in the light of a knowledge of the individuals who make
it up' (Rose, 1989). Particular attention has been paid to the role of
developmental psychology as a technology of normalisation and
governance (cf. Burman, 1994; Walkerdine, 1984) and to its origins
'as a paradigmatically modern discipline', whose emergence 'was
prompted by concerns to classify, measure and regulate' (Burman,
1994, p 18).

... to 'children's spaces'

This chapter now changes tack, by imagining another understanding
of public provisions for children – 'an' other, not 'the' other. It does so

partly as an aid to critical thinking, echoing Foucault's dictum that 'as soon as one can no longer think things as one formerly thought them, transformation becomes both very urgent, very difficult and quite possible' (Foucault, 1988, p 155). What is considered here, however, is not unknown in practice. In *From Children's Services to Children's Spaces*, Moss and Petrie (2002) offered several examples, such as an adventure playground in Wales and the early childhood centres in Reggio Emilia in Italy. But the idea of public provisions as children's spaces is not – like 'children's services' – systemic. Rather it can be seen in operation at the level of particular institutions or communities. The question is whether it can ever be anything more – is it possible to legislate for universal 'children's spaces'?

The concept of 'children's spaces' understands provisions as environments of many possibilities – cultural and social, but also economic, political, ethical, aesthetic, physical – some predetermined, others not, some initiated by adults, others by children. It presumes and values the unexpected and surprising, unpredicted outcomes, the provocation of new thought. These environments are understood as places for children to live their childhoods, paying as much attention to the present as the future, as part of current life, not just preparation for later life. They are spaces for children's own agendas, although not precluding adult agendas, where children are understood as fellow citizens with rights, participating members of the social groups in which they find themselves, agents of their own lives but also interdependent with others, co-constructors of knowledge, identity and culture. Children's spaces are for all children, on a democratic footing across different social groups. They make space for the whole child, not the sectional child of many children's services. Here children co-exist with others in society on the basis of who they are, rather than who they will become.

The concept of 'children's space' does not just imply a *physical* space, a setting for groups of children. It also carries the meaning of being a *social* space, 'a domain of social practices and relationships' (Knowles, 1999, p.241); a *cultural* space, where values, rights and cultures (including children's culture) are created; and a *discursive* space for differing perspectives and forms of expression, where there is room for dialogue, confrontation (in the sense of exchanging differing experience and views), deliberation and critical thinking, where children and others can speak and be heard. In this sense, the concept of 'children's space' implies possibilities for children and adults to contest understandings, values, practices and knowledges.

One of the possibilities of 'children's spaces' understood in this multidimensional way is social inclusion in the sense that they provide opportunities for children to be included in networks of relations with other children and adults, beyond the home. The early childhood centres in Reggio, for example 'opened up [for children] the possibility of a very long and continuous period of children living together [with each other], 5 or 6 years of reciprocal trust and work', where they could 'express their previously overlooked desire to be with their peers' (Malaguzzi, 1993, p 55). Another possibility, explored by Dahlberg and Moss (2005), is that 'children's spaces' may become sites for democratic 'minor' politics (Rose, 1999), thus making the idea of 'discursive space' a reality. Useful leads for this realisation include: the many languages of children (Malaguzzi, 1993); the meaning of listening (Rinaldi, 2001); and tools for challenging dominant discourses and making institutions and practice transparent, such as pedagogical documentation (Dahlberg et al, 1999; Rinaldi, 2005). Viewed and developed in this way, public provision for children might form part of a process of democratic renewal based on new locations, subjects and methods for inclusive politics.

The chapter refers here and throughout to 'child' and 'children', because the author is more familiar with public provisions for this younger age group. However, in principle, the concept could be extended to young people. Indeed, it could be extended to cover public and communal provisions for people of varying ages, including older people. Moreover, the concept can encompass a wide range of provisions, varying, for instance, from provisions with a strong adult presence (such as a nursery or school), to those with minimal or no adult presence. The important and defining criteria are: that the provision is public, in that it is created through collective action and available to all who need or want to use it; and that practices, relationships and ethics are consistent with the understanding or construction of the provision as a 'children's space'. That construction, of public provision as 'children's space', is in turn connected with particular constructions of the child: as a social actor located in a network of relations with other children and adults; as 'a competent and capable child, a rich child, who participates in the creation of themselves and their knowledge' (Dahlberg and Lenz Teguchi, 1994, p 2); and as a citizen with a recognised place in society, with rights and with a voice that should be listened to.

The reconstruction of children's services as children's spaces entails some reconceptualisation of the work and workers in children's spaces. To say we can understand public provisions for children in this way, as 'children's spaces' rather than as 'children's services', is not just a matter of attaching a new label. Calling public provisions 'children's spaces' does not automatically make them different. In this chapter, the term 'children's spaces' in part represents a different way of *thinking* about children and public provisions for them. But it also means *being* different:'children's spaces' require different ethics, relationships and practices.

Rather than a technician, a worker in a children's space is understood to be a reflective practitioner, a researcher, a critical thinker, and a co-constructor of knowledge, culture and identity. But it is necessary to go further, to find a theory and practice for working with children in children's spaces and a type of worker who embodies this theory and practice. The work and worker need to be suited to groups of children of varying ages in many types of setting, to relating to the whole child, and to being open to many and unpredictable possibilities. The worker needs to be comfortable in many fields – from ethics to children's culture, from learning to health – and with adopting varied identities, including reflective practitioner, researcher and co-constructor.

One theory and one worker that have interesting possibilities are pedagogy and the pedagogue – both familiar in many parts of continental Europe, but virtually unknown in the English-language world (not least because 'pedagogy' is usually translated incorrectly as 'the science of education', and 'pedagogue' as 'teacher'). Moss and Petrie (2002) have attempted to give a sense of the pedagogical approach to working with children (or indeed adults, since pedagogy is not age bound):

> Sharing daily life is the stuff of the pedagogic approach; pedagogues and children form a community sharing ideas, activities, learning, meals and outings – depending on the particularities of the setting. Their training aims at producing pedagogues who are reflective practitioners: they think about situations and relationships, bring theories to bear on these, decide how to proceed and review the results of their actions. Their training stresses team work with other pedagogues and with other professionals, as well as with parents and neighbourhood networks. The pedagogical approach to children is holistic. The pedagogue sets out to address the whole child, the child with body, mind, emotions, creativity, history and social identity. This is not the child only of emotions, the psycho-therapeutical

approach, nor only of the body, the medical approach, nor only of the mind, the traditional teaching approach.... For the pedagogue, working with the whole child, learning, care and, more generally, upbringing (the subjects of the original German concept of pedagogy) are closely-related (indeed inseparable) activities at the level of daily work. These are not separate fields needing to be joined up, but inter-connected parts of the child's life. (p 143)

Importantly, the pedagogue does not see himself/herself as an isolated worker, working *for* children, carrying out actions *on* children. The approach is relational. The child is not regarded as an autonomous and detached subject, but as living in networks of relationships, involving both children and adults.

The pedagogue has a relationship with the child which is both personal and professional. S/he relates to the child at the level of a person, rather than as a means of attaining adult goals. This interpersonal relationship implies reciprocity and mutuality, and an approach that is individualised but not individualistic – the pedagogue most commonly works with groups of children and the value of the group and the needs of the group are given prominence. (Moss and Petrie, 2002, p 143)

The profession of pedagogy is found in many countries in continental Europe (Social Education Trust, 2001). It is perhaps most extensive in Denmark. A three-and-a-half-year training in higher education prepares the Danish pedagogue for working with children, young people and adults: indeed pedagogues sometimes describe their occupation as working across an age range from 0 to 100 years. They can be found working in a wide range of settings: nurseries; kindergartens; school-age childcare; youth clubs; residential childcare; services for children and adults with disabilities (Jensen and Hansen, 2002, 2003; Moss and Korintus, 2004).

Ethics and 'children's spaces'

Before leaving the concept of 'children's space' and the worker required for this understanding of public provision, the references to 'children's spaces' requiring a different approach to ethics need some elaboration.

Two sets of ideas about ethics are particularly relevant to the ideal of a children's space: the 'ethics of care' and the 'ethics of an encounter'. The former emerges from feminist scholarship (cf. Tronto, 1993), the latter from the work of Emanual Levinas.

Sevenhuijsen (1998) contrasts the ethical subject in the ethics of care (for example, the pedagogue in a children's space) with the ethical subject of a universalist or Kantian ethics (for example, the technician in children's services) that sees ethics as a universal code, 'a totality of rules, norms, principles equally applicable to everyone and acceptable to every rational thinking person'. The ethical subject:

> ... in the ethics of care stands with both feet in the real world. While the universalist ethicist will see this as a threat to his independence and impartiality, or as an obstacle to creating in his moral imaginary, the care ethicist sees this precisely as a crucial condition for being able to judge well.... The ethics of care demands reflection on the best course of action in specific circumstances and the best way to express and interpret moral problems. Situatedness in concrete social practices is not seen as a threat to independent judgement. On the contrary it is assumed that this is exactly what will raise the quality of judgement.... Rather than an atomistic view of human nature, an ethics of care posits the image of a relational self, a moral agent embedded in concrete relationships with others. (p 59)

The central issue in the 'ethics of an encounter' is the mode of relating, in particular how to relate to the Other without making the Other into the same – a dominating tendency in Western philosophy where 'when knowledge or theory comprehend the Other, the alterity of the latter vanishes as it becomes part of the same' (Young, 1990, p 13). Dahlberg (2003) suggests some of the implications of this for working with children:

> To think an other whom I cannot grasp is an important shift and it challenges the whole scene of pedagogy.... To be able to hear the ungraspable call of the child and to have the capacity to relate to absolute alterity, one needs to interrupt totalizing practices.... Are there other choices than making ourselves masters over the child? How can we open up for radical difference and to 'hear' what children

are saying and doing?... We need spaces where children can speak and be heard. Spaces where we as adults also can become surprised and where we as pedagogues as well as researchers are able to see the possibilities in uncertainty and doubt. (p 273)

These discussions of an ethics of care and an ethics of an encounter contain many ideas that resonate with a construction of children's spaces, illustrating the connections between constructions of provisions for children and ethical concepts and practices: reflection, situatedness, personal judgement, a relational self, interrupting totalising practices, spaces where children can speak and be heard, surprise and possibility. These are ethical approaches that question the instrumental rationality and the 'business ethics' (Bauman, 1995) that permeate the contemporary discourse of children's services. Yet while ethics are always present, they are absent in contemporary discussions of public provision for children, except when ethics becomes a means for governing professional conduct or a curriculum subject, for instance in the early learning goals in the English Foundation Stage, which includes to 'understand what is right, what is wrong, and why' (Qualifications and Curriculum Authority, 2000, p 38). As is the way of modernity, the ethical and political are displaced by the technical and scientific (Dahlberg and Moss, 2005).

Three areas of uncertainty

The chapter concludes by raising three issues, among the many around which there are major uncertainties. First, contrasting 'children's services' and 'children's spaces' risks a lapse into dualistic thinking, implying provisions must either by one or the other. This is not the intention. The aim is rather to suggest that there may be many ways of understanding public provisions for children – just as there are many constructions of children. Others may identify and describe other constructions.

Moreover, the situation is not clear-cut and black and white, but blurred with varying shades of grey. We can see in Britain a variety of ways of thinking and talking about childhood, and many and various images, not all by any means the image of the weak, poor and needy child. Different images jostle each other within the same institutions. In many respects, the New Labour government has been a firm believer in 'children's services' and children as redemptive agents – but it has also given support to a new policy agenda on children's participation.

How far does this reflect ambivalence, an assemblage of different and sometimes contradictory views of the child? Or is the attention to participation a managerial tactic that uses participation as a control technique?

A more general issue blurs some of the distinctions. 'Children's spaces' are places for provocation and confrontation, dissensus and 'indocility', complexity and diversity, uncertainty and ambivalence. For adults and children, they are places where meanings are kept open, where there is space for critical thinking, wonder and amazement, curiosity and fun, learning by adults as well as children, where questions may be asked to which answers are not known. Some of the sense is captured in the following comments on the early childhood services in Reggio Emilia: 'The Reggio practice is rich in paradox and irony ... Reggio Emilia has turned away from the modernist idea of organic unity and encouraged multiple languages, confrontation and ambivalence and ambiguity. Therefore, people favouring a strong modernist idea of organic unity often find their practice too noisy and containing too much "dirt and pollution"' (Dahlberg, 2000, pp 181-2).

However, this does not mean that children's spaces are all spontaneity, with no adult agenda and no predetermined outcomes. The problem arises if the *only* outcomes of interest are those that are predefined and if the importance of processes and relationships is denied. But what of the relationship between closed and open outcomes, the specified and the unspecified? Or put another way, where to draw the line between the regulatory and the emancipatory? The only suggestion at this stage is that this relationship and this line must become an important part of an ongoing 'ethico-politics' discussion (Rose, 1999) around the purposes and practices of 'children's spaces'.

The second issue is especially relevant to questions of social exclusion and inclusion. What can we expect of public provisions for children – whether understood as services or spaces – in solving social problems, in particular those arising from unequal distribution of resources? Can interventions through provisions fix these problems? Can children redeem society? It seems that a degree of scepticism is in order here, for the following reasons:

1. The recurrence of these problems despite a century or more of interventions. Of course, it may be that previous interventions were technically flawed, and we now have more effective technologies, or problems take new forms requiring new forms of intervention. Or it may be that public provisions for children are not effective means of redressing inequality and its attendant ills.

2. The absence of convincing explanatory theories to justify current interventions. For example, Sure Start appears to be based on a cycle of deprivation theory. Yet how can this theory account for a threefold increase in child poverty in 15 years, during the 1980s and early 1990s? How do early intervention strategies engage with the possible causative effects of social dislocation arising from market capitalism?

3. The case of the US, a country that has paid great attention over the years to the possibilities of targeted interventions, especially with children. Despite the claims made for individual US intervention projects, frequently cited when the UK government reviews evidence on service interventions, it is not clear that such interventions have cumulatively had a major widespread impact on children and families in the US. For example, if we compare the US with Sweden, we find that the US is substantially richer materially: per capita GDP (applying Purchasing Price Parity to eliminate differences in price levels) in 2000 was $36,000 in the US and only $24,400 in Sweden (OECD, 2002). Yet on almost all indicators, children fare better in Sweden than in the US: for example, most recent comparisons show that child poverty in the US is five times higher than in Sweden (UNICEF, 2005) while opportunities for social mobility for children are considerably higher in Sweden (Blanden et al, 2005).

It could, of course, be argued that Sweden has a lot of public provision for children, not least an almost universal system of early childhood services, so proving that provision is an effective means of tackling social problems. More plausibly, low poverty and high provision in Sweden can both be seen as consequences of a welfare regime that expresses certain deep-seated political and cultural values. It is in these values, with their emphasis on equality and solidarity, that perhaps we should seek Sweden's relative success. In contrast, the chronic problems in the US may be seen as produced by a different set of political and cultural values, which produce both a liberal welfare regime and persistent inequalities. The UN's *Human Development Report* (UNDP, 2002) notes that:

> OECD countries have increased their incomes over the past two decades but most have seen rising income inequality – most consistently and dramatically in the United Kingdom and the United States. Between 1979 and 1997 US real GDP per capita grew 38% but the income

of a family with median income grew only 9%. So most of
the gain was captured by the very richest people with the
incomes of the richest 1% of families growing 140%....
The income of the top 1% of families was 10 times that of
the median family in 1979 – and 23 times in 1997.

This chapter voices scepticism, not cynicism: it would be good to be
proved wrong and the jury is still out on the latest round of UK
interventions. This is not to say that public provisions for children
have no beneficial effects for children and their families, nor that they
are unable to ameliorate some problems. Access to affordable childcare
ameliorates a major problem for many parents. Nor is to deny the
possibility of making important differences in individual cases (whether
the cases are individual families or individual services).

The uncertainty lies in the ability of public provisions to counter
strong structural forces – economic, social, cultural and political – that
produce material inequalities and social dislocations. When the recent
resurgence of market capitalism (bringing new inequalities of income
and access to resources) is combined with long-standing structural
features (such as excluding systems of education), it seems to be asking
a lot of public provisions in the UK – 'children's services' – to tackle
poverty, let alone the wider and more contentious issue of inequality
(and noting government's greater readiness to target poverty and social
exclusion rather than inequality). At the very least we need more
convincing hypotheses proposing what public provisions may be
expected to achieve, under what conditions and through what
processes.

Finally, to the question 'how do you implement children's spaces?'.
There are no easy answers. 'Children's services' are readily legislated
for and provided as a system, and regulated through a centralised
structure of command and control: they are the provision of choice
for the centralised nation state. The same cannot be said of 'children's
spaces'. They are too complex, too idiosyncratic, too contextually
situated to be universally prescribed. Their workforce cannot be reduced
to technicians. They are the provision of choice for the decentralised
and engaged institution or community. This author recently visited an
Italian city whose services for children have an international reputation.
The head of these services described them, the product of 30 years of
work, as 'a local cultural project on childhood'. This seemed to capture
the idea of local responsibility and local politics within which 'children's
spaces' might flourish.

But this raises major issues about equality of access. The risk is that some children have access to wonderful children's spaces, while others are consigned to poor children's services in communities of political indifference, as in fact happens in Italy (cf. Putnam, 1993). In the UK, the government might argue with some justification that it has to take a centralised and controlling approach to many provisions because they are too weak to be trusted to their own devices and the market as a provider of services frequently fails. Thus a mushrooming childcare sector, with a poorly trained workforce and a fragmented group of business providers, will fail too many children without strong central regulation and clear technical prescriptions. Unless government treats this sector as a quasi-public provision and as a 'children's service' (through regulation and subsidy), it will be no more than a market in a particular product responding to individual consumer demand.

Once again, part of the way forward may be to avoid dualistic either/ or thinking, instead viewing children's services and children's spaces (or other constructions) as in relation, rather than complete opposition. An important policy question would then be what that relationship might be here and now and what we might want it to be in the future. The relationship, now and in the future, is a contestable political issue. Just as some element of predetermined outcomes may be agreed, so too may some element of centralised control. But this may change over time, and recognition and encouragement could be given to institutions and communities who wanted to think and practice differently. A 'local cultural project of childhood fund' springs to mind, but so too does the bowdlerised way this concept could appear under present regimes of managerial regulation. However, the idea is worth playing with: to imagine how local cultural projects, including children's spaces, might be nurtured and sustained over time.

In recent years, we have been provoked into recognising that childhood is a social construct, that social constructions are productive of policy, provision and practice, and that a powerful construction is the 'rich child'. These provocations have come from various directions, including the United Nations Convention on the Rights of the Child, the new social studies of childhood, and the extraordinary global influence of Reggio Emilia. The significance of Reggio Emilia is that it is one instance where this construction of the 'rich child' has thoroughly permeated public provision for children – both in theory and practice (Rinaldi, 2005).

If we are seeing a different image of the child today, the question is what does this mean for the provisions we make for children, the practices in these provisions and the people who work in these provisions. This chapter has tried to suggest one possible direction, from 'children's services to children's spaces'. The analysis has also considered whether a 'social exclusion' discourse leads us in that direction, or away from 'children's spaces' back to 'children's services' or to an innovative blend of the two.

Note
[1] This chapter owes a lot to several years of collaborative work with a colleague at Thomas Coram Research Unit, Professor Pat Petrie. It draws on jointly authored publications in particular a book, *From Children's Services to Children's Spaces: Public Policy, Childhood and Children* (Moss and Petrie, 2002).

References
Bauman, Z. (1995) *Life in Fragments*, Cambridge: Polity Press.
Bauman, Z. (1999) *In Search of Politics*, Cambridge: Polity Press.
Blanden, J., Gregg, P. and Machin, S. (2005) *Intergenerational Mobility in Europe and North America*, London: Centre for Economic Performance.
Burman, E. (1994) *Deconstructing Developmental Psychology*, London: Routledge.
Clarke, J. (1998) 'Thriving on chaos? Managerialisation and the welfare state', in J. Carter (ed) *Postmodernity and the Fragmentation of Welfare*, London: Routledge, pp 171-86.
Dahlberg, G. (2000) '"Everything is a beginning and everything is dangerous": Some reflections on the Reggio Emilia experience', in H. Penn (ed) *Early Childhood Services: Theory, Policy and Practice*, Buckingham: Open University Books, pp 175-83.
Dahlberg, G. (2003) 'Pedagogy as a loci of an ethics of an encounter', in M. Bloch, K. Holmlund, I. Moqvist and T. Popkewitz (eds) *Governing Children, Families and Education; Restructuring the Welfare State*, New York, NY: Palgrave Macmillan, pp 261-86.
Dahlberg, G. and Lenz Teguchi, H. (1994) *Förskola och skola – om två skilda traditioner och om visionem om en mötesplats (Preschool and School – Two Different Traditions and a Vision of an Encounter)*, Stockholm: HLS Förlag.
Dahlberg, G. and Moss, P. (2005) *Ethics and Politics in Early Childhood Education*, London: Routledge Falmer.

Dahlberg, G., Moss, P. and Pence, A. (1999) *Beyond Quality in Early Childhood Education and Care; Postmodern Perspectives*, London: Routledge Falmer.

Deleuze, G. (1992) 'Postscript on the societies of control', October, no 59, pp 3-7.

Fendler, L. (2001) 'Educating flexible souls', in K. Hultqvist and G. Dahlberg (eds) *Governing the Child in the New Millennium*, London: Routledge Falmer.

Foucault, M. (1988) *Politics, Philosophy, Culture: Interviews and Other writings, 1977-1984*, edited by L.Kritzman, London: Routledge.

Gray, J. (1999) *False Dawn: The Delusions of Global Capitalism*, London: Granta Books.

Hatch, J.A. (1995) 'Studying children as a cultural invention: a rationale and a framework', in J.A. Hatch (ed) *Qualitative Research in Early Childhood Settings*, Westport, CT: Praeger, pp 117-34.

Hutton, W. (1995) *The State We're In*, London: Jonathon Cape.

Jensen, J.J. and Hansen, H.K. (2002) 'Care work in Europe: Danish national report for workpackage three (mapping care services and the care workforce)' (www.ioe.ac.uk/tcru/carework.htm, accessed 21 April 2005).

Jensen, J.J. and Hansen, H.K. (2003) 'The Danish pedagogues – a worker for all ages', *Children in Europe*, no 5, pp 6-9.

Knowles, C. (1999) 'Cultural perspectives and welfare regimes', in P. Chamberlayne, A. Cooper, R. Freeman and M. Rustin (eds) *Welfare and Culture in Europe: Towards a New Paradigm in Social Policy*, London: Jessica Kingsley, pp 240-54.

Malaguzzi, L. (1993) 'History, ideas and basic philosophy', in C. Edwards, L. Gandini and G. Forman (eds) *The Hundred Languages of Children*, Norwood, NJ: Ablux.

Moss, P. and Korintus, M. (2004) 'Work with young children: a case study of Denmark, Hungary and Spain (consolidated report)' (www.ioe.ac.uk/tcru/carework.htm, accessed 26 April 2005).

Moss, P. and Petrie, P. (2002) *From Children's Services to Children's Spaces: Public Policy, Childhood and Children*, London: Routledge Falmer.

Moss, P., Dillon, J. and Statham, J. (2000) 'The "child in need" and "the rich child": discourses, constructions and practice', *Critical Social Policy*, vol 20, no 2, pp 233-54.

OECD (Organisation for Economic Cooperation and Development) (2002) *OECD in Figures: Statistics on the Member Countries, 2002*, Paris: OECD.

Popkewitz, T. (1998) *Struggling for the Soul: The Politics of Schooling and the Construction of the Teacher*, New York, NY: Teachers College Press.

Prout, A. (2000) 'Children's participation: control and self-realisation in British late modernity', *Children & Society*, vol 14, no 4, 304-15.

Putnam, R. (1993) *Making Democracy Work: Civic Traditions in Modern Italy*, Princeton, NJ: Princeton University Press.

Qualifications and Curriculum Authority (2000) *Curriculum Guidance for the Foundation Stage*, London: Qualifications and Curriculum Authority.

Readings, B. (1997) *The University in Ruins*, Cambridge, MA: Harvard University Press.

Rinaldi, C. (2001) 'Documentation and assessment; what is the relationship?', in *Making Children Visible: Children as Individual and Group Learners*, Cambridge, MA/Reggio Emilia: Project Zero/ Reggio Children.

Rinaldi, C. (2005) *In Dialogue with Reggio Emilia*, London: Routledge Falmer.

Rose, N. (1989) *Governing the Soul: The Shaping of the Private Self*, London: Routledge.

Rose, N. (1996) 'Governing "advanced" liberal democracies', in A. Barry, T. Osborne and N. Rose (eds) *Foucault and Political Reason: Liberalism, Neo-liberalism and Rationalities of Government*, London: UCL Press, pp 33-64.

Rose, N. (1999) *Powers of Freedom: Reframing Political Thought*, Cambridge: Cambridge University Press.

Sennett, R. (1998) *The Corrosion of Character: The Personal Consequences of Work in the New Capitalism*, London: Norton.

Sevenhuijsen, S. (1998) *Citizenship and the Ethics of Care: Feminist Considerations on Justice, Morality and Politics*, London: Routledge.

Social Education Trust (2001) 'Social pedagogy and social education', Report of two workshops held in Manchester, July 2000 and January 2001 (www.children.uk.co/radisson%20report%20final.htm).

Tronto, J. (1993) *Moral boundaries: a political argument for the ethics of care*, London: Routledge.

UNDP (United Nations Development Programme) (2002) 'Human development report 2002' (www.undp.org, accessed 26 April 2005).

UNICEF (United Nations Children's Fund) (2005) *Child Poverty in Rich Countries 2005*, Florence: UNICEF Innocenti Research Centre.

Walkerdine, V. (1984) 'Developmental psychology and the child-centred pedagogy: The insertion of Piaget into early education', in J. Henriques, W. Hollway, C. Urwin, C. Venn and V. Walkerdine *Changing the Subject: Psychology, Social Regulation and Subjectivity*, London: Methuen, pp 153-201.

Young, R. (1990) *White Mythologies: Writing History and the West*, London: Routledge.

ELEVEN

Child–adult relations in social space

Berry Mayall

Introduction

> In a world where children have few civil rights, the family
> is the one setting where they can aspire to being treated as
> people in their own right. (Neale, 2002, p 468)

This chapter frames children's social relations with adults in the context of socio-political characteristics of child–adult relations in the UK. It argues that these characteristics help explain how children's social relations differ, according to setting. Broadly, children have more chance of respectful relations with adults in the 'private domain' of the home than they do with professionals in the 'public domain'. However, this is a complicated and mixed picture, as the chapter suggests. And the picture is a shifting one, which intersects with changing representations of children.

Chapter One briefly reviewed the development of social exclusion/inclusion policies in the UK. A long-standing aspect of social exclusion relates to behaviour that does not conform to societal norms, often but not exclusively associated with poverty. Policies to tackle social exclusion in this sense have included welfarist, targeted and individualised policies and initiatives, with heavy emphasis on the need to tackle deviants, especially young people. Underlying such policies and initiatives is concern for the appropriate balance between 'the family' and 'the state' as agents of socialisation. Of course, the concept of 'family' implies a norm, whereas families vary in composition and character; this variability underlies discussions in this chapter. Roche and Tucker (2003) note that social exclusion agendas tend to rely on families as the main socialisation arena and to identify as the main governmental role tackling deviance visible in public spheres (for instance, crime, drugs, truancy). Dealing with social exclusion as it affects children in private spheres is more problematic for governments, which hesitate to intervene in families.

Ways of thinking both reify and structure how social trends are perceived. For instance, sociologists reified social life into public and private domains; women, famously, have challenged the very notion of this division, but it has also proved a useful analytic tool for them to challenge male assignment of women to the home, and the complementary notion that what they do there is not work (for example, Stacey and Davies, 1983). Similarly, in enduring functionalist sociology, children at least in their early years are deemed to belong within the socialising domestic, private, domain; and their activities there have not been recognised as contributory to social well-being. Nowadays, institutions of childhood and adulthood outside the family are largely separate – school, childcare centres, paid work. Ideas that describe these institutions and the people that inhabit them carry great weight in defining or constructing childhood – and adulthood. Indeed, 'ways of thinking about children (and adults) fuse with institutionalised practices to produce self-conscious subjects (teachers, parents and children)' (Prout and James, 1997, p 23). A clear example is how both the physical environment and conceptual tradition structure 'the school'; the buildings, lavatories, playgrounds shape how children experience daily life; and definitions of the good schoolchild will shape how children should behave – the good child attends, listens, obeys. A term used only for children is 'truant', which reinforces societal understanding that school is compulsory and non-attending children deviant. Adults cannot truant, though they may 'skive off' or 'call in sick'.

Social exclusion from certain kinds of space is a phenomenon affecting childhoods in many 'developed' countries; and it has a long history. Thus Ariès (1979) argues that the school and the family became in the late middle ages understood as appropriate sites for childhood socialisation. As Judith Ennew (1994, p 125) concluded from a large cross-national project, 'children inhabit spaces within an adult-constructed world'. Furthermore, she described how modern childhood 'constructs children out of society, mutes their voices, denies their personhood, limits their potential' (see also Engelbert, 1994). This chapter examines especially the understandings of, and policies relating to, childhood in the UK: neglect of children's participation rights, definition of children as socialisation projects, and reliance on 'the family' with women as carers (in the private domain and in daycare settings).

Accounting for UK distinctiveness in relation to children and childhood

This chapter suggests three interweaving socio-political strands that together begin to account for the distinctiveness of adult—child relations in the UK (see for fuller account Mayall, 2002, especially Chapters Eight and Nine):

- patriarchy;
- social class divisions;
- emphasis on protection.

As Hood Williams (1990, pp 170-1) stressed, 'we need to begin with a conception of patriarchal authority that even today maintains childhood as a firmly exclusionary status'.

Therborn (1993) has studied the progress of children's rights across a number of countries (see also Pringle, 1998; Kautto et al, 2001). Therborn argues that patriarchy together with the character of religious and legal traditions are three forces that have shaped ideas and policies about children. As regards Europe, the southern countries (broadly) have strong patriarchy, combined with normative and prescriptive Catholic religion and civil law. Northern European (Nordic) countries have weaker patriarchy, less influential and more tolerant religions and common law traditions that are more flexible than those of civil law. This weaker set of powers in the north allowed for the development of women's rights, which, Therborn argues, are a prerequisite for the development of children's rights. The UK, in his vision, lies between the southern and northern traditions. Therborn's arguments are persuasive, for it has proved longer and harder to establish women's rights in the UK than in Nordic societies. This may be because, though UK society is largely secular and has common law, an outstanding feature is the dominance of men at every level, within a class system bolstered and perpetuated by the public school and its associated networks. The strong support for the privacy of families owes its force to patriarchy (see also Wintersberger, 1996, 2005).

These two forces — patriarchy and social privilege — account for women's problems in raising their status. Without effective respect for women's rights, it is hard to upgrade the social status of children and of childhood. Women have challenged gendered relations; but, as a sometimes secondary effort, have also challenged generational relations (Alanen, 1996, 2005). In the Nordic countries, women have gained increasing power to critique and reshape the institutions that control people's lives, notably educational institutions and the families. In the UK from 1997 onwards, the presence of just a few women in top government positions has forced reconsideration of the division of people's time between paid work and home life, and of the need for state provision of daycare. However, most politicians still refuse to face profound issues about what sorts of childhoods we would like to see. Instead (albeit with the laudable aim of reducing child poverty) they promote the unthinking assumption that getting 'parents' (that is, mothers) into paid work is what is needed, and that children's interests and rights are not an issue. The quantity and quality of daycare (mostly private and poorly staffed) available for children is still lamentable.

The third strand, shaping UK ideas and policies about children, concerns the status of children's rights. While rights commentators commonly identify three sorts of rights – protection, provision and participation – policy makers currently think mainly in terms of protecting children; indeed they rarely relate their policies to the United Nations Convention on the Rights of the Child (UNCRC), except in highly specialised areas. This emphasis has deep historical roots. It was England that pioneered the most massive abuse of children (during the early industrialisation period) and also then pioneered child protection organisations (such as Barnardo's, founded in 1866, The Children's Society [1881] and the National Society for the Prevention of Cruelty to Children [1889]); these played a considerable part in the development of protective legislation against child abuse, in the 1908 Children Act (Hendrick, 1994, Chapter 2). The emphasis on protection was taken up with renewed vigour in the 1980s and 1990s, when, under Conservative policies, child poverty had trebled to about one third of the child population. These rising levels of poverty were used by politicians to fuel the idea that people were individually responsible for their own misfortunes; and social services' work for children had to focus almost exclusively on child abuse issues, on an individualistic basis (Holman, 2001). Of course, such child protection work commonly fails, partly at least since it is not accompanied by measures to tackle the root socio-political structures that encourage violence to children.

Today in the UK, adults, including policy makers, still focus on protection as the guiding light for relations between the generations; they rally to the flag of protecting children against the dangers that beset them (Hendrick, 2003) and to some extent of providing support services for children, whereas there is less governmental support for children's participation. The New Labour government has continued with initiatives targeted at the poor (such as Education Action Zones,

Creative Partnerships and Sure Start) and these, in contrast to universalist policies, generally have a poor record of success (Titmuss, 1968).

Whose perspectives matter?

Ideas about children and childhood are powerfully shaped in the UK by men in privileged social positions. It is they who structure social policies. An important recent example is the Green Paper, *Every Child Matters* (DfES, 2003a), which formed the basis for the 2004 Children Act. This paper – spurred on by the murder of a child (Victoria Climbié) by relatives – emphasised child protection as the principal focus for government policy on children; children's participation rights were downplayed.

At policy level, and also at the level of social interactions between children and agents of the welfare state, it is clear that adult behaviour is the key determinant of the character and quality of child–adult relations. Children's social relations in the UK are structured by distinctive UK history and present: the power of men to push aside children's interests and citizenship; the uneasy relation between the state and families, with powerful voices downplaying state responsibility in favour of family responsibility for child welfare; the power of class-based assumptions that families are the authors of their own distress; and the long-held, class-based patriarchal view that, at best, government duty is to protect children in a hostile adult world.

Children's relations with parents at home are affected by public policies that impinge not only on how parents and children order their daily lives, but also on how parents understand child rearing and daily life with children. Immediately we have to gender those parents, and recognise the policy-driven division of labour between them, with mothers generally the principal carers, who continue to live with children after parental separation. My own work with mothers (and some fathers) has indicated that parents' child-related knowledge is distinctive in that it is structured by experiential learning (Mayall and Foster, 1989). For though some parents (like professionals) learn from baby books and other health promotion initiatives, they also learn early on, through experience, that their children are people, who contribute to household maintenance and family relations. Distinctively, it is generally characteristic of parents that they recognise and promote their children's competence and independence; and work over the long term for the children's welfare and happiness (Mayall, 1996).

Children's experiential knowledge and their considered reflections on experience constitute valuable outsider commentaries on how the social order works. In this respect they, like women, are 'valuable strangers', providing critiques of dominant, mainly male, understandings (Harding, 1991; Mayall, 2002). Large numbers of UK children in the past 15 years or so have provided information – through talking with researchers, documenting their activities, responding to questionnaires and conducting their own research. It is not in the remit of this chapter to ask why there has been this volume of research, nor whether and how far it exceeds, per head, that in other countries. But we return later to consider whether making children's voices heard has contributed to the raising of children's status in the UK.

Social arenas for child–adult transactions

Children in private: family relations

To start by considering some examples of children's accounts of relations within families, Neale (2002) noted that children characterise good relations with parents in terms of mutual respect. Though her sample included children whose parents were separating, many of the children found they could still rely on parental respect. This is a general theme that runs through children's accounts. Children may not all, or always, be treated with respect at home, but children say that, at their best, parents think of children as people. The author's own work with children (Mayall, 1994, 2002) found that at home children generally experience flexible relations built on mutual responsiveness. As Morrow (1998) also found, children (aged 8-14) explain this respect in terms of parents' deep-felt, long-term responsibility for their children: their willingness to listen is based on their concern to help solve any problems their children may face.

Within processes of family relations, children learn experientially what participation entails, including its moral dimension. Morrow (1998) found that children think their views should be taken into account. But many also argued that parents should make some decisions for them. They also understood that participation means exactly that: it does not necessarily mean getting their wish; compromise is often required. Relations with siblings provide a fruitful arena for negotiation, choice and compromise.

'Parenthood', according to children, includes the expectation that parents can be relied on to 'be there for you'. In the author's studies (Mayall, 2002), this was most particularly true of mothers in practice, since they were generally the more stable parent in children's lives, both as the main carer and as the remaining parent in case of separation or divorce. Children commonly spoke loyally of 'parents', but their accounts also distinguished between the sexes. Children provided stereotypes of fathers – they are responsible financially for providing for families – and of mothers – they are responsible for caring for family members, including running the household. Their accounts of daily life clearly indicate that, in almost all cases, mothers were the principal parent with whom they talked and shared confidences.

An obvious, but perhaps sometimes overlooked feature of social relations at home, is that they cross the generations. That is, individual children interact with individuals belonging to an earlier generation. This is different from the situation at school, where for the most part children as a social group are under the control of teachers, rather than in personalised interactive relations with them. In some cases, children also maintain and construct relations with the grandparent generation. According to grandmothers in the author's current study, it is not only they who value feeling continuity across time within their families; children also, in some cases, value being part of an entity that reaches back as well as forward in time. A topic that emerges in several studies is that children can confide problems to grandparents in the expectation that they will receive sympathy and support but not intervention, whereas parents, they say, often tend to try to affect events, by moralising or by 'going up to sort out the school' (for example, Hallett et al, 2003).

A further, related theme in children's accounts is their sense of their family as an entity with boundaries, to some extent a private place to be shielded from onlookers. This emerges in connection with a range of topics. In a study about the home as a place of risk or safety, Kelley and colleagues (1997) found that though there might be differences of opinion between family members, they often presented a 'family front', a concerted or unified view, to the researcher. Hallett and colleagues (2003) found that among their sample of young people (aged 13-14), those who lived at home generally told someone about problems – a friend or a parent – but preferred not to approach formal agencies; relatively, children 'in care' and living in children's homes were disadvantaged, for they too disliked approaching formal agencies, but had no informal source of help, so instead they bottled up their problems, acted violently or absconded. Neale (2002) also found that in divorce situations professionals were the last resort, for children preferred to keep problems in their family, or with nearest friends.

These are very general points, which are modified by cross-cutting factors such as children's age, gender and ethnicity. For instance, some parents are more authoritarian than others. But it is important, theoretically and in policy-related terms, to set out commonalities in how children experience 'the family' and child–adult relations. For there is a central paradox here: the privacy of families, supported by patriarchal concepts, may facilitate the oppression of both women and children; yet parental understandings of their children, based on experience, concern and long-term commitment, generally provide children with valuable child–adult relations. However, mothers remain the most reliable parents, and it is to them that children mainly turn; indeed where mothers and children live without the father, they may make common cause to construct a satisfactory life together.

Where private and public cross – the intermediate domain

Across home and school

Key to understanding how children deal with their daily lives is to recognise that they move, every day, between home and school, between the private and the public. One of their tasks is to negotiate distinctive relations with two disparate sets of adults – parents and teachers; their moral status changes as they step into school and when they come home. They also make decisions about what belongs in the world of school, and what in the world of home. Thus one study found that children during their primary school day stored up their troubles until they got home and could tell their mother (Mayall, 1994). This even included a child who did not reveal he had broken his arm until getting home. In particular, it became clear that children did not feel they could rely on the school as a healthcare environment; teachers varied in how seriously they took children's health-related problems; and schools were ill equipped both materially and in staffing to help children.

More generally, study of children's daily lives indicates a profound and probably necessary difference between parent–child and staff–child relations. This is that parents are concerned with every aspect of the child: her bodily and emotional character, her health and her intellectual and social development. During daily interactions, parents deal and have to deal with these interlocking facets of their child. Though they may give one facet priority, at any one time or always, they have to take others into account. This means that children can not only go to parents about any matter that affects them, but can also negotiate on the basis of priorities they think fit parental concerns, for example, 'I can't do the washing up because I've got my homework to do'. Thus, children's relations with parents have a flexibility rooted in daily circumstances, child factors and varying goals. By contrast, teachers, however caring, have a clear set of priorities, made even clearer under 1990s education agendas, to teach children a prescribed curriculum. Individual or group preferences or needs may get some attention, but essentially teacher–child relations are governed by the aims of the institution.

A recent study asked children at primary and secondary schools how they managed home–school relations (Alldred et al, 2002). Schools may ask parents to come to meetings, to talk about their children or to help the school with fundraising. Parents may wish to talk through issues with teachers, about their child or about the school more generally. The researchers found that some children encouraged parental links with the school, but others did not and some actively tried to block contacts. A strong theme was their desire to maintain the privacy of the home and their activities in it from intervention by the school. This point has also emerged in studies of children's and parents' reactions to schools' setting of homework (Mayall, 2002).

Challenges to notions of childhood in 'the private domain'

Some research studies have focused on situations that question what is proper to 'the private domain': for example, where children live at home with domestic violence, and where children act as 'young carers' for relatives. Both cases challenge traditional understandings of children and of childhood. For children are commonly understood as dependants within family relations, to be protected by and provided for by parents. They are also defined through psychological spectacles as vulnerable to damage from events described as 'traumatic'. For agents of social services who see intervention as necessary, these situations may lead to dilemmas.

One argument is that in cases of domestic violence by men to women, children's interests have been poorly considered by agents of the welfare state (Mullender et al, 2003). This is because male violence in the home has been seen as normal, with complementary unease among professionals about whether, when and how to intervene (Wintersberger, 1996). Also children's social work services have prioritised violence towards children (child abuse). The researchers note that children living with domestic violence are often deemed to be 'silent witnesses' or 'passive victims'; that their coping abilities or competences have not been recognised or fostered; and that how they manage when faced with violence to their mother has not been addressed. As in other studies, it seems that the children turned mainly to mothers, siblings and friends for support. A study of children in refuges found that, apart from refuge workers, most other professionals either ignored them or did not take them seriously (Dickson, in press).

The case of children who care for a disabled or ill family member also raises issues about models of childhood, and about what intervention into domestic affairs the state is willing to support. According to one estimate, 175,000 people under 18 years are carers, and the work they do adversely may affect their school attendance and achievement (Smithers, 2005). Roche and Tucker (2003) state that most social exclusion policy agendas focus on young people 'doing' deviancy in public places; yet young carers at home also face social exclusion, if professionals fail to help them. One factor making communication difficult is that parents and children may not disclose their problems for fear of the family being broken up. Second, professionals may fail children because, when faced with complex situations, their assumptions about childhood lead them to prioritise child protection and children's rights to education. Furthermore, some may think that children who 'care' may be adversely affected in terms of their emotional and social development (Aldridge and Becker, 2002).

Both these cases suggest that children's rights to participate in decision making could be better respected, to their advantage. Such participation might also help them and professionals to reach child-appropriate and case-appropriate solutions to or compromises for the particular situation. Young people have made useful suggestions about how agencies could improve their services (Hallett et al, 2003): staff could provide better information to young people, could listen sympathetically, could maintain confidentiality and could avoid moralising. Other small-scale qualitative work has suggested the importance of considering all the people in a family and their wishes and needs, rather than identifying 'young carers' as necessarily carrying an inappropriate burden (Banks et al, 2001).

Children in public places

We turn now to situations where children are more unequivocally acting in the public domain. We should note initially that children at home and school are generally thought to be in the right place, whereas children anywhere else offer challenges to many adults' assumptions. A dramatic example is young people who meet and talk together in shopping malls; they find themselves approached by 'authority', challenged and 'moved on' – notably, boys more than girls (Matthews et al, 2000). As discussed elsewhere (Mayall, 2002), it is especially common for children outside the home to be ascribed low moral status; they find themselves regarded as unreliable, feckless, lying, opportunistic and even dangerous.

Contacts with professional services are another site for child–adult relations. I think it is fair to say that in the UK, social workers, closely followed by health workers, were the first in statutory agencies to regard it as right to listen to children (Page and Clark, 1977). This may be because adults recognised that children 'in care', and children faced with health-related interventions, have a legitimate interest in their own welfare and health, in the present. In the health field, especially, issues of ethics and consent as they affect children have been seriously addressed (British Medical Association, 2000). On the other hand, there is plenty of evidence that social workers, doctors and other professionals have time and time again failed to take account of the evidence – children's accounts, as well as bruises, cuts, burns – presented to them. Reports on child abuse cases document with disgraceful regularity how professionals have failed in their duties to children (Lansdown, 2002).

Alderson's study of children's consent to surgery (1993) provides an interesting discussion of the question, is children's competence to decide about surgery age-related? At the time of the study (1989-91), the researcher found considerable variation within the groups she studied: children, parents and health staff (nurses and doctors). Children themselves showed considerable competence and wisdom in discussing the implications of surgery for their lives now and in the future. Where staff sought and respected children's views, joint decision-making led to satisfactory action.

Of the three main statutory services relating to children (welfare, health and education), it is education that has most signally and deliberately failed to respect children's rights, in particular their participation rights. There is evidence going back many years that, as has been flagged up throughout this chapter, what children most want is respect, at school as elsewhere. This was shown, for instance, in two surveys of children's views (Blishen, 1969; Burke and Grosvenor, 2003). Essentially, it seems that governmental resistance to children's rights in schools rests on the argument that education is for the future and therefore that children lack knowledge and experience to judge education agendas and curricula (whereas they do have a direct interest in their own current health and welfare). Yet currently government ministers have to recognise that unless children participate actively and enthusiastically in educational agendas, they are unlikely to achieve, academically and practically (DfES, 2003b), and disaffection among teenagers is likely to continue.

In recent years, much debate has occurred about the welfare of young people in the hands of the youth justice system. Smith (2003) suggests there is a need for more empirical evidence of how it works, especially as regards children's interests. However, many studies have investigated children's contacts with family law workers, especially in cases of parental divorce and separation. Neale (2002), in the study referred to earlier, found that children often were not given a choice whether or not to talk with a professional – they just found themselves 'referred'; and children also reported that they were not always given a chance to give their views, or to give their views confidentially. Essentially, their views were not respected. Similarly, in an overview of children's views in cases across the UK, Australia and New Zealand, Cashmore (2003) showed that while children wanted to know what was happening, to have their views taken into account and to have flexible working arrangements that could change over time as they themselves wished, in general their wishes were not fulfilled. This was so both for uncontentious cases – where parents agreed and the case was informally decided – and for cases that went through formal court procedures.

Conclusion

This chapter has outlined some powerful reasons why it is hard for the socio-political status of childhood to be advanced in the UK. Our society has in place a unique combination of barriers to full recognition of children as citizens: patriarchy, social class divisions and the principle of protection as the driver of child-related policy. In some areas of social life, children have a very hard time. They are not accorded respect as citizens, who contribute to the social good. They are, in brief, socially excluded from full participation in social relations. As has been suggested, their current best chance of respect as persons is within the private domain of their family – though is must also be recognised that families present dangers to some children.

The issues discussed in this chapter require consideration of the division of responsibility for children between the state and families.

Each party has interests in the welfare of children and many of these interests overlap or coincide. But, according to some commentators, there will always be conflict between families and the state, regarding measures relating to children. A key area where conflict seems to be unavoidable is education, where the state's legitimate interests may clash with children's own interests. Some commentators argue that if a child is defined as not yet an adult, and therefore not accorded adult rights, then the control exercised over children, in varying ways, by families and the state, will always mean that children are a subordinate social group (for example, Shamgar-Handelman, 1994). Moreover, respect for children's rights may increase children's dependency on adults, since it is adults who have to take responsibility for respecting those protection, provision and participation rights.

This pessimistic view has considerable force, but it can perhaps be countered, somewhat, by the appeal to practice. Some changes are under way, though interpretations of them vary. First, the UNCRC is in itself an important step forward, though much remains to be done (Freeman, 2002). Some commentators in the UK argue that, despite all the difficulties and barriers, children's rights have increasingly been recognised over the 15 years since the UK signed the UNCRC (Franklin, 2002). Government departments as well as non-governmental organisations (NGOs) are proposing as a goal the principle of children's participation in service planning, delivery and evaluation, for instance in health (DH, 2004). Second, we have massive evidence from research studies – with more in process – that children have experience and knowledge relevant to commenting on matters affecting them. These two movements, which both respect children as people, may in themselves go some way to raising the status of children in the UK.

Some further promising trends are visible. Childhood studies courses at schools and universities are helping to broaden knowledge; conferences on children's participation proliferate; children's NGOs continue to pressurise governments; the appointment of children's rights officers in local authorities and of children's commissioners in the four areas of the UK may help to change thinking and practice. As knowledge is internationalised and as Europe and the United Nations pressurise the UK, for instance to end physical punishment to children and more broadly to implement the UNCRC, we may see some glimmers of hope for our children.

However, it is argued here that without profound shifts in ideas about the status of childhood in society, such trends and initiatives are not likely fundamentally to shift child–adult relations. Rethinking childhood is an essential ingredient in the process of respecting children and conceptualising them as citizens. This is difficult work in a society structured by patriarchal attitudes intersected by social class divisions, for deeply entrenched models of the child as dependent, as a being in process, adversely affect our adult behaviour towards children and also structure child-related policies. But these models can be countered through the approaches pioneered by Qvortrup (1985, 1994) and others. He proposed that we include children in the division of labour: that we reconceptualise children as contributors to the workings of society – in the past through their work in field, factory and household; now through their work in school, acquiring knowledge and skills. Add to this the 'people work' that children (like women) do in the private domain, and across the private and the public (Mayall, 2002). The challenge is how to make such ideas part of the common currency of understandings of children, and how to move such ideas onto public agendas.

References

Alanen, L. (1996) 'Social policy and generational relations: child policy in a Nordic landscape', Paper presented at the Politics for Children, with Children or against Children colloquium at the Deutsches Jugendinstitut, Munich, May.

Alanen, L. (2005) 'Women's studies/childhood studies: parallels, links and perspectives', in J. Mason and T. Fattore (eds) *Children Taken Seriously: Theory, Policy and Practice*, London: Jessica Kingsley, pp 31-45.

Alderson, P. (1993) *Children's Consent to Surgery*, Buckingham: Open University Press.

Aldridge, J. and Becker, S. (2002) 'Children who care: rights and wrongs in debate and policy on young carers', in B. Franklin (ed) *The New Handbook of Children's Rights: Comparative Policy and Practice*, London: Routledge, pp 208-22.

Alldred, P., David, M. and Edwards, R. (2002) 'Minding the gap: children and young people negotiating relations between home and school', in R. Edwards (ed) *Children, Home and School: Regulation, Autonomy or Connection*, London: Routledge Falmer, pp 121-37.

Ariès, P. (1979) *Centuries of Childhood*, Harmondsworth: Penguin.

Banks, P., Cogan, N., Deeley, S., Hill, M., Riddell, S. and Tisdall, K. (2001) 'Seeing the invisible children and young people affected by disability', *Disability and Society*, vol 16, no 6, pp 77-814.

Blishen, E. (1969) *The School That I'd Like*, Harmondsworth: Penguin.

British Medical Association (2000) *Health Care for Children and Young People: Consent, Rights and Choices*, London: BMA.

Burke, C. and Grosvenor, I. (2003) *The School I'd Like: Children and Young People's Reflections on an Education for the 21st Century*, London: Routledge Falmer.

Cashmore, J. (2003) 'Children's participation in family law matters', in C. Hallett and A. Prout (eds) *Hearing the Voices of Children: Social Policy for a New Century*, London: Routledge Falmer, pp 158-76.

DfES (Department for Education and Skills) (2003a) *Every Child Matters*, London: DfES.

DfES (2003b) *Excellence and Enjoyment: A Strategy for Primary Schools*, London: DfES.

DH (Department of Health) (2004) *National Service Framework for Children, Young People and Maternity Services*, London: DH.

Dickson, K. (in press) 'Children's experiences of domestic violence'.

Engelbert, A. (1994) 'Worlds of childhood: differentiated but different. Implications for social policy', in J. Qvortrup, M. Bardy, G. Sgritta and H. Wintersberger (eds) *Childhood Matters: Social Theory, Practice and Politics*, Aldershot: Avebury, pp 285-98.

Ennew, J. (1994) 'Time for children or time for adults', in J. Qvortrup, M. Bardy, G. Sgritta and H. Wintersberger (eds) *Childhood Matters: Social Theory, Practice and Politics*, Aldershot: Avebury, pp 125-44.

Franklin, B. (2002) 'Children's rights: an introduction', in B. Franklin (ed) *The New Handbook of Children's Rights: Comparative Policy and Practice*, London: Routledge, pp 1-12.

Freeman, M. (2002) 'Children's rights ten years after ratification', in B. Franklin (ed) *The New Handbook of Children's Rights: Comparative Policy and Practice*, London: Routledge, pp 97-118.

Hallett, C., Murray, C. and Punch, S. (2003) 'Young people and welfare: negotiating pathways', in C. Hallett and A. Prout (eds) *Hearing the Voices of Children: Social Policy for a New Century*, London: Routledge Falmer, pp 123-38.

Harding, S. (1991) *Whose Science? Whose Knowledge? Thinking From Women's Lives*, Buckingham: Open University Press.

Hendrick, H. (1994) *Child Welfare: England 1872-1989*, London: Routledge.

Hendrick, H. (2003) *Child Welfare: Historical Dimensions, Contemporary Debate*, Bristol: The Policy Press.

Holman, B. (2001) *Champions for Children: The Lives of Modern Child Care Pioneers*, Bristol: The Policy Press.

Hood Williams, J. (1990) 'Patriarchy for children: on the stability of power relations in children's lives', in L. Chisholm, P. Büchner, H-H. Krüger and P. Brown (eds) *Childhood, Youth and Social Change: A Comparative Perspective*, London: Falmer, pp 155-71.

Kautto, M., Fritzell, J., Hvinden, B., Kvist, J. and Uusitalo, H. (2001) *Nordic Welfare States in the European Context*, London: Routledge.

Kelley, P., Mayall, B. and Hood, S. (1997) 'Children's accounts of risk', *Childhood*, vol 4, no 3, pp 305-24.

Lansdown, G. (2002) 'Children's Rights Commissioners for the UK', in B. Franklin (ed) *The New Handbook of Children's Rights: Comparative Policy and Practice*, London: Routledge, pp 285-97.

Matthews, H., Taylor, M., Percy-Smith, B. and Limb, M. (2000) 'The unacceptable *flaneur*: the shopping mall as a teenage hangout', *Childhood*, vol 7, no 3, pp 279-94.

Mayall, B. (1994) *Negotiating Health: Children at Home and Primary School*, London: Cassell.

Mayall, B. (1996) *Children, Health and the Social Order*, Buckingham: Open University Press.

Mayall, B. (2002) *Towards a Sociology for Childhood: Thinking from Children's Lives*, Buckingham: Open University Press.

Mayall, B. and Foster, M-C. (1989) *Child Health Care: Living with Children, Working for Children*, Oxford: Heinemann.

Morrow, V. (1998) *Understanding Families: Children's Perspectives*, London: National Children's Bureau.

Mullender, A., Hague, G., Farvah Imam, U., Kelly, L., Malos, E. and Regan, L. (2003) '"Could have helped but they didn't": the formal and informal support systems experienced by children living with domestic violence', in C. Hallett and A. Prout (eds) *Hearing the Voices of Children: Social Policy for a New Century*, London: Routledge Falmer, pp 139-57.

Neale, B. (2002) 'Dialogues with children: children, divorce and citizenship', *Childhood*, vol 9, no 4, pp 455-76.

Page, R. and Clark, G.A. (eds) (1977) *Young People's Working Group: Who Cares? Young People in Care Speak Out*, London: National Children's Bureau.

Pringle, K. (1998) *Children and Social Welfare in Europe*, Buckingham: Open University Press.

Prout, A. and James, A. (1997) 'A new paradigm for the sociology of childhood? provenance, promise and problems', in A. James and A. Prout (eds) *Constructing and Reconstructing Childhood: Contemporary Issues in the Sociological Study of Childhood* (2nd edn), London: Falmer, pp 7-33.

Qvortrup, J. (1985) ' Placing children in the division of labour', in P. Close and R. Collins (eds) *Family and Economy in Modern Society*, London: Macmillan, pp 129-45.

Qvortrup, J. (1994) 'Introduction', in J. Qvortrup, M. Bardy, G. Sgritta and H. Wintersberger (eds) *Childhood Matters: Social Theory, Practice and Politics*, Aldershot: Avebury, pp 1-24.

Roche, J. and Tucker, S. (2003) 'Extending the inclusion debate: an exploration of the family lives of young carers and young people with ME', *Childhood*, vol 10, no 4, pp 439-56.

Shamgar-Handelman, L. (1994) 'To whom does childhood belong?', in J. Qvortrup, M. Bardy, G. Sgritta, and H. Wintersberger (eds) *Childhood Matters: Social Theory, Practice and Politics*, Aldershot: Avebury, pp 249-68.

Smith, D. (2003) 'New Labour and youth justice', *Children & Society*, vol 17, no 3, pp 226-35.

Smithers, R. (2005) '175,000-strong hidden army of school-age carers', *The Guardian*, 13 April, p 13.

Stacey, M. and Davies, C. (1983) *Division of Labour in Child Health Care: Final Report to the SSRC*, Warwick: Department of Sociology, University of Warwick.

Therborn, G. (1993) 'Children's rights since the constitution of modern childhood: a comparative study of western nations', in J. Qvortrup (ed) *Childhood as a Social Phenomenon: Lessons from an International Project*, Report 47/1993, Vienna: European Centre, pp 105-38.

Titmuss, R.M. (1968) *Commitment to Welfare*, London: Unwin University Books.

Wintersberger, H. (1996) 'The ambivalence of modern childhood: a plea for a European strategy for children', in H. Wintersberger (ed) *Children on the Way from Marginality towards Citizenship: Childhood Policies: Conceptual and Practical Issues*, Eurosocial Report 61/1996, Vienna: European Centre, pp 195-212.

Wintersberger, H. (2005) 'Work, welfare and the generational order', in J. Qvortrup (ed) *Studies in Modern Childhood: Society, Agency Culture*, Basingstoke: Palgrave Macmillan, pp 201-20.

TWELVE

Participation with purpose

Liam Cairns

Introduction

The past 20 years have seen a change in the language and the rhetorical framework within which the debate about social policy for children and young people is conducted. There is a growing acceptance, in principle at least, that children and young people are not simply objects of adult concern, but should be seen as citizens with rights. The most obvious manifestation of this change can be seen in the near-universal ratification of the United Nations Convention on the Rights of the Child (UNCRC, endorsed by the UK Government in 1991).

Many of the rights contained in the UNCRC are based on predictable and well-accepted ideas about welfare and protection, but the UNCRC also recognises that children are in possession of the political right to participate in decisions that affect them, and this represents a significant and qualitatively different dimension (Foley et al, 2001). It has been argued that failure to recognise the legitimate political rights of children and young people to contribute to the debate about the construction of social policy is an important factor in understanding the marginal position and social exclusion of particular groups of children and young people (Brown, 1998; Badham, 2004; Brannen and Cairns, 2005).

It has to be said that, although there is evidence of a change in the *rhetoric*, it is less easy to provide evidence of a change in the extent to which the participation rights of children and young people are respected in *reality*. If, as is argued below, some of the mechanisms that have been adopted are ineffective, that is, they create an impression of participation without the contribution of children and young people having any actual impact upon the outcome of the debate, then it is reasonable to question the depth of the commitment to the human rights of children. Osler and Starkey (2003) summarise the rights of citizens to 'participate in and influence government'. Without the influence, participation would be tokenistic. It is in reference to this relationship – between the rhetoric and reality of children's involvement in decision making – that the debate about the purpose of participation is particularly relevant.

This is partly because it is possible to promote the participation of children and young people for a number of purposes (Crimmens and West, 2004; Sinclair, 2004). Not all of these are necessarily exclusive, but nor are they always complementary. However, in discussions about practice, the purpose of particular initiatives are often assumed rather than made explicit. Participation is generally seen as 'a good thing', and different participation projects are uncritically accepted as making a positive contribution to the (undefined and assumed) purpose. The gap between rhetoric and reality is in part explained by a reluctance to critically evaluate different approaches to practice.

It is sometimes assumed that change in the rhetoric will inevitably be followed, in due course, by a change in reality. However, part of the argument advanced here is that the commitment in principle to participation can be seen as a double-edged sword. It can be argued that the political act of formal endorsement of the UNCRC creates a 'permissive environment' within which imaginative and effective models of children's participation can be developed. At the same time, however, the endorsement of the UNCRC can also create pressure on government (at every level) to show progress in the creation of mechanisms through which children's voices can be heard. This has led a number of commentators, in the UK and also in Europe, to question whether the priority is to be *seen* to be promoting the participation of children and young people rather than participation *per se* (Crimmens, 2004; Mori, 2004; Henricson and Bainham, 2005). In this context, Swiderek refers to the problem in Germany of 'political stage-management', and suggests that on occasions, participation serves as 'an alibi for adults' (2004, p 90).

Given this situation, it is at least reasonable to ask whether all of the practice initiatives that have been developed under the banner of participation reflect a genuine commitment to promoting the citizenship rights of children and young people. Phillips and Prout sound a note of caution, commenting: 'That few now claim to oppose young people's participation should not be seen as a victory for anyone' (2003, p 2). They suggest that a more critical analysis is needed. Clarity about the purpose of participation is a key starting point for this analysis.

The argument put forward here is that, first and foremost, the participation of children and young people in decisions that affect them needs to be seen as a human right. Assessing the extent to which the human rights of children and young people are promoted by this or that initiative becomes a matter of efficacy and democratic legitimacy.

The following section outlines what might be described as the 'human rights-based' perspective on the purpose of participation. The rest of the chapter then considers how the main practice models measure up against this perspective.

Participation: a fundamental human right

Participation is the fundamental right of citizenship (Hart, 1997) , the means by which democracy is built (Crimmens and West, 2004) and the 'axial' principle of post-industrial liberal democracies (Swiderek, 2004). If we consider the position of children and young people in society from this perspective, the purpose of participation can be described as the assertion of one of their fundamental human rights. Through participation, children and young people lay claim to the status of 'citizens' within the community, and all that goes with it. As Osler and Starkey observe: 'In democratic states, citizens are constitutionally entitled to equal rights to participate in and to influence government' (2003, p 255). This represents a radical departure from the conventional view of children and young people (Storrie, 1997; Roberts, 2001; Prout, 2002; Cairns and Davis, 2003).

If this claim to citizenship status is accepted (and surely in this country that is a reasonable interpretation of the implication of the endorsement of the UNCRC by the UK government), then children and young people can legitimately put forward their views, and represent their interests, in the expectation that they will be listened to and respected. (This does not assume that the interests of all children and young people are the same but that, like any other citizen, each child or young person is entitled to be heard.)

This is not to suggest that the views of children and young people should be afforded any special status – only that they should be accepted as being as valid as the views of other citizens. The adoption of a rights perspective simply asserts the entitlement of children and young people to take part in political dialogue. Henricson and Bainham described it like this:

> Rights provide a framework and points of reference for
> handling interests. Interests sometimes elide, but also

> compete, and their reconciliation, or in some cases, the championing of one side or another is the stuff of politics. (2005, p 178)

From this perspective, then, the purpose of participation is the assertion of the right of children and young people to be accepted as legitimate contributors to political debate. This is of crucial importance because, although they are part of the community, and are affected by political processes, they currently have little means to influence these processes. Thus they are being denied a fundamental human right. Furthermore, a number of commentators have argued that the absence of the authentic voice of children and young people themselves in the public discourse about childhood has left them in a vulnerable and marginal position (Brown, 1998; Brannen and Cairns, 2005; Cairns et al, 2005), and less able to assert and claim the other more conventional welfare and protection rights guaranteed under the UNCRC (Badham, cited in Sinclair, 2004).

Participation in practice: from an establishment standpoint

> Principles are one thing; practice is another. Too often the aim of engaging young people is vitiated by existing structures of professional power and cultural attitudes that devalue the opinions and skills of young people. (Williamson and Cairns, 2005, p 2)

That there is a commitment in principle to participation, not least from the government, is undeniable. From the endorsement of the UNCRC, to the early publications of the Children and Young People's Unit (CYPU, 2001a, 2001b, 2001c), to the guidance on the creation of the Connexions Service (Connexions, 2001), to *Every Child Matters* (DfES, 2003) and the National Service Framework for Health Services for Children (DH, 2003), the exhortation to consult with and involve children and young people is an ever-present theme.

At the same time, a number of collections of examples of participative practice have been published over the past few years that seem to suggest that there has been significant progress in the development of effective participative activity (Cutler, 2002; Willow, 2002; Kirby et al, 2003; Oldfield and Fowler, 2004). However, these tend, in the main, to describe an increase in the volume of activity, rather than analyse the quality or effectiveness of this activity. Part of the problem is that there is little or no discussion on the purpose of the described activity – it (whatever it is) appears to be taken for granted. Without clarity about purpose, of course, analysis would be pointless.

Sinclair (2004), reflecting on this growth of activity, acknowledges that an evaluation of this or that approach depends on understanding the reason(s) *why* the approach was taken. She puts forward the following list of possibilities: to uphold rights; to fulfil legal responsibilities; to improve services; to improve decision making; to enhance democratic processes; to promote child protection; to enhance children's skills; and to enhance self-esteem. All of these, Sinclair believes, can be justified, although she acknowledges that she 'speaks both from and to an adult perspective', and she suggests that there is a need for 'greater honesty about the purpose of participation activity and whose agenda it is serving' (Sinclair, 2004, p 107).

This combination of circumstances, that is, the explicit commitment of government to the rhetoric of participation, and a lack of clarity about the purpose of some approaches to participation practice, presents its own formidable challenge. Having made the commitment in principle to engage with children and young people, the key institutions of the state (at local and national level) are under pressure to demonstrate how this commitment is being discharged. Effectively, this has resulted in the creation of practices designed to show how adult organisations, on their terms, are involving (some) children and young people. This is not, of itself, problematic – given that the engagement of children and young people is a policy requirement, it is perfectly reasonable, and indeed commendable, that policy implementation is accompanied by standards against which the extent of its implementation can be measured.

However, this is not necessarily the same as recognising the right of *all* children and young people to engage, on their own terms, as citizens, with the institutions concerned with them, and to have a say in decisions that affect them. The situation does become problematic when the satisfaction of the adult institutional agenda is uncritically assumed to also satisfy the human rights entitlement of children and young people. In relation to social inclusion, this becomes crucial. If the mechanisms through which adults choose to hear the voice of children and young people favour some groups to the exclusion of others, then the excluded groups are even less likely to be heard.

This is, at heart, a question of *standpoint*. The debate about the extent to which the UK (or almost any other western society) is respecting the political rights of children and young people, and thus conforming to the requirements of the UNCRC, is conducted almost exclusively from an adult standpoint. The power rests with adult institutions, not only to determine the nature, extent and range of 'participative practice', but also to evaluate and determine the effectiveness of such practice.

If the premise is accepted that this should be seen, first and foremost, as a debate about the human rights of children and young people, it seems at least reasonable to attempt to consider the situation from the standpoint of children and young people themselves.

Two models: representative versus participative democracy

The practice of most initiatives designed to engage children and young people can be divided into two categories: those that work with a small group of children and young people as representatives of a wider population, and those that create opportunities for children and young people to be participants on their own behalf. Both approaches bring their own particular challenges. We shall attempt to analyse these, from the perspective of the extent to which they promote participation as a human right.

Representative democracy

Across Europe, a common response to Article 12 of the UNCRC (which guarantees children and young people a voice in matters that affect them) has been the creation of structures modelled on, and often attached to, adult representative democratic institutions. Thus in schools, school or student councils are common, and beyond the school, often on a local authority or municipality basis, youth councils can be found. For example in Norway, over 300 local authorities have established Children's Councils (Begg, 2004, p 126). In Porsgruun, one of the most celebrated Norwegian models, the Joint Pupils' Council has been in existence since 1991 (Mjaavatn, 2000). Beyond that, sometimes using the local youth councils as a building block, some countries have created national representative bodies, for example Dáil na nÓg (National Children's Parliament) in Ireland, Funky Dragon in Wales and The Children's Parliament of Slovenia (Pinkerton, 2004; Dekleva and Zorga, 2004; Hayes, 2004; Jones, 2004).

For many of these structures, the starting point is the school council, and this immediately raises some difficult questions. Various commentators have remarked on the irony of promoting the concept of young people's citizenship rights in an institution that is singularly ill equipped to treat young people as citizens (Pilcher and Wagg, 1996; Alderson, 1999; Prout, 2000; Cairns, 2003).

This is not a criticism of teachers and others who work in schools, but of the education system. In England, the 1996 Local Education Act states that local authorities must observe the principle that 'pupils should be educated in accordance with their parents wishes'. Monk observes an 'almost total absence of legal recognition of children's rights in education' (cited in Henricson and Bainham, 2005, p 36). Reflecting on the situation in Ireland, Hayes quotes Hart thus:

> There is no nation where the practice of democratic participation in schools has been broadly adopted. The most fundamental reason seems to be that, as the primary socialising instrument of the state, schools are concerned with guaranteeing stability, and this is generally understood to mean preserving the very conservative system of authority. (2004, p 50)

This, Hayes suggests, could certainly be said of Ireland.

Clearly, a process that attempts to create a genuinely rights-based participative structure for children and young people within an institution geared up to promote stability over change, and within which parents, but not children and young people themselves, are seen to have a legal right to have a voice, is going to be fraught with difficulties.

The result seems to be a process that is heavily proscribed at each stage. First, the system seems predominantly to involve only young people with particular skills. It 'scoops up all the "good" children' in Slovenia, (Dekleva and Zorga, 2004, p 145); 'only the resourceful ones get involved' in Norway (Begg, 200, p 131). Once involved, there may also be a process that determines who stays involved. Begg notes that a criticism of the Norwegian system is that it is conducted on adult terms, which may not suit all children and young people. She notes that 'children and young people are praised when they behave like small adults and put in their place when they do not' (p 131).

Second, there are restrictions on what is deemed to be appropriate to discuss. Alderson, in a study of school councils in the UK, reported that: 'Some teachers told us that school councils were not useful because pupils want to talk only about uniform *and other forbidden questions*' (emphasis added) (Alderson, 2000, p 132). Recent guidance from the Department for Education and Skills in England advises schools to be very clear about what issue it may want to consult students about. The guidance suggests that: 'Pupils could also be involved in deciding *whether* to change the school uniform and *what* the new one should be' (DfES, 2004, p 12). Note that whether there should *be* a school uniform in the first place is not part of the sanctioned agenda.

In a recent piece of work around evaluating the public services they receive, a group of young people in Durham have adopted the principle of *equivalence* to measure quality. Put most simply, they ask the question: 'Would adults, in an equivalent situation, find this or that provision acceptable?' (Cooke et al, 2005). They suggest that the closest equivalence to school, for adults, is employment. The most common mechanism by which employees' interests are represented is the trade union or staff association.

Applying that principle here, it seems reasonable to ask how many adults would find it acceptable to be a member of a trade union, when what the union could discuss was determined by the management.

The third issue concerning the representative model of participation concerns its *effectiveness*. Does the representative model create opportunities for children and young people to intervene in the decision-making process in a way that makes any difference to them? Again, there is a stark difference between the rhetoric and the reality. Although, from the perspective of adult institutions, representative models may well provide evidence that children and young people have been *consulted,* there is little evidence that this process has led to any significant *change* (Alderson, 2000; Wyse, 2001; Cairns, 2003).

Finally, and from a rights perspective, the most problematic issue concerning representative structures is democratic legitimacy. In this case, it is necessary to consider the standpoint of two groups of children and young people – those who represent, and those who are assumed to be represented. At best, it can be assumed that being a member of a representative body (bearing in mind the limitations noted above) may well present opportunities to participate, and be heard, for those who are members of the school council, youth council or youth parliament.

However, it is unclear how this process can be described as a means through which the individual rights of the *represented* are acknowledged and promoted. Largely because representative approaches tend to be more concerned with the purpose of demonstrating how the adult agencies have consulted *some* children and young people, the standpoint of this group is rarely considered. In a recent piece of work carried out by some young researchers in Durham, young people who were questioned were unaware of the existence of a local youth council, and that their interests were being 'represented' by other young people (Cooke and Walton, 2005). In a similar vein, in a critique of the situation in Wales, Jones notes that Funky Dragon, the Welsh national representative youth forum, draws its members from existing local youth councils, organisations that cannot be considered as inclusive of all children and young people (Jones, 2004). In a study for the Scottish Parliament on the best ways of obtaining children's perspectives, Hill and colleagues report the tendency of young people not invited to participate to have a different perspective than those who were included, and that the uninvited thought that it wasn't right that only the views of a minority are taken into account (Hill, 2004, p 12).

This is not to deny that the young people who participate in structures such as youth fora are exercising their *individual* rights as citizens, but to suggest that the claim to collective representation is an empty one. Unlike adult representative structures (which are by no means perfect), the infrastructure does not exist to first of all ensure that everyone who is to be represented is enfranchised, and to allow for the represented to regularly express their views to their representatives.

If those who are being represented have not given their consent to the process, it is reasonable to conclude that there is a serious democratic deficit in this model of participative practice.

Participative democracy

The alternative practice model sets out to create opportunities for children and young people to be participants in dialogue in their own right, and to intervene directly in decision-making processes. We can illustrate this model by considering a number of initiatives that have developed participative practice from slightly different perspectives.

The first initiative, centred on a particular group of children and young people in particular circumstances, is the Keeping the Family in Mind project in Liverpool. The project, run by Barnardo's, aims to support children and young people who are living in families affected by adult mental health issues.

The project created space for the young carers to express themselves, in particular by producing a video entitled 'Telling it like it is', a powerful account of the challenges faced by children and young people whose parents have mental health problems. An important principle was that everyone who was involved in Keeping the Family in Mind had a right to be part of the video project: 'They all had a choice whether or not they wanted to get involved and if they did, it was to be on their level and in ways that they found meaningful to them' (Wardale, 2003, p 5).

The young people involved were very clear about what they were setting out to achieve: 'We all wanted the video to raise awareness of some of the issues we face when our parents have mental health problems, as we all felt that this was important to us' (Wardale, 2003, p 2). The Corporate Audit and Inspection Unit of Barnardo's clearly believed that they had succeeded, commenting that they had found 'a voice that influences and affects professional practice' (Wardale, 2003, p 7).

Evidence of this influence can be seen at a number of levels. At a local level, it has led to the adoption of training and protocols across the local Specialist Mental Health Trust that include the needs of young carers and their parents; the development of family visiting rooms across the same trust; and the involvement of young people in monitoring and evaluation of adult mental health services and in providing training across child and adolescent mental health services.

At a national level, it raised the importance of family visiting facilities with the government's Social Exclusion Unit, with the result that this was included in the government's Mental Health and Social Exclusion Action Plan 2004; there was collaboration on the establishment of a national implementation group, Better Support for Parents and their Children – Action 16; and direct involvement in the work of the SCIE (Social Care Institute for Excellence) Parental Mental Health and Child Welfare Network.

In addition, because of the development of mature and confident cross-sectoral relationships that have been established by the project in Merseyside, the locality has now received recognition as an 'organisational case study' of important learning potential. The project is currently lead local coordinator for two such national studies, one about young carers' assessments in mental health settings, the other about care pathways and service response.

This may seem like a relatively small-scale example, but it usefully demonstrates a number of key principles. The young people who took part did so in their own right, not as representatives of others. They also took part on their own terms, and were not required to comply with an adult-determined process. They decided what they wanted to say, and how they wanted to say it (by making a video).

They were then able to negotiate access to appropriate technical expertise to achieve their objectives. Adults were partners in the venture, but the young people were in control. Their participation has led to significant change, both locally and nationally.

From the standpoint of the children and young people receiving a service from Keeping the Family in Mind, it is reasonable to conclude that this process provided a genuine opportunity for meaningful participation.

The second initiative is a community development project in the US, Making Connections in Hartford. Despite being located in the state with the highest per capita income in America, Hartford has the second highest national poverty rate of all American cities with a population over 100,000 (Annie E Casey Foundation, 2004). The Making Connections project focuses on two of the poorest neighbourhoods in the city. Its aims are to 'improve the outcomes of disadvantaged children and their families by documenting conditions, raising awareness about core issues, and developing practice and policy recommendations for sustainable change' (Liu and Garcia, 2004).

The operating principles of the project can be summed up under the heading 'resident engagement and leadership'. There is a recognition that, for people living in poverty, the way forward lies in a process that engages 'residents (parents, young people, elders and other community partners) who are being tapped as contributors to the analysis, planning and implementation of the family and community strengthening agendas' (International Initiative for Children, Youth and Families and the Centre for the Study of Social Policy, 2004, p 7).

Of particular interest here is the inclusion of children and young people as active partners in the political process of community development. In one particular initiative, City Scan, young people, using modern technology (hand-held computers, Global Positioning Satellite receivers and digital cameras) collected information on the state of their environment. In partnership with others, they used this to prioritise desired improvements, and monitor how well local government services delivered results (Annie E Casey Foundation, 2004). As a result, the city authorities have been persuaded to take action on specific environmental issues, such as the removal of abandoned cars, and the maintenance of derelict property, which were identified as having a damaging effect upon the neighbourhood.

At the heart of Making Connections is the principle that engaged citizens, acting in their own right, and coordinating their activity with others, can achieve improvements in the circumstances of their community. In this case, young people are seen as fellow citizens, who share a common cause with other residents. As with the first example, the project is participative and inclusive, and does not impose a preordained structure, but works to support efforts by local people to create their own solutions. And as with the work of the young people in Liverpool, it has resulted in tangible changes.

The third example that illustrates this 'participative democracy' model is Investing in Children (IiC) in County Durham (a project managed by the author).

This is a multi-agency public service initiative concerned with the human rights of children and young people. Over the past eight years it has developed a range of practices designed to create opportunities for a wide range of children and young people to contribute to debate, primarily about the public services used by them. It is based on the following explicit principles:

- IiC is a *universal* project, concerned with the human rights of all children and young people.
- IiC believes that children and young people are *knowledgeable* about their lives, and *competent* to take part in discussion about them.
- IiC believes that it is for children and young people themselves to determine both what they want to say, and how they want to say it.
- IiC is based on the concept of *participative democracy* – opportunities are created for young people to take part in their own right, not as representatives of others (Brannen and Cairns, 2005, pp 79-80).

In an evaluation of Investing in Children, Williamson notes:

> Investing in children is a successful, innovative project that has pioneered a model of active citizenship that engages young people … [it] has been a catalyst for change in many areas of service provision for young people. The working models of the project have been largely consistent with the principles of engagement and social inclusion on which it is built. (2003, p 5)

Although, as Williamson points out, there is evidence of children and young people, by their actions, having brought about significant change (in relation, for example, to public transport, access to leisure services in particular communities, and the provision of medical services to young people with diabetes (Cairns, 2003)), it must also be acknowledged that there are many examples of young people, working through IiC, failing to achieve the changes they have been seeking. The approach depends on supporting the developing capacity of children and young people to be active and effective participants in dialogue, and in creating an environment in which their contribution is valued. Paradoxically, success in the first area can make it more difficult to succeed in the second. Williamson (2003) notes:

> A consultative, representative model of how to involve young people in decision-making does not lead to situations where mainstream institutions or their managers feel challenged to change what they do or how they work. Investing in Children almost invariably will challenge them for it brings into the open perspectives that might otherwise remain in the shadows expressed as grumbling and dissatisfaction rather than as something to be openly debated and changed. (p 27)

Not all managers have responded positively to being challenged by young people, and this, on occasion, has led to increased resistance.

So although children and young people, working with IiC, have achieved some significant change (Cairns, 2003; Williamson, 2003), there are as many examples where their influence on the outcome of particular debates is negligible. In terms of efficacy, this highlights a potential political weakness in this approach, but, it could be argued, also draws attention to the traditional differential distribution of power. Supporting young people to be able to say what they want to say is (relatively) straightforward, but ensuring that key adults listen to what is said is much more challenging. It is always going to be an uphill struggle for children's voices to be heard – the dominant discourse (the default position) is that adults know best.

A further issue for IiC lies in its universal aspiration. It is designed to be available to all children and young people, and the evidence suggests that the inherent flexibility of the model has made it accessible to a wide range of children and young people from different backgrounds (Williamson, 2003). However, in order to claim to be truly universal, the project would have to be able to ensure that every child and young person in County Durham was kept fully informed of their right to become involved, and the resources are not available currently to do this.

This leads to an important conclusion about the significance of approaches like those described above. They have legitimacy if they can be shown to provide an effective vehicle for the children and young people who use them, without claiming to speak on behalf of other children and young people. But from the standpoint of *all* children and young people, this participative approach can only be seen to be promoting their individual human right to be heard when it has been adopted effectively by the mainstream institutions with which they come into daily contact.

To an extent, the IiC Membership Scheme is a limited attempt to address this issue. The Membership Scheme is a kitemark project, through which individual agencies can apply for membership by demonstrating that they are engaged in a dialogue with the young people who use their service, and that significant change has occurred as a result. The evidence required to support the application must be provided by children and young people themselves. The Membership Scheme has been running since 1999, and there are currently 180 members, and 90 applicants, ranging from schools and youth clubs to GP practices and leisure centres.

The IiC approach (and the Liverpool and Hartford examples) can also be seen as significant if, by achieving real social change, they contribute generally to an emancipatory discourse about children's political status in society. Again, progress lies in this approach being adopted across a wide range of situations where children and young people interact with the state. In a report on a series of seminars with children's services professionals in England, Williamson and Cairns note: 'Obstacles in the way of the development of children's services that respect their human rights as citizens and engage them in defining how those services should be run, are not inadequacies in resources or in staff shortages. They lie in the ways in which the prevailing, dominant discourse in public policy disempowers young people because they are not seen as citizens' (2004, p 14).

Conclusion

Despite progress in the rhetorical commitment to the political rights of children and young people, in terms of their ability to influence the political agenda, little has changed in reality. It is part of the argument presented here that in order to make progress in promoting change in reality, greater clarity is needed about the purpose of initiatives that purport to promote children and young people's participation.

This chapter has argued that it is important to consider purpose from the standpoint of children and young people themselves. From this perspective, the standards that apply are a mixture of democratic legitimacy, inclusion and efficacy.

Models based on adult representational democracy have dubious democratic legitimacy. Whereas there is (notionally at least) universal adult suffrage, there is no equivalent children's suffrage, so building structures that mimic adult structures (although they can be useful in so far as the children involved develop certain skills as a result) cannot meet the requirements of a system of universal participation rights.

The models examined in this chapter that are based on participative democratic principles do not suffer from this democratic deficit, but they have other limitations, in terms of their reach and scope.

This leads to the conclusion that processes that are most likely to promote the political/human right of children and young people to be recognised as citizens in their own right are not representational but based on individual participative principles, but they need to be widespread, right across the interface between the adult world and the world of children and young people.

Acknowledgement

I would like to thank Brian Davis and Ashleigh Greathead, two young colleagues from Investing in Children, for their comments on this chapter. I would also like to acknowledge the contribution of Louise Wardale to the section on Keeping the Family in Mind.

References

Alderson, P. (1999) 'Human rights and democracy in schools – do they mean more than "picking up litter and saving whales"?', *International Journal of Children's Rights*, vol 7, no 3, pp 185-205.

Alderson, P. (2000) 'Children's rights and school councils', *Children & Society*, vol 14, no 2, pp 121-34.

Annie E Casey Foundation (2004) *Effective Resident Engagement and Leadership. International Learning Exchange Nov 2004*, Study Tour Site description, Hartford: Annie E Casey Foundation.

Badham, B. (2004) 'Participation – for a change', *Children & Society*, vol 18, no 2, pp 143-54.

Begg, I. (2004) 'Participation rights in Norway', in D. Crimmens and A. West (eds) *Having their Say. Young People and Participation: European Experiences*, London: Russell House Publishing.

Brannen, M. and Cairns, L. (2005) 'Promoting the human rights of children and young people: the Investing in Children experience', *Adoption & Fostering*, vol 29, no 1, pp 78-87.

Brown, S. (1998) *Understanding Youth and Crime*, Oxford: Oxford University Press.

Cairns, L. (2003) 'Young people as citizens. A case study of participation and change in County Durham', Unpublished MA thesis, University of Durham.

Cairns, L and Davis, J. (2003) 'Issues in the practice of children and young people's participation', Paper presented at the ESRC Seminar Series, Challenging Social Exclusion: Perspectives for and from Children and Young People, Stirling, November.

Cairns, L., Kemp, P. and Williamson, B. (2003) 'Young people and civil society: lessons from a case study of active learning for citizenship', in D. Wildemeersch, V. Stroobants and M. Bron Jr (eds) *Active Citizenship and Multiple Identities in Europe*, Frankfurt: Peter Lang.

Connexions (2001) *Connexions Service Business Planning Guidance*, London: Department for Education and Skills.

Cooke, J. et al (2005) *Every Child Matters*, Durham: Investing in Children Archive.

Cooke, J. and Walton, J. (2005) *A Draft Report on Young People's Opportunities to Participate*, Durham: Investing in Children Archive.

Crimmens, D. (2004) 'The role of government in promoting youth participation in England', in D. Crimmens and A. West (eds) *Having their Say. Young People and Participation: European Experiences*, London: Russell House Publishing.

Crimmens, D. and West, A. (2004), 'Introduction', in D. Crimmens and A. West (eds) *Having their Say. Young People and Participation: European Experiences*, London: Russell House Publishing.

Cutler, D. (2002) *Taking the Initiative: Promoting Young People's Involvement in Public Decision-making*, London: Carnegie.

CYPU (Children and Young People's Unit) (2001a) *Building a Strategy for Children and Young People*, London: CYPU.

CYPU (2001b) *Learning to Listen. Core Principles for the Involvement of Children and Young People*, London: CYPU.

CYPU (2001c) *Children's Fund Guidance*, London: CYPU.

Dekleva, B. and Zorga, S. (2004) 'Children's parliaments in Slovenia', in D. Crimmens and A. West (eds) *Having Their Say. Young People and Participation: European Experiences*, London: Russell House Publishing.

DfES (Department for Education and Skills) (2003) *Every Child Matters*, London: DfES.

DfES (2004) *Working Together: Giving Young People Their Say*, London: DfES.

DH (Department of Health) (2003) *Getting the Right Start: The National Service Framework for Children, Young People and Maternity Services – Emerging Findings*, London: DH.

Foley, P., Roche, J. and Tucker, S. (2001) 'Foreword', in P. Foley, J. Roche and S. Tucker (eds) *Children in Society: Contemporary Theory, Policy and Practice*, Oxford: Oxford University Press.

Hart, R. (1997) *Children's Participation: The Theory and Practice of Involving Young Citizens in Community Development and Environment Care*, New York, NY: UNICEF.

Hayes, N. (2004) 'Children's rights in Ireland: participation in policy development', in D. Crimmens and A. West (eds) *Having Their Say. Young People and Participation: European Experiences*, London: Russell House Publishing.

Henricson, C. and Bainham, A, (2005) *The Child and Family Policy Divide*, York: Joseph Rowntree Foundation.

Hill, M. (2004) 'Children's voices on ways of having a voice', Paper presented at the ESRC Seminar Series, Challenging Social Exclusion: Perspectives for and from Children and Young People, Glasgow.

International Initiative for Children, Youth and Families and the Centre for the Study of Social Policy (2004) *Resident Engagement and Leadership to Improve Results for Children, Youth, Families and Communities – An International Toolkit*, Hartford: Annie E. Casey Foundation.

Jones, B. (2004) 'Beyond rhetoric in the search for participation in youth work in Wales', in D. Crimmens and A. West (eds) *Having Their Say. Young People and Participation: European Experiences*, London: Russell House Publishing.

Kirby D. et al (2003) *Building a Culture of Participation*, London: DfES.

Liu, I. and Garcia, A. (2004) *The High Cost of Being Poor in Hartford*, Hartford: Annie E Casey Foundation.

Mjaavatn, P. (2000) 'Children and their environment', in *Consolidated Report for 'Children at the Dawn of a New Millennium'*, Council of Europe Conference, Nicosia, November, Council of Europe.

Mori, L. (2005) 'Young people as outsiders: the Italian process of youth inclusion', in D. Crimmens and A. West (eds) *Having Their Say. Young People and Participation. European Experiences*, London: Russell House Publishing.

Oldfield, C. and Fowler, C. (2004) *Mapping Children and Young People's Participation in England*, London: National Youth Agency/DfES.

Osler, A. and, Starkey, H. (2003) 'Learning for cosmopolitan citizenship: theoretical debates   and the realities of young adults', in D. Wildemeersch, V. Stroobants and M. Bron Jr (eds) *Active Citizenship and Multiple Identities in Europe*, Frankfurt: Peter Lang.

Phillips, B. and Prout, A. (2003) 'Issues in the theory of young people's participation. A discussion brief, Paper presented at the ESRC Seminar Series, Challenging Social Exclusion: Perspectives for and from Children and Young People, Stirling, November.

Pilcher and Wagg (1996) *Thatcher's Children*, London: Falmer Press.

Pinkerton, J. (2004) 'Children's participation in the policy process: some thoughts on policy evaluation based on the Irish National Children's Strategy', *Children & Society*, vol 18, no 2, pp 119-30.

Prout, A. (2000) 'Children's participation: control and self-realisation in British late modernity', *Children & Society*, vol 14, no 4, pp 304-15.

Prout, A. (2002) 'Researching children as social actors: an introduction to the Children 5-16 programme", *Children & Society*, vol 16, no 2, pp 67-76.

Roberts, M. (2001) 'Childcare policy', in P. Foley, J. Roche and S. Tucker (eds) *Children in Society: Contemporary Theory, Policy and Practice*, Milton Keynes: Open University Press.

Sinclair, R. (2004) 'Participation in practice', *Children & Society*, vol 18, no 2, pp 106-18.

Storrie, T. (1997) 'Citizens or what?', in J. Roche and S. Tucker (eds) *Youth in Society*, London: Sage Publications.

Swiderek, T. (2004) 'The relevance of children's policy and the participation of young people in decision-making in Germany', in D. Crimmens and A. West (eds) *Having Their Say. Young People and Participation: European Experiences*, London: Russell House Publishing.

Wardale, L. (2003) *Barnardo's Action with Young Carers and Keeping the Family in Mind*, Liverpool: Barnardo's.

Williamson, B. (2003) *The Grit in the Oyster: Final Report of the Evaluation of Investing in Children*, Durham: University of Durham.

Williamson, B and Cairns, L, (2005) *Working in Partnership with Young People: From Practice to Theory*, Report on two Research in Practice Seminars, Durham: Investing in Children Archive.

Willow, C. (2002) *Participation in Practice: Children and Young People as Partners in Change*, London: Save the Children.

Wyse, D. (2001) 'Felt tip pens and school councils: children's participation rights in four English schools', *Children & Society*, vol 15, pp 209-18.

THIRTEEN

Conclusion: social inclusion, the welfare state and understanding children's participation

Alan Prout and E. Kay M. Tisdall

This book is one of the fruits of a three-year-long, extremely rich and productive dialogue between scholars, practitioners and policy makers[1]. Given the rich experience of this group, not to mention their personal commitments to extending and deepening children's participation, it is to be expected that we want this book to make a contribution to those tasks. At the most basic level, the contributors have demonstrated a point fundamental to arguments in favour of children's participation: that children are not simply empty containers, to be filled and moulded by adult knowledge. Ridge (Chapter Two), for instance, shows how children actively participate in family economics by being aware of financial restrictions and seeking to tailor their needs accordingly. Mayall demonstrates how, at home, children engage in flexible, mutually responsive relationships. Gallagher (Chapter Nine) and Moss (Chapter Ten) show how children negotiate, form and change educational and early childhood settings. Taken together, these and other chapters build up a picture of children who, like humans in general, have needs but also have resources. More than this, as Edwards (Chapter Four) and Pinkerton (Chapter Seven) argue, they have an enormous potential contribution to make to their communities, a potential that can be realised through their active participation.

That this is still not fully and widely accepted in academic research and policy, or in much day-to-day practice in the institutions and organisations that children live in, is a shame. That it is not comprehensively incorporated into social inclusion/exclusion policy, functioning as one of its founding assumptions, stretches credulity. Social inclusion/exclusion should logically entail questions of participation. If children are excluded and there is a need to include them, then creating conditions for active participation must be at the core of any solutions proposed or attempted. However, in these concluding reflections, the intention is not to rehearse and rehash old arguments, but rather to consider how research, policy and practice around children's participation can be developed by considering three related themes running through the various contributions. These are: social inclusion/exclusion and children; the implications of children's participation for the welfare state; and understandings of children's participation.

Social inclusion/exclusion and children

Starting with the first of these, it is clear that the meaning of social inclusion/exclusion has evolved since the time when New Labour first borrowed these concepts from European social policy debates. At first, the terms communicated very little but as the rhetoric led to new policies, initiatives and funding streams, concepts that were arguably imprecise and ill defined gained more concrete and contextualised meanings. As the Introduction to this volume suggests, one important aspect of this process was the way that the language of inclusion/exclusion became a fashionable way of recasting much older concerns about poverty that had traditionally dominated UK social research and policy. Many chapters in this book remind us that poverty is not so easily sidelined. Ridge (in Chapter Two), for example, shows through empirical research with children themselves, that low income creates difficulties for children's participation in social activities and shared leisure opportunities, sustaining and negotiating social networks and friendships, and particular dimensions of inclusion and exclusion within the school environment. Hill and colleagues (Chapter Three) add to this list material limitations, the paucity of social capital, and territorial restrictions to the impact of poverty on children. From an international perspective, Lansdown (Chapter Eight) reports how children may well echo adults' concerns about housing, clothing, education and health but children often prioritise issues around emotional well-being, safety and protection over material needs. The contributions from Cairns (Chapter Twelve) and Edwards (Chapter Four) underline the importance of leisure opportunities and local transport, which children report as frequently being difficult to access both in terms of sheer availability as well as cost.

Exclusion due to lack of access to community space, to shared space with peers and other community members, is thus a common finding about childhood poverty gained from direct work and consultation with children. It shows that environmental poverty is often closely linked to financial poverty, but not inevitably and with different implications. The issue of space is given further depth with the conceptual challenges presented by Gallagher (in Chapter Nine) and Moss (in Chapter Ten). In the former, we are drawn to the mutual constitution of spaces, bodies and identities. Thus, children's exclusion from community and shared spaces is more than a deficit; it creates and recreates particular conceptualisations, identities and ways of being for children and adults. This idea chimes with Moss's challenge to rethink children's services as children's spaces, creating possibilities for mutual recognition of child and adult contributions to these spaces. Again, spaces are not seen solely as physical, but also being social, cultural and even discursive. Mayall (in Chapter Eleven) reminds us that (at least some) children's services, and their associated professionals, are frequently the last resort for children and their families in difficulty; perhaps if they functioned more as children's spaces, and professionals as co-facilitators, children and their families might themselves take on different (and less problematic identities) and wish to use these spaces more.

The work reported in this book reminds us, therefore, that the concepts of social inclusion and exclusion have a considerable potential to camouflage and divert attention from what are arguably more fundamental issues. While recognising the agency, resilience and resources of those at risk of social exclusion is valuable, it can also lose sight of the systematic realities that create an increased risk for some. Ridge (Chapter Two) and Hill and colleagues (Chapter Three) remind us that 'traditional' concerns remain about child poverty and multiple disadvantage, concerns that predate today's concentration on 'social inclusion' and 'social exclusion'. More than 3.5 million children in the UK still live below the poverty line. And this does matter.

However, the complementary concepts of social inclusion/exclusion do have some potential advantages over an exclusive focus on poverty. These operate in at least two ways: they help recognise the different dimensions of disadvantage beyond material deficits; and they emphasise the *process* of social exclusion and inclusion, the interactions between different elements, rather than emphasising static categories (like 'the poor'). Edwards (Chapter Four) takes us further, in showing how children's participation locally can lead to collective, community regeneration and thus children not only address their own social exclusion but that of their whole community. With a recognition of process, the issues of participation, voice and children's active engagement gains salience.

The welfare state

This brings us to our second main theme: the implications of the research and debate represented in this book for the welfare state. It is important to recognise that the shift from poverty to social inclusion/exclusion came at the end of a period in which 'class' was displaced from its central place in UK academic and policy discussions. In part, this happened because the broadly social democratic agenda faced a powerful political challenge from the right. In response, the social democratic left sought a way to counter the wave of neo-liberal economics and social conservatism that defined the Thatcher period, a wave that, it is often forgotten, had won a significant level of popular support in parts of the UK, even if this was not strictly proportional to its parliamentary majorities. Social inclusion and exclusion provided a language and framework through which to reconstruct a centre-left alternative. This move had the added political and fiscal advantage to the New Labour government of creating a wider and more flexible policy agenda around social disadvantage, one that could supplement, or even displace, income redistribution and central government spending programmes as policy instruments and open the field to other possibilities.

The Social Exclusion Unit (SEU) was at the centre of this approach in Westminster (with its equivalents in other parts of the UK), as it investigated and recommended wide-ranging responses to problems of social disadvantage that were often concerned less with new policy or spending and more with 'joining up' existing provision and reducing obstacles to accessing existing services. Importantly, too, this new flexibility allowed much more room for the identity politics and social movements that had grown up and flourished over the previous period: race, gender, disability and age could all be encompassed in the capacious categories of inclusion and exclusion, as well as in the local initiatives constructed through them. Interestingly, children and young people were among the first groups to be looked at through the lens of social inclusion/exclusion. For example, as part of its concern with neighbourhood renewal, the SEU's Policy Action Team (PAT) 12 Report (SEU, 2000), while recognising the role of macro-policy such as that on eliminating child poverty, stated its goals in terms that would become very familiar over the next years:

> The PAT believes a more effective and coherent approach nationally needs to be matched locally. The key roles for local co-ordination include: identifying the local needs of young people; promoting a common assessment framework for young people; sharing information between agencies; identifying public, private and voluntary resources which could help young people; and developing a local youth strategy, based on effective consultation. (p 11)

These themes, especially the need for integrated services open to the voices of users, were later to re-emerge through the English Green Paper *Every Child Matters* and the 2004 Children Act, and similar policy developments in all parts of the UK. In fact, the welfare state has been one of the main arenas in which children's voice and participation has found recognition and through which a (limited) place for them in public policy has been assembled. Throughout the 20th century, childhood has functioned as the gateway for state (and other) interventions in the family. It has been both a target of, and a means for, achieving innumerable national projects. In the post-war welfare settlement, support for the family was the government's main instrument in ensuring the health and development of children. In the UK (more than in the Nordic countries but less than in the USA), this settlement was based on a relatively strong and high boundary between the private sphere of the family and the public concerns of government. Parents were assumed to work in harmony with the government and to voice their children's interests. From the 1970s onwards, however, this post-war settlement was increasingly troubled. Three parallel tendencies caused this. First, a continuous stream of public scandals (starting with the death of Maria Colwell in 1973) eroded faith in the capacity of the state to safeguard children. Services were judged to be fragmented, riven by interprofessional rivalries, dominated by producer interests and undermined by communicative inefficiencies.

Second, dissatisfaction with the state as a means of delivering services was not confined to those for children. It grew significantly and became more general throughout the 1970s and was one of the sources of popular support for the Thatcher government. The transition to neo-liberal economic policies in the 1980s initiated a process through which the bureau-political organisation of the classic welfare state was modified by introducing market-driven providers, various hybrid and quasi-market innovations and the integration of voluntary sector and informal community networks. At the same time, concerns about the disintegration of civil society and the disengagement of communities from public life gave rise to new attempts to install mechanisms for creating and hearing the voice(s) of public service users.

Third, the ideal of the family as a unitary entity and a safe haven for children (or, for that matter, women) was eroded. Changing patterns of family formation and dissolution diversified parenthood and childhood, rendering them less comprehensible in terms of an imagined standard model. This was underpinned by a series of social, economic and technological changes (including labour market flexibilisation, the growth of women's participation in paid employment outside the home and the growth of information and communication technologies) that weakened the boundary between the private and the public (Prout, 2005). These contributed to the disaggregation of the family as a unit. The interests of men, women and children became recognised as (partially) distinct and in need of representation through separate voices. Taken together, these changes modified the post-war welfare settlement, creating a shift from a dyadic relationship between the family and the state towards a triangular relationship between parents, children and the state (Dencik, 1989).

However, if the processes discussed above set the scene for the emergence of children's voice, this does not mean that the welfare state has ceased to see children primarily as a target for national economic and social projects. On the contrary, especially during the years since 2000 there has been an immense investment in children's services, traditionally defined, and particularly an unprecedented investment in the early years. The word 'investment' is constantly used by government when debating its policies towards children. Despite the shift to voice and participation, these continue the 20th-century welfare state vision of preparing children as future adults, citizens and workers. However, there is a potentially important tension between this focus on children 'as the future' and listening to children in the present. It risks marginalising children's own concerns, views and definitions of social inclusion and exclusion, and their own resources for addressing social exclusion and fostering participation.

In one respect this underlines the importance of the social and policy trend, noted above: children are increasingly recognised as separate entities from their parents, families and households. Children's concerns, needs and rights can be different from adults, even their parents and family members, in relation to poverty, social inclusion and exclusion. Indeed all the chapters of this book beg recognition of children outside of their families, when they are out in public spaces and institutions. As Edwards shows in relation to community regeneration, children participate and contribute to communities where they need recognition not as future but as current investors, workers and resources, and as creators as well as beneficiaries.

At the same time, however, certain authors highlight just how complex, ambiguous and shifting the boundary between the state and the family has become. For, while children and parents (as well as men and women) are now recognised as having distinct voices, this separation is not complete. As testament to this, a number of chapters of this book suggest that policies must recognise the interconnections between children and significant others. Chapters by Ridge, Hill and colleagues, and Mayall (Chapters Two, Three and Eleven, respectively) emphasise the importance of family, particularly parents, to children; children's social inclusion is deeply entwined with that of their parents. Thus, for example, Ridge recommends a much more child-centred approach to the agenda for 'welfare to work' for unemployed mothers, which takes into account the (in)stability and (lack of) quality of parental employment in relation to its very real impact on children's needs and experiences. Mayall shows homes to be spaces of intergenerational interaction, demonstrating how children experience more egalitarian relationships with adults than those found in schools and other institutional settings.

This focus on the importance of community complements concerns about the relationship between national and the local initiatives. Edwards (Chapter Four) sees community development, a 'grass-roots', ground-up approach, as an essential means to address social inclusion. Moss (Chapter Ten) questions what children's services can achieve from national uniformity rather than through the local co-construction of children's spaces. Implicit in these examples is the tension between the desire for a basic level of equality of provision and outcome for all and the creativeness, dialogue and participative process of the local that can result in national patterns of inequity. Without participation, policies may be misguided and ultimately unsuccessful at addressing social exclusion. Finding the optimum combination may, therefore, involve trading off national uniformity against local participation.

Understanding children's participation

Finally, we turn to our third theme, that of understanding children's participation. As children's participation has become an increasing policy demand, both internationally and in the UK, it too has been tested in its translations into practice. These tests have raised questions on at least two fronts: whether participative activities are tokenistic gestures that, in fact, have little impact on decision making (see, for example, Tisdall and Bell (Chapter Six), and Cairns (Chapter Twelve)); and whether children's participation takes place through 'adult' forms and practices into which children are required to fit themselves. It is argued that such ways of working actually exclude many children, especially those who also risk social exclusion by other means (see, for example, Gallagher (Chapter Nine) and Cairns (Chapter Twelve) on school councils, and Lansdown (Chapter Eight)). These are important issues and it is clear that the fate of many participation initiatives turns around them. There is an ongoing need for well-designed research and evaluation that examines the process and outcomes of particular initiatives in these terms. Such work can only benefit from a well-developed dialogue between researchers, practitioners and policy makers.

Nevertheless, it is also clear that the rapid expansion of children's participation in recent times has revealed the limits not only to its practice but also to its current theorisation. It is to these that we now turn. The isolation of the literature on children's participation from wider discussions about participative democracy is noted in several chapters. It is central to Prout and colleagues' argument (Chapter Five) for a general model of participation based on four key factors: motivations; resources; mobilisation; and dynamics. This model is analytically symmetrical between adults and children and makes no *a priori* assumption of differences between them. Other chapters also seek to break through the isolation and learn from adult-centred research and concepts. For example, Tisdall and Bell (Chapter Six) explore conceptual ideas from the political literature, to see how ideas of civic society, governance and policy networks can illuminate the influence of children's participation on national decision making. Pinkerton similarly uses concepts of policy communities and issues networks to conceptualise the development of the Irish National Children's Strategy.

Such efforts to deploy (and perhaps contribute to) wider theory through work on children's participation should, we think, be extended. This need not be an abstruse exercise with no practical or policy implications. On the contrary, as we show below, the concepts of relationality and power are deeply implicated in practical questions about how children's participation can be further developed. In particular, they are important to thinking about creating alliances for children's partners. The relational dimension of participation is a theme that surfaces in many contributions to this book. Lansdown (Chapter Eight) argues that participation requires information sharing and dialogue between children and parents, based on mutual respect and power sharing. Mayall (Chapter Eleven) contrasts the fullness of parent–child relations, which encompass the interlocking facets of the child, with the narrowness of many adult professional–child relations. Moss (Chapter Ten) takes this further by arguing that professional adults should inform their relationships with children through practising 'ethics of care' or 'ethics of the encounter'. These terms index intrinsically relational ways of thinking and being that move beyond rules and rights and emphasise the importance of mutual interdependence and inter-subjective understanding. Peer relations also appear in several contributions: Prout and colleagues (Chapter Five) point to the role of peers in encouraging participation; Hill and colleagues (Chapter Three) and Ridge (Chapter Two) suggest they are a source of resilience and safety, as well as a vital component of social inclusion itself; Gallagher (Chapter Nine) suggests, meanwhile, that relations between peers are not always benign because they may – and often do – work to perpetuate social exclusion. What all of these contributors do, however, is shift attention from children *per se* to children in relation to others, suggesting that children's participation cannot be understood outside of the set of relationships that constitute all the actors.

Such a conclusion is not unexpected when one considers our second concept of power. Power is a central concept for social analysis and one that is periodically revisited in social theory. One influential account of power was given by Lukes (2004). Strongly influenced by research on decision making by North American political scientists, Lukes argues (in the 1974 edition) that power can be seen as having three dimensions. The first dimension concerns the overt process of making decisions, such as might be gained by observing a committee meeting. The second dimension looks deeper by examining the often-covert influences, such as behind-the-scenes persuasion or coercion, and the hidden processes by which some items get on to the agenda while others do not. It is, however, the third dimension of power that is particularly relevant in considering children's social inclusion and participation. This concerns those norms, values and ideologies that keep some issues out of political processes altogether, not because there is covert activity but precisely because none is needed. They are excluded from discourse by their taken-for-granted quality such that few even think about them. The struggle for children's participation has in part been a fight against the expectation, invisible and hardly worth expressing, that children do not have the right, competence or capacity to take part in decision making. Generally speaking, children have no direct voice, not because they have been manoeuvred off the agenda but because few even think it might be a question to ask. Asking whether children are stakeholders, among others, and whether children's own dimensions of social inclusion are included in conceptualising and evaluating interventions has been, and to some extent still is, a radical challenge to such normative assumptions. For, as Tisdall and Bell in Chapter Six amply show, one of the weaknesses of children's participation activities is that they are not seen as essential 'business' by civil servants and tend to be given low priority when and if they come into conflict with the interests of other stakeholders.

However, while Lukes' third dimension of power is clearly a useful analytical resource, it is unduly based on a conception of power as something exercised over others. Borrowing from the post-structuralist ideas of Foucault and Giddens, he now (in the 2004 edition) argues that power should be seen as a dispositional concept, identifying an ability or capacity that may or may not be exercised. In the earlier conceptualisation, power was seen as a zero-sum game in which a fixed quantity of power is asymmetrically distributed – so that there are winners and losers. In his later formulation, however, power is productive and cumulative. Rather than there being a fixed amount to be shared (or not shared), the quantity depends on the strategy and tactics of the players: it is not a zero-sum game. Nevertheless, it is commonplace in childhood studies to see differentials in power as a zero-sum game and, therefore, as a major contribution to the division between children and adults, and to the difference between childhood and adulthood. To put it another way, if power is a zero-sum game, then children and childhood are largely defined by their dependency and lack of power, while adults and adulthood are defined by their respective power over children.

The two questions of relationality and power come together when we consider the need to build alliances between children and other interest groups. If power, in at least some contexts of children's participation, is not a zero-sum game, then children's relationships with adults might open the way to mutually beneficial outcomes in which both increase their power. This is a question that emerges in many contexts discussed in this book. Pinkerton (Chapter Seven), for example, suggests that children's groups now need to make alliances with other rights groups. The movement for children's participation needs to capitalise on the collective strength that can be created by linking with other constituencies demanding participation and voice. It is at the heart of Edwards' promotion of children's participation in community development activities (Chapter Four). Tisdall and Bell's chapter (Chapter Six), however, is more uneasy about the role of supporting adult organisations. It recognises that their involvement is not purely benign and humanitarian – they gain particular status and resources from facilitating children's participation. Prout and colleagues (Chapter Five) suggest that the role adults may (or may not) play in expanding the resources for participation, acting as mobilising agents for it and facilitating its dynamics, are all-important research questions. Discussion of children's relationship with parents by Mayall (Chapter Eleven) and Ridge (Chapter Two) suggests that, although parent and child interests are not identical, parents can also be key people in listening to children and facilitating their participation and agency. Moss (Chapter Ten) suggests that such activities should be core to adult facilitators in children's spaces and Lansdown (Chapter Eight) makes clear that, based on her overview of international activities, adults will have continuing responsibilities in participation processes and sustained autonomous activity by children is in most instances not a realistic goal. A relational view of children, linked to a productive interpretation of power and its flows, seem, therefore, to be key to understanding policy and practice developments over the next period.

Notes

[1] As recorded in the acknowledgements, the seminars were organised by the editors of this volume with financial support from the Economic and Social Research Council (seminar grant R451265206), The Children's Society and participants' individual organisations.

References

Dencik, L. (1989) 'Growing up in the post-modern age: on the child's situation in the modern family, and on the position of the family in the modern welfare state', *Acta Sociologica*, vol 32, no 2. pp 155-80.

Lukes, S. (2004) *Power: A Radical View* (2nd edn), London: Palgrave Macmillan.

Prout, A. (2005) *The Future of Childhood: Towards the Interdisciplinary Study of Children*, London: Routledge Falmer.

SEU (Social Exclusion Unit) (2000) *National Strategy for Neighbourhood Renewal: Report of Policy Action Team 12: Young People*, London: Crown Stationery Office.

Index

Also available from The Policy Press

Children these days
Nicola Madge

"*Nicola Madge has done a great service to childhood studies in the UK through this fascinating snapshot of children's lives, experiences and views. Discussing many important issues, and illuminating them with valuable evidence drawn from a large sample of children, it should be a standard reference for future debate.*" **Alan Prout, Institute of Education, Warwick University**

What is it like to be a child growing up in Britain these days? What are the best and worst aspects of being a child today? *Children these days* draws on the accounts of over two thousand children, and five hundred adults, to examine the present day meaning of childhood and its implications for policy and practice.

PB £17.99 ISBN 978 1 86134 783 1 **HB** £45.00 ISBN 978 1 86134 784 8 192 pages
February 2006

When children become parents
Welfare state responses to teenage pregnancy
Edited by *Anne Daguerre* and *Corinne Nativel*

"*An extremely useful review of the literature on the various faces teenage pregnancy has in several nations and welfare regimes. This book is an enormous step forward that will set a trend for future research in teenage reproductive health issues.*" **Gijs Beets, Netherlands Interdisciplinary Demographic Institute (NIDI)**

Teenage parenthood is recognised as a significant disadvantage in western industrialised nations. It has been found to increase the likelihood of poverty and to reinforce inequalities. This book explores, for the first time, the links between welfare state provision and teenage reproductive behaviour across a range of countries with differing welfare regimes.

PB £24.99 ISBN 978 1 86134 678 0 **HB** £55.00 ISBN 978 1 86134 679 7 264 pages
November 2006

Beyond listening

Children's perspectives on early childhood services

*Edited by **Alison Clark**, **Anne Trine Kjørholt** and **Peter Moss***

"Beyond Listening will be of great interest to a wide audience. It draws together theory and practice from an international perspective comprehensively and accessibly - a valuable contribution to raising the status of children's perspectives within early childhood services."
Penny Lancaster, Listening to Young Children Training and Consultancy Service

This book is the first of its kind to focus on listening to young children, both from an international perspective and through combining theory, practice and reflection. With contributions and examples from researchers and practitioners in six countries it examines critically how listening to young children in early childhood services is understood and practiced.

PB £17.99 ISBN 978 1 86134 612 4   **HB** £50.00 ISBN 978 1 86134 613 1   208 pages October 2005

Children of the 21st century

From birth to nine months

*Edited by **Shirley Dex** and **Heather Joshi***

"With major changes underway in and across children's services, large cohort studies such as this are essential for assessing and analysing outcomes for children. the contributors to Children of the 21st Century *draw upon their widespread expertise to enable crucial evaluation of policy and practice."* **Pam Foley, School of Health and Social Welfare, The Open University**

This book documents the early lives of almost 19,000 children born in the UK at the start of the 21st century, and their families. It is the first time that analysis of data from the hugely important Millennium Cohort Study, a longitudinal study following the progress of the children and their families, has been drawn together in a single volume. The unrivalled data is examined here to address important policy and scientific issues.

PB £24.99 ISBN 978 1 86134 688 9 **HB** £50.00 ISBN 978 1 86134 689 6   296 pages October 2005

Child welfare and social policy
An essential reader
Edited by **Harry Hendrick**

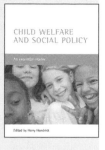

"... this reader is rich in fascinating and thought-provoking accounts and cannot fail in its aim to encourage thinking theoretically and politically about child welfare."
Children & Society

This book provides an essential one-stop introduction to the key concepts, issues, policies and practices affecting child welfare, with particular emphasis on the changing nature of the relationship between child welfare and social policy. No other book brings together such a wide selection of material to form an attractive and indispensable teaching and learning resource.

PB £25.00 ISBN 978 1 86134 566 0 **HB** £55.00 ISBN 978 1 86134 567 7 576 pages March 2005

Child welfare
Historical dimensions, contemporary debate
Harry Hendrick

"Hendrick has provided us with a book to be appreciated and savoured, one offering students and the general reader a shrewd and intelligent overview of child welfare policy. Here is a standard text, one unlikely to be bettered for a long time." **Youth & Policy**

This book offers a provocative account of contemporary policies on child welfare and the ideological thrust behind them and provides an informed historical perspective on the evolution of child welfare during the last century.

PB £18.99 ISBN 978 1 86134 477 9 304 pages February 2003

The EU and social inclusion
Facing the challenges
Eric Marlier, Tony Atkinson, Beatrijs Cantillon and *Brian Nolan*

This book provides an in-depth analysis of the EU Social Inclusion Process, the means being used to attain social cohesion and reduce the level of poverty and social exclusion. Providing a unique theoretically-informed analysis of policy formulation and EU social processes the book explores the challenges ahead at regional, national and EU levels, setting out concrete proposals for moving the Process forward.

HB £65.00 ISBN 978 1 86134 884 5 320 tbc pages November 2006

To order copies of this publication or any other Policy Press titles please visit **www.policypress.org.uk** or contact:

In the UK and Europe:
Marston Book Services, PO Box 269,
Abingdon, Oxon, OX14 4YN, UK
Tel: +44 (0)1235 465500
Fax: +44 (0)1235 465556
Email: direct.orders@marston.co.uk

In the USA and Canada:
ISBS, 920 NE 58th Street,
Suite 300, Portland, OR
97213-3786, USA
Tel: +1 800 944 6190
(toll free)
Fax: +1 503 280 8832
Email: info@isbs.com

**In Australia and
New Zealand:**
DA Information Services,
648 Whitehorse Road Mitcham,
Victoria 3132, Australia
Tel: +61 (3) 9210 7777
Fax: +61 (3) 9210 7788
E-mail: service@dadirect.com.au